THE JOY OF
FAMILY TRADITIONS

THE JOY OF
FAMILY
TRADITIONS

*A Season-by-Season Companion to
Celebrations, Holidays, and Special Occasions*

JENNIFER TRAINER THOMPSON

CELESTIAL ARTS
Berkeley | Toronto

Celestial Arts
an imprint of Ten Speed Press
PO Box 7123
Berkeley, California 94707
www.tenspeed.com

Distributed in Australia by Simon and Schuster
Australia, in Canada by Ten Speed Press Canada,
in New Zealand by Southern Publishers Group,
in South Africa by Real Books, and in the United
Kingdom and Europe by Publishers Group UK.

Cover and text design by Katy Brown

"Speaking of Greenberg" © 1934 by Edgar A. Guest.
Printed with permission by Steve Greenberg.

Library of Congress Cataloging-in-Publication Data

Thompson, Jennifer Trainer.
    The joy of family traditions : a season-by-season
companion to celebrations, holidays, and special occasions/
Jennifer Trainer Thompson.
        p. cm.
    Includes bibliographical references and index.
    ISBN 1-58761-114-7 (978-1-58761-114-8 : alk. paper)
    1. Holidays. 2. Fasts and feasts. 3. Family. 4. Manners
and customs. I. Title.
    GT3930.T477 2008
    394.269—dc22

                    2007041142

Printed in China
First printing, 2008

1 2 3 4 5 6 7 8 9 — 12 11 10 09 08

This book is dedicated to my mother,
Elinor Burnett Trainer, who never baked
a brownie, forgot my nineteenth birthday,
and stapled my Girl Scout badges onto
my sash because she refused to learn how
to sew, yet was deeply committed to her
big brood of a family and our heritage,
closeness, and future.

Acknowledgments

Traditions are communal, and I am grateful to the many friends and family members who gave me traditions, ideas, and support during the course of writing this book, including Cathy Dow, Concepcion Montalvo, Jose Sanchez, Alison Kolesar, Jonquil Wolfson, Audrey Werner, Alison Benjamin, Steve Swoap, Victoria Rock, Richard and Jeanne Besser, Joyce Bernstein, Eric Widing, Bobbie Crosby, Morty and Mimi Schapiro, Judy and Jenny Raab, Andrea Fox Jensen, Jack Wadsworth, Melissa Greene, Magnus Bernhardsson, Irving Tanzman, Judy Cummings, Jeffrey Burnett, Stephanie Mouse, Laurie Werner, Paulette Wein, Jennifer Ma, Judy Huber, Reverend Carrie Bail, Robin Brickman, Carole Schultze, Everton Sylvester, Julie Applegate, Darra Goldstein, Hans Morris, Steve Greenberg, Deborah Rothschild, Cristin Marandino, Shelley Jurs, Molly Polk, Lincoln Russell, Holly Mines, Diane Cooper, Deborah Coombs, Richard Criddle, Jody Fijal, Kathi Duble, Kaarin Lemstrom-Sheedy, Merritt and Mary Sue Colaizzi, Barry Olsen, Becky Acquaye, Sue Hamilton, Peter Bruun, Katherine Myers, Erik Bruun, Deborah Rothschild, Laura Heon, Dick and Sandy Bisson and the Bisson clan, Gary Flynn, Linda Becker, Linda White, Reverend Peter and Diana Elvin, Chris Howard, Geoff Strawbridge, Richard and Mary Beth Kerns, Darlie Kerns, Elizabeth Kerns, Stephanie Francis, JoAnn Noyes, Melissa Matuscak, Don and Andy Ovans, Jonathan Secor, Jude and Dick Sabot, Mary Saloschin Hubbard, Janette and Will Dudley, Julie Solomon, Alex Fox Coakley, Diana Walczak, David and Jeannie Aplin, Nancy Duble, Cecilia Vogtand, and Hanne Guri Belgau.

To the Ten Speed crew, for their longstanding support and good humor, especially my editor Veronica Randall, who was so patient while I took the time to live and enjoy these traditions, and Katy Brown, who did a beautiful job of designing this book. To Dennis Hayes, Lorena

Jones, Jo Ann Deck, and Phil Wood, dear Phil: you are more than one could possibly hope for in a publisher.

To Eric Kerns, who helped enormously with the research, writing, and shaping of the manuscript while adding a vital male perspective. Eric shares my feelings about the profound role traditions play in family life as he and his wife Molly raise their girls Darlie and Zoe, but he also sees life through a humorous lens and is slightly irreverent about anything overly sentimental. My heartfelt thanks to Eric for all his help.

To my families—Trainers, Thompsons, Burnetts, Harveys, and Dubles—who have always shown me know how much family matters.

To my cousins (especially Doug and Lee), who continue the traditions begun at 1 Everett Street, the Cottage, and Camp, and who, as our children grow, do what comes naturally: staying close.

To my three "sisters"—Sarah Purcell, Jeannie Aplin, and Sue Hamel—as well as my dear friend Janette Dudley, who keep me entwined in the sisterhood and are so much fun to experience motherhood with.

To Mary Jane and Jim and the rest of the Thompson clan, who welcomed me into the family with a cow pie and love and who dish up family gatherings with humor and deep affection.

To my dear father, who made me a Swamp Yankee and is one of the brightest stars in my sky. And to Peg, who keeps him shining.

Lastly, to my beloved husband Joe—Big Joe Daddy-O!—and to our children, Trainer and Isabel. You give these traditions value and have taught me so much. I couldn't have done it without you, nor would I want to.

CONTENTS

INTRODUCTION · 12

PART ONE · 19

Spring

Welcoming Spring │20│ St. Brigid's Day and Candlemas │22│ Groundhog Day │23│ Valentine's Day │24│ Tu B'Shvat │27│ Ramadan │30│ Carnival │31│ Mardi Gras │33│ Calle Ocho │35│ Pancake Tuesday │35│ Maslenitsa │36│ Purim │37│ International Women's Day │39│ Pi Day │40│ The Ides of March │40│ St. Patrick's Day │41│ Norouz │44│ Vernal Equinox │44│ Spring Cleaning │47│ Sham al-Naseem │49│ Passover │50│ Easter │54│ April Fools' Day │59│ Daylight Savings Time │60│ Take Our Daughters and Sons to Work Day │61│ May Day │62│ Cinco de Mayo │65│ Kentucky Derby Day │66│ Mother's Day │66│ Vesak │70│ Memorial Day │70│ Acts of Remembrance │73│ Last Day of School │78│ Father's Day │79│

PART TWO · 81

Summer

Welcoming Summer │82│ Summer Solstice │82│ Independence Day │83│
Baseball Season │84│ Summer Vacation │86│ Once in a Lifetime Trip │89│
Repeat Trips │90│ Back Home │94│ Celebrating a Birth │95│ In the Beginning │95│
Preserving Memories │98│ Ceremonies │99│ Godparents │101│ Unusual Baby
Gifts │101│ Happy Birthdays │104│ Recording the Years │105│ Other Birthday
Rituals │106│ The Party │108│ Milestone Birthdays │109│ Your Own
Birthday │110│ Making Your Child Feel Special │111│ As They Grow │114│
Family Communication │116│ Kids Rule │117│ Bedtime │117│ Coming of
Age │119│ Bar Mitzvah and Bat Mitzvah │121│ Turning Thirteen │122│ Native
American Rites of Passage │123│ La Quinceañera │126│ Male Rites of Passage │127│

PART THREE · 129

Autumn

Welcoming Autumn | 130 | Lammas | 131 | Sukkoth | 132 | Autumnal Equinox | 133 | Back to School | 134 | Earth's Bounty | 135 | Blessing of the Animals | 136 | Oktoberfest | 136 | Moon Festivals | 137 | Feast Days | 139 | National Hunting and Fishing Day | 141 | Rosh Hashanah | 142 | Yom Kippur | 143 | Halloween | 146 | Dia de los Muertos | 150 | Election Day | 153 | Weddings and Anniversaries | 154 | The Date | 155 | The Dress | 157 | Tossing the Bouquet | 158 | Bridesmaids | 159 | The Best Man | 159 | The Cake | 160 | Throwing Rice | 161 | The Rings | 162 | Wedding Customs Around the World | 164 | Encore Weddings | 167 | Wedding and Anniversary Gifts | 168 | Happy Anniversaries | 170 | Anniversaries of the Heart | 171 | Home and Hearth | 172 | Guess Who's Coming to Dinner? | 174 | Symbols of the Hearth | 175 | Shabbat | 177 | Sunday Nights | 178 | Home Nights | 180 | Family Homestead | 181 | Walk When the Moon Is Full | 182 | Thanksgiving | 184 | The First Thanksgiving | 185 | Giving Thanks | 187 | What to Do with the Rest of the Day | 190 |

PART FOUR · 193

Winter

Welcoming Winter │194│ Winter Solstice │194│ Doing the Winter Around
the World │196│ Festivals of Light │198│ Hanukkah │199│ Christmas: The Glitter and
the Sacred │202│ The Birth of Christmas │203│ Advent │206│ The Tree │209│
Decking the Halls │211│ Holiday Performances │216│ Caroling │217│ The Nativity
Scene │218│ Yours, Mine, and Ours: New Traditions for Stepfamilies │219│
Christmas Music │220│ Christmas Movies │221│ Christmas Stories for
Children │223│ Christmas Cards and Letters │223│ Gift Giving │224│ Letter to
Santa │227│ It Is Better to Give │229│ Giving When There's a Crowd │230│ Giving to
Others │231│ Christmas Morning │233│ The Pageantry of Food │234│ Twelve Days of
Christmas │238│ Epiphany │241│ Kwanzaa │243│ A New Year │248│ New Year's
Resolutions │249│ Old Celebrations │250│ New Celebrations │251│ Throughout the
World │252│ New Year's Day │254│ Chinese New Year (Gong Hey Fat Choy) │256│
Super Bowl Sunday │257│ After the Holidays │259│ A Season of Giving │260│

CONCLUSION 265 · SELECT BIBLIOGRAPHY 266 · INDEX 269

INTRODUCTION

This book was written because it was a book I wanted to read.

Though I've always been inclined towards perpetuating traditions—organizing family parties and marching with my cousins and kids in the same small-town Fourth of July parade that my mother marched in as a child—it wasn't until our son Trainer was born in 1998 that I began thinking consciously about the importance of traditions in our lives. Soon I was asking friends and acquaintances about their traditions as well, and I was startled by the responses.

Almost universally, people first professed to have no traditions. Then several days later they'd contact me and reminisce about the private rituals their family indulged in—be it celebrating a milestone birthday or clipping the first rhododendron blossom or putting a baby in the family clock (really). There were some doozies as well as some terrific ideas that I wanted to try out on my family. I started jotting down the ideas I liked in a notebook, in an attempt to remember them in the haze of early motherhood and to incorporate them into our lives. After a while, I realized I had a book.

And then came Isabel.

I had been gathering book notes and interviewing people as Trainer explored his way through preschool, trying out new ideas on him and my husband Joe as well as dusting off ones I remembered fondly from my own childhood. In October, we'd go apple picking in the orchards up the road in Vermont. In December, I'd embroider the date and some scene relevant to that year on Trainer's Christmas stocking. At the beach, we'd collect sand dollars, decorate them with glitter, and give them away as tree ornaments to family and friends. And then, when Trainer was four, we got a call that a baby had been born—a Christmas baby!—and soon the three of us were flying to Guatemala to pick up the newest member of our family. Isabel was in our arms by March 27.

With two young children, the book got sidelined for a couple of years. And what a good thing that was, for many reasons, not the least of which was that it allowed me to explore the role traditions play in our lives, especially as our family grew. Like my friends' traditions, many of mine were handed down to me, and their origins were a mixed bag, inspired by ethnicity, religion, heritage, or simply circumstance. A tenth-generation Yankee married to an Okie, I thought it'd be interesting to incorporate a sprinkling of traditions from around the world in the book. But as my own family expanded and I had the amazing opportunity to embrace a different culture and ethnicity, I found myself drawn to a larger worldview that reflected the needs and interests of our growing family. I think this is true of many families: as a people, we are migrating culturally and becoming a lot less "separate." Indeed, as our view gets bigger, the world gets smaller. What a great opportunity to savor old traditions and also to create some new ones.

Take, for example, a tradition that starts at the moment of birth: naming. It was easy for me to imagine naming my son "Trainer" after his grandfather H. Potter Trainer.

When I looked at my infant son, it was like looking in a mirror, for I could see distinct features of my father, my grandmother, as well as my own reflected in his wide blue eyes, high temples, and reddish-blonde hair. It made sense to name him J. Trainer Thompson. (Another family tradition: give your firstborn male your maiden name as a middle name.) For my daughter Isabel—a feisty streak of a comet—she deserved something different. It seemed ludicrous to saddle this beautiful Mayan baby with her inky dark eyes and black hair that shimmered ("Like a halo, Mom," said Trainer) with a hardscrabble Yankee name that tumbled from your mouth like nuts from the basket of my family tree: Burnett . . . Harvey . . . Easton . . . Sherlock . . . Coffin. No, she was Isabel Rose, and when we strolled with her as an infant through the streets of the colonial Guatemalan city of Antigua as Easter preparations were underway, and the women selling their tapestries on the sidewalks gently asked her name, they cooed, "Isabel*ita*," Little Isabel.

That became her beautiful name, underscoring the fact that we all bring threads to the fabric of our family, and what a precious gift we received from this infant to inherit the culture of her birth, and what a powerful and overwhelming sense of responsibility I felt to do right by this little one in my arms. Looking at her beautiful skin and hair, I was also reminded that, although she didn't physically resemble her brother or parents, physical characteristics aren't what make a family. Or as Trainer put it soon after she was born, "Mommy, if you forget the color of our skin, our hair, and our eyes, I think we look just alike, don't you?" You betcha. And then, of course, at age three-and-a-half Isabel rejected Isabelita. ("It's only for babies, Mommy.") And that's an important lesson, too: traditions are successful only as long as they work for you, and sometimes they need to die a graceful death on the vine.

It also became evident to me as I wrote this book that traditions are important as we parent our children. At first I collected big, fat, obvious traditions (weddings, birthdays, first day of school), but soon it became apparent that traditions do so much more than commemorate a milestone; they can serve as guideposts along the way, helping us to shape our daily lives and foster values—indeed, they can be an oasis in an increasingly hectic and busy world. How do traditions and ritual help our children learn about nature or charity or differences (but also of the power of clan)? Rituals are also helpful as single-parent families, transracial families, and other nontraditional families forge ahead into uncharted territory. According to *Newsweek*, there are more than 22 million "step" (I've never liked that word) families in the United States today. How can children of divorce navigate holidays or weddings through the minefield of ex-spouses, stepsiblings, a new home (with new traditions), and inherited in-laws? How does a stepmother deal with Mother's Day? How might you instill ethnic pride when a child can't absorb the culture of her heritage from her environment? Traditions can help us grow and flourish; they reflect and inspire the way we parent and how we honor the passage of time, achievement, and meaningful moments in our lives. In a society that is increasingly chaotic, wired, and weird, they offer a way to connect with a spiritual dimension, a way to feel the embrace of a quieter world, and a chance to teach your children well.

The search for meaning through ritual is ancient, though perhaps more important now than ever before. Often, people live great distances from their families. Children with older parents don't always have the advantage of knowing their grandparents. Divorce is commonplace. One out of three parents is a stepparent. People work—a lot. Many kids are in extended daycare after school, not home baking cookies and making ornaments. Many good parents simply don't have as much time as they'd like to dedicate to their kids.

Traditions are comforting and predictable. They involve a sense of history—sometimes generational—that affords a strong sense of self and one's place in the family and the world, both morally and spiritually. They ground us. Think of one simple act: sharing a family meal. According to the *Journal of Pediatric Psychology*, children of alcoholics are much less likely to become alcoholics themselves if, while growing up, they take part in the simple act of eating with their parents as a family.

Traditions are also a great way to make everyone in your family feel included. Inclusiveness is a key to comfort in any environment, be it at home, work, or in the community. "Rituals foster a sense of belonging and provide comfort and security," said Barbara Fiese, chair of the psychology department at Syracuse University and lead author of a study on family routines and rituals published in *Journal of Family Psychology*. "We know we can count on them." Indeed, according to Fiese, rituals lower stress because they reassure us and add to our well-being. Certainly little kids revel in tradition, and as they get older, these memories can serve as anchors. Adolescents may pooh-pooh family traditions, but they absorb them and, from what I've observed, secretly desire them. The National Longitudinal Study of Adolescent Health, a study of ninety-thousand youth completed in 1997, indicated that children who feel connected to their families are far less likely to abuse drugs or engage in other risky behavior even if both parents are working.

The traditions in this book aren't just for children, though. They are a way to mark passages, be it a birthday, holiday, marriage, or death. We impart them to our children, but we also partake in them for our own sake. My mother was one of six children, and her father—who had grown up the product of divorce in the early 1900s—was adamant that Sundays were family days; the kids couldn't even leave the yard. My aunts still reminisce fondly about those Sundays; they played games in the grass, took care of their two grandmothers who lived with them, and after dinner clustered on the braided rug in the parlor listening to the evening radio broadcast. Indeed, at my mother's funeral sixty years later, one of her childhood friends talked about Sundays at the Burnett house on Clifford Street and how as a kid he wanted to be a Burnett more than anything else in the world. We all know families like that—big, boisterous, spontaneous clans—and we want to be part of them.

There's also a lot of yearning inherent in traditions, especially for those who live alone or are in crisis. Can you imagine Christmas while going through a divorce? You'd want to hightail it to the High Atlas Mountains where no one will jingle at you with false cheer. A friend of mine whose parents died when he was young found winter holidays depressing until he and others at his Wall Street firm started a phone-a-thon, using company phones to wish shut-ins a happy holiday, an idea that became a fulfilling annual tradition. My hope is that this book can help people forge satisfying new traditions. Though I miss my mother every Thanksgiving, I know she's there in spirit when I make her Grand Marnier turkey stuffing from the *Silver Palate* cookbook—and I know my father's there in the flesh when he grouses about how much it costs.

So how do you distinguish between a tradition and a rut? Sometimes you do things because you've always done them (like going to the same place every summer) and hope they will eventually become cherished memories. Often they do. Sometimes they don't. Starting a tradition is like growing a garden: you plant the seed, water it, and wait. Sometimes it takes root, sometimes it doesn't. You'll know by the flowering whether it was successful. As you read this book, I urge you to keep several thoughts in mind:

✳ Don't wait—until next year, next month, or even tomorrow—to start a tradition. Think about the rest of today. There are dozens of ideas in this book that take just a few minutes to try. We don't need special occasions to celebrate our lives.

✳ Don't feel obligated—the tradition should never overshadow the spirit of an event. Especially during the winter holidays, there's no need to host or attend every single event or include every possible ritual every year. Save your sparkle and participate when you have the health, energy, and inclination. Otherwise the fatigue and stress of living up to obligations will kill the fun, and you'll either do them grudgingly or not at all. I have some Christmas traditions that, rather than attempting annually, I enjoy every two or three years at best. And why not? A tradition doesn't have to be annual, and when I feel up to it (and have begun to miss a particular ritual) I pick it up, and it feels fresh and fun again. If a tradition feels like a chore, don't do it.

✳ Don't hesitate to banish the traditions you never liked—it's liberating! Everyone outgrows certain rituals just like we outgrow clothing, and a periodic review of what works and what doesn't in your family is a good idea. There is no dishonor in letting go of traditions that no longer (or never did) suit you.

✳ Lastly, have fun. You probably don't have time to make an exquisite needlepoint keepsake for every friend's newborn, but there are plenty of others ways to mark the milestones for your kids, parents, spouse, siblings, friends, and colleagues. I promise you that whatever effort you put in will come back to you tenfold. Guaranteed.

The beauty of traditions is that they endure, in our lives and in our memories and, long after we're gone, in the memories of our children.

Spring

There is no time like Spring,
When life's alive in everything. . . .

CHRISTINA ROSSETTI

❧ Welcoming Spring ❧

Spring begins at the first sign that winter is loosening its grip, whether it is a garden shoot poking up through the snow, the grace of a warm breeze on your cheek after a cold morning, the lengthening days, or the change in the light . . . all are small, intimate signs of spring.

In a world that is increasingly governed by the clock, it's easy to miss the rhythm of the seasons and get caught up in our daily lives, but I find it hardest to ignore the advent of spring. This season of rejuvenation in the natural world gives rise to a spiritual rebirth where we are delivered from the dark depths of winter to walk again on warm soil, to breathe deeply the scent of green, and to hear the music of returning birds. What better time to start a year of traditions than in the spring?

Personal rituals abound, and, for many people, spring flowers have a way of both heralding the future and commemorating the past. My friend Jeannie Aplin always cuts the first rhododendron blossom, making it a centerpiece on her kitchen table in the cut glass bowl that belonged to her husband's grandmother, knowing how much it pleases him to see this ritual carried on that he enjoyed as a child. For photographer Lincoln Russell, spring takes him back to when his now grown son was a toddler and would ride on his dad's shoulders, "catching" the buds of the flowering trees along Boston's Commonwealth Avenue. It remains a distinct memory for both father and son. For my friend Audrey Werner, the first scent of opening lilacs wafting across the lawn reminds her of her father, for although she can't remember the man who died when she was two, her mother told her that he passed away when the lilacs were in bloom. A vase of lilacs on the table is both a memorial and a fragrant way to greet the season.

Indeed, scent is a powerful reminder. You might think about what your home smells like, and what you'd like your kids to remember it smelling like . . . wood fires, fresh flowers, baking bread, orange-scented wood polish, garlic sautéing . . . For years I kept a big rosemary pot by the back stoop, and whenever it rained the raindrops would pelt the bush and for hours the air was laced with the scent of rosemary.

Although spring doesn't technically begin until March 21, the Romans and Celts considered February the start of spring, and I think they had the right idea; February and March are full of rituals that seem more suited to awakenings than to the dormancy of wintertime.

> It is the first mild day of March:
> Each minute sweeter than before
> The redbreast sings from the tall larch
> That stands beside our door.
>
> WILLIAM WORDSWORTH

St. Brigid's Day and Candlemas ✤ February 1 and 2

In ancient times in Ireland, the beginning of February was the halfway point between the winter solstice and spring equinox and signaled that winter was finally coming to an end. Yet with food supplies dwindling and the harvest six months away, the early Celts worried about survival and staged a festival of light (one of four major Celtic festivals) to conjure a bit of divine energy for the speedy return of spring. Held on February 1 or at the first sign of spring, the festival was called Imbolc, which means in the belly, although it's sometimes translated as ewe's milk, and involved enormous bonfires and torch-lit processions into the farmers' fields.

As Christianity spread through Europe, many pagan festivals were transformed into Church-sanctioned holy days. Thus, Imbolc evolved into two holidays. One was St. Brigid's Day, in which the Celtic goddess of fire and fertility was canonized as St. Brigid (today the second patron saint of Ireland, after St. Patrick). According to Church legend, St. Brigid was born around 450 AD, the daughter of the King's poet laureate and a servant. The poet's jealous wife sold the child to a Druid family. Converting to Christianity as a young girl, Brigid became a nun and founded a convent in Kildare. Today in Ireland St. Brigid's Day (held from sunset on February 1 until sunset on February 2) is traditionally the first day of spring.

The second holiday to evolve was Candlemas, a candle-lit mass conducted on February 2 to commemorate when Jesus was presented in the temple forty days after his birth. A precursor to Groundhog Day, it also prognosticated the coming of spring.

Although Christian in origin, the spirit of Candlemas is easily adapted to a secular celebration of the turning of the season:

- Make your own candles with your children. Craft stores stock easy-to-use kits.

- Illuminate your home exclusively with your handmade candles on this night.

- Have a bonfire in your backyard. (Be sure to check your local fire ordinances.)

If Candlemas day be fair and bright,
Winter will have another flight.
If Candlemas day be shower and rain,
Winter is gone and will not come again.
OLD SCOTTISH RHYME

Groundhog Day ❧ February 2

Early Christians embraced the folklore that animals had supernatural powers and their behavior could foreshadow the length of winter and other events. (Even Aristotle admired the hedgehog's weather-predicting talents.) According to legend, a creature will come out of hibernation on Candlemas Day, and if he sees his shadow (that is, if the sun is shining), he will be frightened by it and go back to sleep for six more weeks (until the spring equinox). If the sky is cloudy and he can't see his shadow, he will emerge from his burrow, figuring that winter is over. In Germany and France, the animal of choice was a bear or badger, but German immigrants who brought the custom to Pennsylvania in the late 1800s found no badgers (there weren't any east of the Mississippi) and so used woodchucks or groundhogs for the task. On the weekend closest to Groundhog Day, have a Family Hibernation Day. Fun rituals include:

- Sleep late and stay in your pajamas all day.

- Read aloud, play board games, watch a favorite movie, take a collective nap.

- Make a decadent chocolate dessert, or do whatever activity will turn the day into a mini-retreat from the world for your entire family.

Valentine's Day ❧ February 14

The Romans honored Juno, goddess of marriage, with a feast on February 14, followed the next day by the boisterous Lupercalia, a festival dedicated to Lupercus (the god of fertility) that involved purification rituals and animal sacrifices. One feature of the festival was a kind of lottery: the names of young unmarried women were placed in a large urn, single young men were invited to draw a name, and the couple would pair off for the duration of the festival. Many such partnerships resulted in marriage.

The early church scowled on such behavior, and in 486 AD, Pope Gelasius invented a story to discourage the custom. There are several versions, but the basic narrative begins in Rome around 270 AD with Emperor Claudius II, a fierce ruler whose bloody military campaigns were legendary. When his soldiers balked at going to war, Claudius assumed it was because they didn't want to leave their wives and children. So he cancelled all pending marriage contracts and made marriage illegal. A priest called Valentinius (Valentine) defied the tyrant's decree and secretly officiated at Christian marriages. Enraged, Claudius threw the priest in jail, where Valentine fell in love with the jailor's daughter. Not realizing she was blind, he sent her love notes "from your Valentine." Claudius had Valentine beheaded on February 14, 270. Two centuries later, as the story goes, Pope Gelasius canonized the priest as a martyred saint and created St. Valentine's Day in an effort to replace the Lupercalian tradition.

The English later adapted a more romantic version of the Lupercalian lottery: a soldier or knight would select a maiden's name from a jar or basket, draw hearts around it, and pin the badge to his sleeve, hence the phrase, "to wear your heart on your sleeve."

The romance associated with St. Valentine's Day came a bit later; the earliest evidence is thought to be a poem from the early 1300s by Geoffrey Chaucer written to commemorate the engagement of Richard II in which the author linked St. Valentine's Day to birds and romance. People thought that birds (especially lovebirds) chose their mates on this day, and it became common to pen verses about one's sweetheart using this metaphor.

Valentine's Day went into full swing in Victorian England, when love symbols such as cherubs, cupids, hearts, hands, and roses supplanted the religious icons of the day. The first commercial American valentine cards were printed in the 1840s, when Esther Howland, a Mt. Holyoke graduate who was a contemporary of poet Emily Dickenson, sent her salesman brother off with a dozen samples and was shocked when he returned with $5,000 in orders. (Today, according to greeting card industry reports, 25 percent of all cards are sold for Valentine's Day.)

China tea, the scent of hyacinths, wood fires and bowls of violets—that is my mental picture of an agreeable February afternoon.

CONSTANCE SPRY

As a mother of young children, I often find it easier to make a big deal out of minor holidays such as Valentine's Day. There are many ways to celebrate beyond going out to dinner and buying your family chocolates.

Serve up love at every meal: oatmeal with red hot candy hearts for breakfast, or a heart-shaped sandwich in your child's lunchbox.

Make your own cards: let your kids go to town with fancy papers, doilies, ribbon, glitter, snapshots, and markers. I still have the cards my nieces and nephews made for me when I was single, and I still treasure them.

When your kids come home on February 13 with a list of everyone in their class they *have* to give cards to (and, trust me, they will) buy a few packs of commercial cards and ask your children to personalize each one with stickers and markers. This allows you to concentrate guilt-free on the homemade cards for best friends or family.

My friend Jeannie hosts a Valentine's Day tea party for her daughters and their friends. She serves pink rosehip tea, pink sandwiches, and pink cookies.

Author and illustrator Tasha Tudor made miniature valentines for her children's dolls and stuffed animals. You can adapt this charming tradition by addressing a valentine card to your child from his or her favorite toy.

When one of my co-workers and her boyfriend were on a tight budget, he hit upon the idea of giving her a heart-shaped pizza for lunch instead of a pricey restaurant dinner. She still looks forward to this tasty gesture from him—except that now he's her husband.

❋ Ask each family member to memorize a love poem or sonnet to recite at the dinner table. John and Caroline Kennedy would write or choose a poem for their mother and paste it into a scrapbook. Of this family ritual, Caroline has said, "A few days before Valentine's Day or Mother's Day, there would be a mad scramble for the poetry books and a mild sense of competition to see whose poem was longer or more famous. It wasn't like a school assignment, but an infinite wandering that took us out of our world and into so many others." She has since edited two compilations of poetry, *The Best-Loved Poems of Jacqueline Kennedy Onassis* and *A Family of Poems: My Favorite Poetry for Children.*

Tu B'Shvat ❋ January or February

Celebrated on the fifteenth day of the Hebrew month of Shvat (January or February on the Gregorian calendar), Tu B'Shvat is known as the New Year for Trees, not unlike Arbor Day. In ancient times, farmers planted trees and blessed their orchards on Tu B'Shvat, and in Israel today, children have parades, plant seedlings, dance, sing, and eat fruits and nuts. It is a day dedicated to environmental and ecological awareness and beautification, with an emphasis placed on trees, which have a place of honor in the Old Testament and in the Torah. You can celebrate Tu B'Shvat and help the environment at the same time:

❋ Have a Tu B'Shvat seder at home that features the seven "fruits," praised by the Torah and cited in Deuteronomy, that flourish in Israel: pomegranates, olives, dates, figs, grapes, barley, and wheat. (It can be structured like a Passover seder, or more freestyle.)

Set a Tu B'Shvat table with three kinds of fruit: one with a skin or peel that must be opened before eating (oranges or bananas, for example), one with an inedible seed or pit (apples or pears), and one that is entirely edible (such as grapes).

Plant parsley, basil, scallions, and onions (they're fast growers and can be planted in late winter or early spring if you live in a temperate climate) in time to serve at your seder.

Discuss how your family might become more environmentally aware around your home. Then set up a playful way to keep track: If someone forgets to shut off the lights when she leaves a room or leaves the water running while he's brushing his teeth, they pay a fine of 25 cents. At the end of the year, take the accumulated fines to your local nursery, buy a tree or shrub, and plant it in your yard (if you have one), or work with your school to select a spot that's crying out for some greenery. Or donate the funds to a nonprofit that offers energy assistance to those in need.

Best time to plant tree, one hundred years ago.
Second best time, today.

CHINESE PROVERB

THE JOY OF FAMILY TRADITIONS

THE CHRISTIAN CALENDAR grew out of the Jewish lunar calendar and the Roman solar calendar, and as a result, some important celebrations and feasts can float to different dates while others remain constant. Before AD 325, Easter was celebrated by some Christians on Passover (a Jewish lunar holiday) and by others the following Sunday. In 325, the Council of Nicaea set the date of Easter to get everyone on the same page and, possibly, to sever its chronological association with the Jewish Passover. Since then, Easter has been observed on the Sunday following the first full moon after March 21—the vernal equinox—and the dates of all other moveable feasts are calculated using Easter as a reference point. It seems simple enough, but in practice the methods are a bit imprecise, in part because, due to leap years, the vernal equinox doesn't always fall on March 21 and because the church still uses traditional tables (rather than modern astronomical data) to determine the dates of full moons.

Ramadan

A period for spiritual reflection and prayer, the month of Ramadan celebrates the time when the verses of the Koran were revealed to the prophet Mohammed. Reading the Koran is an important aspect and many Muslims will attempt to read the entire text at least once during this period. Many will also go to mosques to attend special services during which the Koran is read aloud.

The exact dates of Ramadan change yearly because Islam uses a lunar calendar, which means the start of Ramadan happens approximately eleven days earlier each year according to the Gregorian calendar and consequently is not associated with any particular Western month. The ninth month of the Islamic calendar, Ramadan is a time when Muslims fast during daylight hours. It is common to have one meal, known as the *suhoor*, just before sunrise and another, called the *iftar*, directly after sunset.

The fasting is intended to enhance self-discipline, self-restraint, and generosity. The fast may be comparatively short if Ramadan falls during the winter months or much longer if it occurs during the summer. At the end of the month, once fasting has been completed, there is a celebration called Eid ul-Fitr, the Festival of the Breaking of the Fast. During this celebration it is traditional for Muslims to dress in their finest clothes, decorate their homes with strings of colored lights, give gifts to children, visit with their friends and family, and donate money to charity.

For non-Muslims, foregoing meals all day long every day for a month or more would be daunting, but there are ways to adapt and incorporate these mindful rituals into your life:

North African nomads determine sunrise and sunset by holding a black thread up to the horizon. In the morning, when the thread is discernable from the pre-dawn darkness, fasting begins. In the evening, when the thread can no longer be distinguished from the night sky, the feasting begins. Instead of watching the clock, try this (dare I say timely tradition?) with your kids.

❋ Consider asking your family to observe one day of fasting in honor of Ramadan, choosing a day when everyone can sit down together before dawn for breakfast and again after sunset for supper.

Carnival ❋ February or March

For Christians, spring brings Lent, a reflective period of forty days that begins on Ash Wednesday and leads up to Easter. The day before Ash Wednesday is Shrove Tuesday (still a legal holiday in Alabama), which gets its name from parishioners who, centuries ago, asked their priest to "shrive" or absolve them of their sins before entering the Lenten season.

Also known as Fat Tuesday, Shrove Tuesday can occur between February 3 and March 9, depending on when Easter falls. Because Shrove Tuesday is the last night that Catholics eat meat before giving it up for Lent, on that day people would slaughter and eat their fattened calves or lambs. They would also "let the good times roll" before embracing the rigors of Lent, beginning on Twelfth Night and ending on Shrove Tuesday. The period between Twelfth Night and Fat Tuesday (or *Mardi Gras* in French) is known the world over as Carnival (from the Latin *carne vale*, meaning farewell to the flesh).

And what is Twelfth Night, other than a comedy by William Shakespeare? In some churches, Twelfth Night is a holiday that concludes the twelve days of Christmas. Exactly when Twelfth Night falls is open to interpretation; to those who believe a day starts at sunset, it's the eve of January 5 (preceding the twelfth day), whereas to others, it's the eve of January 6 (the twelfth day).

Like many modern holidays, Carnival has pre-Christian roots. The Roman festival of Lupercalia (see page 24) was most likely recast as Carnival by the early church, thus allowing the recently (and, perhaps, reluctantly) converted populace to let off a little steam before accepting forty days of Lenten austerity. Indeed, the power of the Catholic Church endures; to this day in New Orleans, Mardi Gras concludes at the stroke of midnight on Shrove Tuesday.

Medieval carnivals often included elaborate theatrical spectacles that sometimes invited ribald audience participation. At the Florentine Carnival of 1496, the crowds were especially loud and frenzied, boldly demanding that the nobility give up their vanities, which they apparently did, stripping off their clothing, jewels, shoes, and wigs and tossing them into a heap in the Piazza della Signoria where they were torched into a blazing bonfire. (This incident gave rise to the expression "bonfire of the vanities.") In the 1500s when Charles IX hosted Carnival at the Louvre in Paris, he invited ten professional pickpockets to join the party then watched in delight as they relieved the bejeweled guests of their baubles, swords, and fans. This was relatively tame when compared to his predecessor, Louis XI, whose invited guests were forced to dance with exhumed corpses (with great effort expended to ensure that each reveler was paired up with a deceased relative.)

Today, Carnival season runs from January 6 through Shrove Tuesday in North America, Europe, Latin America, and even parts of New England (Dartmouth College, for example, has had a winter carnival since 1911). The spectacular Carnival in Rio de Janeiro takes place three days before Ash Wednesday, while in New Orleans it begins on Twelfth Night and ends with Mardi Gras on Shrove Tuesday.

American Mardi Gras possibly has its roots in the Feast of Fools, a medieval French carnival that was imported to New Orleans in 1699 but banned in the mid-1700s by the Spanish colonial government. The tradition was restored in the 1820s by American students, home from their studies in Paris, who wanted to recreate the fantastic parades, buffoonery, and costumed frivolity they had witnessed in France. The idea took hold with wealthy Louisiana plantation owners, and by 1833, there was a masked Mardi Gras Ball and the festival's colors had been established: purple for justice, green for faith, and gold for power. The first official Mardi Gras Parade was staged in 1837.

Mardi Gras ❄ February or March

In New Orleans, Mardi Gras foods include thick soups of pig's feet, beans, and peas, and of course the Kings Cake, which was a crown-shaped confection served on Kings Day (January 6) to represent the Three Kings who traveled to Bethlehem to see the baby Jesus. Historically, a prize or bean was placed inside the cake before baking (wealthy Louisiana plantation owners often used a jewel), and whoever found the prize got to be king for the day, and was required to host the next year's party and provide the cake.

The king could select his queen, or sometimes a pea was baked into the cake, and the woman who was served the slice with the pea became the king's consort. Latin Americans and New Orleanians often bake a toy infant (for baby Jesus) into the cake. The traditional Kings Cake is made with twisted braids of cinnamon dough, not unlike a coffee cake, dusted with green, purple, and golden sugar.

If you can swing it, take a family trip to New Orleans for Mardi Gras. There's no better way to support the post-Katrina recovery efforts of this soulful city. But if travel isn't in the cards, an annual Mardi Gras party is a bodacious way to enjoy our American melting-pot heritage:

🌼 Set your table with a centerpiece piled with masks and beads. Because food is a huge part of New Orleans culture, serve a Fat Tuesday feast featuring gumbo, crawfish étouffée, or jambalaya (and don't forget the hot sauces).

🌼 Discover the fabulous musical heritage of New Orleans and work off those Fat Tuesday calories with the incomparable rhythms of jazz, Cajun, and zydeco that will get your group on its feet. *Laissez les bon temps rouler!*

🌼 A Mardi Gras potluck is a great way to meet your neighbors. Consider expanding your party by including folks in your building, on your block, or at your school. Hold a raffle with a small prize (a Cajun cookbook, a few bottles of hot sauce, or some CDs) and donate the proceeds to a charity dedicated to rebuilding New Orleans.

> *If ever I cease to love,*
> *If ever I cease to love*
> *May the fish get legs and the cows lay eggs,*
> *If ever I cease to love!*
>
> FROM "IF EVER I CEASE TO LOVE" BY GEORGE LEYBOURNE (1871),
> MARDI GRAS THEME SONG SINCE 1872

THE JOY OF FAMILY TRADITIONS

Calle Ocho ❀ March

Carnival in Miami is held at the beginning of March along Calle Ocho (Eighth Street), which forms the heart of Little Havana, the neighborhood where Cubans settled after fleeing Castro's government in the late 1950s. A giant street party that stretches for twenty-three blocks, Calle Ocho features Latin music, food, and dance. It begins with Noche de Carnaval (Carnival Night) and concludes ten days later with Carnaval de Calle Ocho. Not just for Cubans, it draws over a million people and has become the largest Latin cultural celebration in the United States. Can you imagine thousands of people forming a conga line or doing the mambo in the streets? This is not to be missed.

Pancake Tuesday ❀ February or March

In addition to foregoing meat, people weren't allowed to eat dairy products during Lent, and one way to use up (and avoid wasting) a family's lard, butter, and eggs was to make pancakes on Shrove Tuesday. Determined not to sit by and watch his foodstuffs rot for a month, one nineteenth-century English aristocrat famously invited all the farming families on his Nottinghamshire estate to make pancakes. He not only provided the frying pans and the fire, he gave each man a quart of ale, each woman a pint, and each child a gill (a quarter of a pint). As my English friend Richard Criddle quipped, "There's always beer attached to British traditions."

The Shrove Tuesday Pancake Race in Olney, England, which requires that a pancake be tossed a specified number of times over a length of 415 yards, dates back to 1445. Since 1950, the women of Liberal, Kansas, have competed in another race against the ladies of Olney. Wearing an apron and head scarf and holding a skillet, each competitor runs along a prescribed route in her respective town, all the while flipping pancakes. The mayors of Liberal and Olney are connected by telephone, and the winning town holds the title until the following year. Prior to the race, each town hosts a parade and pancake breakfast, of course.

Knick-knock, pan's hot, I'm come a-shroving. . . .
OLD ENGLISH NURSERY RHYME

Maslenitsa ❧ February or March

Most Catholic countries have a version of carnival, and in Russia it's called Maslenitsa (from *maslo*, or butter), a week of festivities celebrated during the Lenten fast. Although it also heralded the coming spring, Maslenitsa was based on the Russian Orthodox calendar, so it often arrived in February, and gave the faithful an opportunity to fatten up before the prolonged lean time. Essentially a butter festival, Maslenitsa promoted the foods that were forbidden during the fast, such as pancakes, whose round golden shape had been symbolic of the sun since pagan times. Blinis (Russian-style pancakes made with buckwheat flour) are often served with caviar, herring, salmon, sour cream, or sweet jam. In the late 1800s, Maslenitsa was a grand affair, with colorful *troika* (sleigh) races, ice slides (similar to toboggan runs), bonfires, and snowball fights on a massive scale staged from ice forts. On the final day of the festival, a straw scarecrow, called Lady Maslenitsa, was thrown into a bonfire and burned to symbolize winter's end.

Purim ❊ March

This raucous holiday, held on the fourteenth day of Adar (mid-March), is sometimes referred to as the Jewish Mardi Gras. Purim commemorates a biblical legend of redemption: 2,400 years ago, King Ahashveros of Persia consolidated his empire, stretching from Ethiopia to India, and celebrated with a six-month feast. One night the increasingly dissipated monarch commanded his wife to dance before a drunken crowd wearing nothing but her crown. She declined, and the king's advisors urged him to hold a beauty contest for a new wife. The winner was a lovely Jewish woman called Esther, whose powerful uncle, Mordecai, counseled her to conceal her religious identity. One of the royal ministers, Haman, persuaded the king to order all the Jews in the empire executed. But when Esther revealed to Ahashveros that she was Jewish, her people were spared, Haman was hanged, and Esther's triumph is celebrated today as Purim. (The Hebrew word *purim*, which means lots, commemorates the execution date Haman had drawn from a lottery—the fourteenth day of Adar).

The hallmark of the service is that everything is topsy-turvy: kids can make fun of grown-ups, anyone can make fun of the rabbi, and most people (including rabbis) wear costumes. Since the fifteenth century, many synagogues have presented a Purim *shpiel* (play or skit in Yiddish) that recounts the events in the book of Esther. The shpiel always encourages audience participation: the crowd gets to stomp and cheer the heroes (Mordecai and Esther) and boo the villains (Haman).

The service is followed by a feast or party that encourages a continuation of the zany carnival-like atmosphere. The wife of a rabbi once told me of a Jewish saying that attempts to sum up most Jewish holidays: They tried to kill us. They failed. Let's eat. "And you can say that about Purim more than any other holiday," she quipped. Purim is a joyful holiday, with numerous rituals both religious and secular:

🌸 Give small gifts of food (called *mishloach manot*) to friends and people you'd like to reach out to (especially those from whom you may be estranged). A traditional item is the *hamantaschen* (the hat of Haman), a three-cornered cookie filled with prunes, chocolate, or poppy seeds.

🌸 Make at least two charitable donations to those in need on the day of Purim. (This is called *matanot l'evynim*.)

🌸 Stage a Latke vs. Hamantasch debate. The University of Chicago has hosted this annual event since 1946, and various colleges across the country have followed suit. Usually four professors bring their academic rigor to bear as they argue the merits of the potato pancake versus the triangular pastry. A psychology professor might discuss the psychological profile of the potato versus a cookie, while a public policy professor might counter with an argument about the "liberating" qualities of the *hamantasch* versus the "binding" qualities of latkes. The debates are so popular on the Williams College campus that professors consider it an honor to be asked to participate.

International Women's Day ❀ March 8

In 1909, socialist activists in several European countries declared March 19 International Women's Day to call attention to women's suffrage, which spurred more than a million people to attend rallies across the continent. Less than a week later the tragic Triangle Shirtwaist Factory fire in New York took the lives of 146 female immigrants, highlighting the abysmal working conditions endured by women. In 1913, the first International Women's Day was observed in Russia. Four years later, with more than two million Russian casualties as World War I dragged on, women in St. Petersburg went on strike on March 8, 1917, for "bread and peace." Several days later the Czar abdicated, and a provisional government gave women the right to vote. Today in Russia, women are still honored on March 8 with small gifts and flowers. It would take almost thirty years, but in 1945, the United Nations Charter proclaimed gender equality to be a fundamental human right, and in 1975 the U.N. began promoting March 8 as International Women's Day.

There are simple but discussion-provoking ways to acknowledge the day:

❀ Choose a memoir or biography of someone you admire to read with your children.

❀ Watch a film that has women's issues at its heart that you can discuss afterwards, such as *Norma Rae, Iron-Jawed Angels, 9 to 5, A League of Their Own*, or *Yentl*.

Pi (π) Day ❋ March 14

Pi Day (also Einstein's birthday) is celebrated in college math departments across the country on 3/14 at 1:59 P.M., which reflects the first six digits of the infinite non-repeating decimal expansion of pi (3.14159 . . .). Events sponsored on various campuses range from pi(e)-eating contests to writing "pi-ku" poems to debates on the merits of Pi versus E. M.I.T. even coordinates the mailing of its acceptance letters with Pi Day.

Thanks to the Internet, it's easy to brush up on both Einstein and pi (the ratio of a circle's circumference to its diameter) and use the day to launch a light hearted discussion with the kids about either subject . . . and don't forget the pie.

The Ides of March ❋ March 15

"Beware the Ides of March." Leave it to Shakespeare to turn an innocuous phrase into an iconic expression of impending doom. It's not clear why this line has achieved such notoriety since even to an Elizabethan audience the phrase would have held no more significance than "Beware next Tuesday" would today. The phrase comes from the complex Roman calendar: *kalends* was the first day of every month; *nones* was the seventh day in March, May, July, and October, and the fifth day in all other months; and *ides* was the fifteenth day in March, May, July, and October, and the thirteenth day in the other months.

So, although there is an ides of every month, the significance of the Ides of March offers an opportunity to brush up on your Shakespeare, not to mention Roman history (Gaius Julius Caesar was murdered in the Roman Senate House on March 15, 44 BC). Pick up a copy of *Julius Caesar* or *Illustrated Tales from Shakespeare* to read with your kids or, what the heck, throw an all-ages toga party. Just be sure to hide the steak knives.

St. Patrick's Day 🌱 March 17

"America celebrates St. Patrick's Day like no other country," says Dublin brewer Fergal Murray, "even Ireland." With 34 million Americans claiming Irish ancestry, it's hardly surprising. The first St. Patrick's Day parade was organized on March 17, 1766 in New York City (not Ireland!) by Irish soldiers serving in the English army a decade before the American Revolution. By the mid-nineteenth century, after the potato famine had driven almost a million Irish to the United States, immigrants began to organize. Their political support, known as the "green machine," was often critical to a candidate's success, and many astute politicians used the parade to enhance their campaigns. Irish Americans watched with pride when President Harry Truman attended the 1948 St. Patrick's Day parade in Manhattan, and to this day the parade is a major event with 150,000 marchers and two million spectators.

The history of St. Patrick himself is sketchy. Born to a wealthy family at the end of the fourth century, he was abducted at sixteen, shipped to Ireland, and sold to a landowner. After herding sheep for six years, he escaped to a monastery in Gaul (France). Returning fifteen years later to Ireland as a missionary, the enterprising Patrick used creative techniques to convert the locals to Christianity; to celebrate Easter, for example, he lit a bonfire at the top of a hill, knowing that the largely pagan peasantry was accustomed to honoring its gods with fire. Legend has it that he attached an image of the sun (an ancient pagan symbol) over a Christian cross, creating a Celtic cross to encourage a newly converted Celtic population. Patrick is alleged to have founded 365 churches and today is the patron saint of Ireland.

Originally a Catholic holy day (pubs throughout Ireland were closed on St. Patrick's Day until the 1970s), the anniversary of his death on March 17 has evolved into a secular celebration of all things Irish. The day is rich with symbols, including the four-leaf clover, whose use as a lucky talisman predates Christianity most likely due to its rarity (the chances of finding one are one in ten thousand). St. Patrick came to be associated with the common three-leaf clover, or shamrock, which, according to legend, he used to explain the holy trinity to his converts as he traveled the countryside. Another enduring icon is the leprechaun, a mischievous character that has inhabited Irish mythology since pre-Celtic times.

Growing up on the outskirts of Boston, the only St. Patrick's Day tradition I knew as a child was to wear orange (if you were Protestant) or green (if you were Catholic) and failing to do so meant you got pinched at school. I've since discovered better traditions you can launch with your family on this day.

Visit the Irish Hunger Memorial in New York City. Located near Ground Zero, this lovely garden memorial in lower Manhattan is a down-to-earth tribute (constructed with imported Irish sod and stones) to the million-and-a-half people who lost their lives during the great famine of 1846–1850. From a roofless stone cottage, a winding path leads up a small hill with stunning views of the Statue of Liberty and Ellis Island. This half-acre site is a tranquil (and free) introduction to Irish history and the story of immigration to the United States.

Attend a big, no-holds-barred St. Patrick's Day parade: New York's may be the largest, but Chicago not only has a parade but dyes the Chicago River emerald green, and Boston's Southie parade is the second largest in the U.S. with a turn out of more than a half-million spectators. Among the oldest are Atlanta's parade, inaugurated in 1881, and Savannah's, in 1824.

Diana Porter and her sons make a playground for the leprechauns who might visit their garden on the eve of St. Patrick's Day. Using Popsicle sticks, copper pennies, plastic bowls, and shoeboxes, they fashion tiny swing sets, swimming pools, slides, and teeter-totters. If the leprechauns find the garden, they leave small gifts of chocolate coins for the boys to discover in the morning.

The Kelly family, who owned Brodie Mountain Ski Resort in western Massachusetts for decades (and gave their trails names like "Long Way to Tipperary"), celebrated St. Patrick's Day with an Irish Olympics Festival that included a limbo-on-skis contest, three-legged downhill races, a slush jump, and a three-mile run on green snow. If you could prove your name was Kelly, you got a free lift ticket, too.

The Swoap family children know when they have been visited by leprechauns because on St. Patrick's Day morning, when they're not looking, the milk in their cereal turns green.

While I prefer homemade decorations (I still hang the paper four-leaf clover my son made that says, "I'm lucky. I have Isabel."), sometimes I buy small seasonal kitchen items. Last year, I brought out two small plates for the kids decorated with four-leaf clovers and Isabel exclaimed, "Oh, our lucky plates!"

Norouz ❀ March 20 or 21

For thousands of years, those living in what was once Persia (today Iran and Afghanistan) have celebrated the first day of spring with Norouz (new day), a Persian New Year Festival celebrated on March 20, or whenever the vernal equinox falls. In preparation for this thirteen-day festival, modern Iranians still practice *khooneh takouni*, which means shaking the house or spring cleaning, for several weeks before the festival.

Norouz is a time for gathering with friends and relatives, the highlight being *haft sin*, a beautiful table that is set with seven symbolic foods, each beginning with the letter "s" (*sin*). Opinions differ, but some believe they represent seven creations or attributes: *sabzeh* (green sprouts representing rebirth); *samanu* (a pudding made from wheat germ to symbolize affluence); *senjed* (the dried fruit of the oleaster tree symbolizing love); *sir* (garlic for medicine); *sib* (apples for beauty); *somaq* (sumac berries to represent the color of the sunrise); and *serkeh* (vinegar for patience).

Other symbolic items are placed on the table, such as coins for wealth, goldfish in a bowl to acknowledge the sign of Pisces which the sun is leaving, an orange afloat in a bowl of water to represent the earth floating in space, a bowl of milk to nourish the children, painted eggs for fertility, or candles for enlightenment and happiness. It is customary for the head of the household to say a prayer at the moment the vernal equinox occurs.

Vernal Equinox ❀ March 20 or 21

What exactly is the vernal equinox? A review of the astronomical year might be helpful. The longest day of the year is the summer solstice, which occurs on June 21 when the sun reaches its northenmost point in relation to the equator. The winter solstice occurs six months later on December 21 or 22 and is recognized as the first day of winter in the northern hemisphere. During the solstices, the sun appears to hover for six days, seeming to rise and set at the same point in the sky. It is called the solstice from the Latin *sol stetit* (standing-still-sun). Halfway between the solstices are the two equinoxes, which occur when the sun crosses the equator from south to north, and day and night throughout the world are of equal length. The spring (vernal) equinox occurs on or about March 20 and the fall equinox, on or about September 22.

The Celts divided the year into eight cycles by including halfway points between the solstices and equinoxes. Called cross-quarter days, these occur approximately on November 1, February 1, May 1, and August 1. One way to think of it is that if the solstice and equinoxes each start a season, then the cross-quarter days mark the season's high point.

In pre-Christian times, people feared that evil spirits would descend on these dates. Would the sun return? Would the crops yield or fail? So they created events around these

ANCIENT PEOPLES built their temples and observatories around the alignment of the sun to the earth. New Grange, for example, is a megalithic site in Ireland consisting of a large circular stone structure thought to be 5,000 years old. At dawn on the winter solstice, a sliver of light peeks through a slot above the entrance and passes down an eighty-foot-long tunnel, striking the back wall of a chamber and illuminating its carvings. Another prehistoric burial chamber is Maeshowe (2,700 BC) on one of Scotland's Orkney Islands. Constructed from local flagstones and clay, it is aligned so that on the solstice, winter sunlight shines through a small aperture above the entry passage and hits the tomb wall. One of the most famous is an astronomical stone at the Peruvian citadel of Machu Picchu, known as the Intihuatona, which means "Hitching Post of the Sun." Resembling a sundial, it is a precise indicator of the dates of the equinoxes.

SPRING EQUINOX
MARCH 20 OR 21

SUMMER SOLSTICE
JUNE 21

WINTER SOLSTICE
DECEMBER 21

FALL EQUINOX
SEPTEMBER 22 OR 23

BELTANE

IMBOLC

LUGHNASAD

SAMHAIN

Easter
Passover
Tu B'Shvat
Candlemas
Groundhog Day
Valentine's Day
New Year
Hannukah
Saturnalia
Christmas
May Day
Midsummer's Eve
St. John's Day
Summer Harvest Festivals
Fall Harvest Festivals
Halloween
All Saint's Day
All Soul's Day
Day of the Dead

benchmarks. (That the church repackaged these as religious holy days is part of the fascinating story.) Today, many popular holidays are derived from these eight seasonal dates, paying indirect homage to their ancient pagan roots.

There is no shortage of rituals surrounding the coming of spring, and you'll find many in the following pages, plus a few fun ones here:

Try balancing an egg on its oblong end—legend has it that it can be done on the vernal equinox, when the days and nights are of equal length and the world is in balance.

Fix a dinner of seven foods that begin with "s" in honor of the Persian New Year (for more information about Norouz, see page 44).

Take the opportunity with your kids to bone up on the Great Sphinx, which the Egyptians built so that it would face the rising sun on the vernal equinox.

Spring Cleaning

Annual spring cleaning was not invented by your mother just to get you to scrub the floors and wash the drapes every April. With its roots in the Persian Norouz, the tradition of spring cleaning can also be traced to the ancient Jewish practice of cleansing the home in anticipation of Passover. In America, it was primarily a cold-climate tradition. Back when homes were heated with wood or coal and lit with whale oil or gas, interiors got grimy and sooty. After five months of tracking in winter slush and spring mud, it was time for a clean sweep when April rolled around.

Believe it or not, transitioning from winter to warm weather can be a family activity. The key is to make it fun:

Set aside a weekend day and seal off the borders. Make sure everyone knows his or her duties beforehand and play to the strengths of your crew. Let everyone take turns choosing the CDs for your spring-cleaning soundtrack, and be sure to have plenty of snacks and beverages on hand. Celebrate your achievement on Sunday night by going out for dinner and a movie.

Help clean up your town. Each year, an organization called Keep America Beautiful sponsors the Great American Cleanup, a three-month event from March through May to encourage communities to beautify public spaces. There are local affiliates nationwide that can recommend activities and locations in your area.

Give spring cleaning an added dimension by subtly incorporating your values into the activities. You might have everyone clean their rooms and select items for a yard sale (the proceeds of which will go to charity), or switch all household cleansers to non-toxic brands.

Make soap with your children. This springtime activity dates back to colonial times, when women would combine the leftover winter ashes with lard to make soap for the following year.

Sham al-Naseem 🌸 March 21

In Egypt, both Muslims and Christians honor the beginning of the spring season with a national holiday on March 21 that has the delightful name Sham al-Naseem (Smell of Spring). Although there is no equivalent holiday in the United States, I've always thought there should be. Some joyful traditions to smell the spring:

🌸 Plant a garden. It doesn't matter whether you have a yard, balcony, or just a window-sill that can hold a planter box. Children love to dig in the dirt, but sustaining a garden is something that is learned. Give each child a small plot, or even just a flower pot or planter, and begin with fast-growing nasturtiums, cosmos, or basil.

🌸 Create a garden journal. Collect leaves or blossoms from plantings and press and paste them into a book with their botanical names. If you're feeling ambitious, you could mark changes as the seasons change: What blooms first? How long do the flowers last? Is it native to your area? I treasure the pressed flower diary that my great aunt Aggie made as she traveled the world on a clipper ship in the late 1800s with a pistol in her petticoat, and it will be a unique heirloom for my children.

🌸 Start a bird album. Get a good bird identification guide, and mark the date and location as you spot each bird. My family has continued a bird album that was begun by my great aunt Rutty. I know that she spotted a vermilion flycatcher in Africa in 1957, a wild turkey in Buffalo, Wyoming, in 1972, and a lesser scaup duck in Southport, Connecticut, in 1973. We've added our own observations and recently expanded with a regional guide.

🌸 Make maple syrup. When I was a child, my entire school was allowed to skip classes in March to tap the maple trees in the woods, boil down the sap, then eat pancakes garnished with our own syrup. Sugar making, as it's called, was taught to early settlers by Native Americans and is unique to the United States and Eastern Canada. There's a wonderful rural tradition, still adhered to by French Canadians, to cap the maple harvest in early spring with a Sugaring-Off Party that includes music, food, and snow cones flavored with maple syrup. Today there are many sugarhouses throughout New England that welcome visitors. Just look for the galvanized buckets or plastic tubing by the roadside and watch for the steam rising from a nearby shack.

Have an annual spring picnic. When I was a teenager, we always picked a Sunday in early spring to drive to the dunes of Cape Cod. The weather was still cold and blustery, but we'd race along the beach with our dog, then take shelter among the dunes to escape the wind and enjoy our lunch.

*In the spring, at the end of the day,
you should smell like dirt.*

MARGARET ATWOOD

Passover　Late March or April

According to Judeo-Christian tradition, some three thousand years ago, the Israelites migrated to Egypt following a terrible drought in their homeland. The Jews prospered in Egypt for several centuries until a new pharaoh enslaved them to build his pyramids and other monuments. Moses tried to convince Pharaoh to free the Jews, but Pharaoh refused, and God sent the first of ten nasty plagues upon the land. Pharaoh still didn't budge. After several more plagues, he promised to free the Jews but didn't, which angered God further. The tenth and final plague was that every firstborn male from every household in Egypt would be killed. Moses warned his people, instructing them to mark their doorposts with lamb's blood so that God's angel of death would "pass over" their homes and slay only the Egyptian children. When Pharaoh finally released them, the Jews fled so quickly that they didn't wait to let their bread dough rise. Instead, it was rolled into thin wafers and placed on boards where it baked into cracker-like sheets (*matzoh*) in the desert sun. Pharaoh's army gave chase all the way to the shores of the Red Sea, which parted for the fleeing Jews, then closed and drowned the Egyptian soldiers.

If people observe only one Jewish holiday in the year, it's often Passover, which lasts eight days starting at sundown on the first full moon following the spring equinox. The first two evenings are celebrated with a highly ritualistic meal called the *seder*, which means order in Hebrew and references Moses' warning. There are many rich traditions associated with Passover:

Prior to the Passover seder, homes are swept scrupulously clean, especially of any traces of *chametz* (leavened bread) since only unleavened bread may be eaten during Passover. Sometimes the crumbs are taken outdoors with a prayer.

Prior to the meal, celebrants take turns reading from the Haggadah, a book that contains songs, legends, chants, and parables pertaining to the Passover story. A special moment during this portion of the celebration occurs when the youngest child at the table (who is able to do so) reads four questions aloud to his or her parent. The answers teach those present about the Israelites' deliverance from Egypt and slavery.

❋ Some families place three matzohs on the table. The head of the house takes the middle one, breaks it in two before dinner, and hides one half. The last item to be eaten that evening is the hidden piece, which the children hunt for during the meal. Often the child who finds it gets a prize.

❋ Set an extra wine glass at the table and keep the front door open for the prophet Elijah, who, it is believed, visits families during Passover. When the children return to the table after the matzoh hunt, Elijah's glass is less full.

❋ In some homes, guests recline at the table to remind them of ancient times when free people reclined during a meal while being served by slaves. (Jews were not permitted to adopt this posture during their enslavement in Egypt.)

❋ Although an important holiday on the Jewish calendar, many Passover seders are leavened with lightheartedness, humor, and fun. At the wonderful seders my family has attended at Mimi and Morty Schapiro's home, readings are interspersed with religious lyrics sung to the tune of popular television theme songs, such as *Gilligan's Island* and *The Brady Bunch.*

The seder itself is rich in culinary symbolism that corresponds to the Passover story. A plate in the center of the table includes six items, some of which are eaten, others ceremonial:

ZEROA (shank bone) symbolizes the sacrifice of the lambs and the blood left on the doorways. (Some vegetarians I know substitute roasted beets or dog biscuits.)

MAROR AND CHAZARET (bitter herbs, such as horseradish) signify the bitterness of slavery.

BEITZAH (hard boiled egg) symbolize spring, fertility, and life's continuity.

CHAROSET (a mixture of apples, nuts, and other fruits) represents the mortar used by Jewish slaves to build the Pharaoh's monuments.

KARPAS (fresh greens, such as parsley) are dipped in salt water to represent tears.

Four wine glasses filled with kosher wine complete each place setting, to symbolize the joy of life, and to represent God's four promises: freedom, deliverance, redemption, and release.

According to Rabbi Jeffrey Goldwasser, the Passover seder, with its emphasis on freedom, has become a magnet for contemporary rituals. Some families place an extra glass of water at the table to represent Miriam (the sister of Moses) at the well and other historic Jewish heroines. At some seders, a seventh item—an orange—is placed on each plate to honor the fact that there are now many female rabbis. Why an orange? An ortho- dox rabbi once said that a woman had as much right to be a rabbi as an orange had being on the seder plate.

Easter ✲ March or April

There's an argument to be made that both Passover and Easter evolved from ancient spring festivals that heralded the return of the sun. The word "Easter" evolved from Eostra, goddess of spring, the dawn, and fertility, who was honored every year in a secular Germanic festival bearing her name. Ancient Saxons brought the festival to the British Isles, calling it Eastre. Early Christian missionaries in the second century folded these rituals into a story about the resurrection of Christ, and Eastre eventually became Easter. It's interesting to note, too, that in non-Teutonic countries, Christians used the word Pesach (Hebrew for Passover) to commemorate Christ's resurrection: Spaniards call the holiday Pascua, Italians call it Pasqua, and so on.

With Easter falling on the first Sunday after the first full moon that follows the vernal equinox, many Easter customs can be traced back to these archaic rites of spring. The egg, for example, is an ancient symbol of the origins of life and the earth's fertility. Egyptians, Romans, and Greeks all dyed eggs and ate them at spring festivals. During Eostra, eggs were exchanged as a gesture of friendship and romance, much as valentine cards are exchanged today.

Omne vivum ex ovo. (All life comes from an egg.)
LATIN PROVERB

As missionaries and crusaders spread Christianity across Europe, the egg became a symbol of the resurrection. At medieval church services, eggs were tossed among choir members while hymns were sung. In nineteenth-century Russia, elaborately decorated eggs (egg painting is still a Russian specialty, particularly in the Ukraine) were carried to church in a basket on Easter and exchanged with the words "Christ is risen." At the end of the service, worshippers would tap their eggs together, much as we clink glasses for a toast. In France, children once rolled eggs down a slope in remembrance of the stone being rolled away from Christ's tomb, the object being to keep the eggs from breaking. In the early 1800s, First Lady Dolley Madison introduced an Easter egg roll in Washington, D.C., during her husband's presidency.

As silly as it is to think of a rabbit bringing eggs, the Easter bunny endures as an Easter icon. One theory speculates that Eostra's favorite animal was the bird, but one day in a fit of anger the goddess made the hare her earthly symbol. Another theory suggests that the story originated in the 1500s from a Germanic children's tale about a hare leaving eggs. Over the centuries, the Easter hare has figured almost as prominently as St. Nicholas, and it is believed that on Easter Eve she sneaks into the homes of well-behaved German children while they sleep and leaves colored eggs for them. German immigrants brought the Easter bunny to America where the tradition took off after the Civil War.

On Good Friday throughout the British Isles, hot cross buns are still served for breakfast or afternoon tea. This likely originated with the Saxons who made sacramental cakes in honor of Eostra. Wily monks, recognizing the pastry's appeal, decorated them with a cross and developed a story about St. Clare of Assisi, an abbess who was visited by a pope. According to legend, the pope asked her to bless the buns they were about to eat. She made the sign of the cross in the air, and this emblem magically appeared on the buns. Bakers have decorated these yeasty buns with crosses of white icing for centuries.

In Guatemala, as in many Latin American countries, Easter festivities begin with Semana Santa (Holy Week) and conclude with Pascua (Easter). In many cities, including the colonial city of Antigua, there is a magnificent processional through the streets on Good Friday. Shopkeepers wash and paint the walls of the buildings along the route, and the streets are covered with a carpet of flower petals.

On Easter Sunday in Florence, Scoppio del Carro (explosion of the cart) is enacted. Dating back to 1099, an ox-drawn cart is pulled through the city to the cathedral of Santa Maria del Fiore in the Piazza del Duomo. The oxen are unyoked, and a rocket resembling a white dove is ignited by the Archbishop of Florence. This launches a spectacular fireworks display, and legend holds that if the pyrotechnics go off smoothly, the coming year will be prosperous for Florentines. And no Easter menu would be complete without *la columba*, a confectionary bread baked in the shape of a dove.

Easter is the most important holiday on the Russian Orthodox calendar. The Easter feast might include roast ham or suckling pig, *pashka* (cheesecake), *kulich* (saffron bread), and desserts such as *mazurka* (rich cookies) and *babki* (sweet cakes), not to mention an elaborately carved or molded butter lamb (symbolizing Jesus as the Lamb of God). Week-long feasting means that hosts continually replenish their tables while guests travel from home to home, enjoying the hospitality.

For many Armenians, eggs dyed red to represent the blood of Christ are a vivid childhood memory. A traditional Easter meal includes trout (the fish being a Christian symbol since Roman times), rice pilaf, dried fruits, nuts, and hard-boiled eggs.

Since the early 1900s in Mexico, and among many Mexican-American families, children have enjoyed decorating *cascarones* (eggshells). First, the eggs are drained and the shells saved. (The hole where the yolk escapes can be up to a half inch in diameter.) Once the eggshells are cleaned and dried, they are decorated with vivid paints and glitter. When the decoration has set, the eggs are filled with confetti. The rim of the hole is edged with glue then covered with a square of tissue paper. The fragile cascarones must be protected until the big day. On Easter morning, first the children hunt for eggs left by *la coneja de Pascua* (the Easter bunny), then have a ball running around and cracking their cascarones on each other's heads.

For many people, Easter is a secular holiday associated with fun traditions, not the least of which is the egg hunt:

In the Carver family, the Easter bunny always leaves a note, indicating which plastic colored eggs belong to which person (including adults). Several of the eggs contain clues as to where each Easter basket is hidden.

In the Swoap family, a different colored ribbon is tied to each child's bedpost; by morning each ribbon has wended its way through the house—under furniture, around toys—to one of the treasured Easter baskets. (Of course, the ribbons intersect, especially when you have four kids.) Everyone hunts for eggs that are the same color as their ribbons.

Dick Bisson saves his spare change, and every year when Easter rolls around he fills dozens of plastic eggs with the coins, placing a $20 bill in one egg. After the eggs are hidden all over his yard he invites his grandchildren over for an egg hunt.

Every year David Aplin's grandmother served Eggs-in-a-Nest for dessert: the nest was a baked white meringue, the eggs were three scoops of pastel-colored sherbet, and it was topped with homemade raspberry sauce.

Judy Cummings always asks guests to bring a hand-decorated egg to her Easter dinner. The egg can be real, plastic, or papier mâché—the only requirement is that it be decorated by the person who brings it. The eggs form the table's centerpiece. After dinner, guests find a number under their plates that determines the order in which they get to select an egg.

One of the loveliest egg hunts I've seen is hosted every year by a friend of my father's who invites everyone she knows with young children to her seaside farm (last year there were more than forty kids). The children are grouped by age; when the adults say "Go!" the older children run into the woods, where the eggs are harder to find, while the little ones head to a field, where foil-wrapped eggs are cupped in easily visible straw nests. For each age group, there is one golden egg, which is the hardest of all to find. The child who discovers it is given a silver dollar.

Oh, give us pleasure in the flowers today;
And give us not to think so far away
As the uncertain harvest; keep us here
All simply in the springing of the year.

ROBERT FROST

April Fools' Day 🌿 April 1

There are loads of foolish traditions, but the granddaddy of them all is April Fools' Day, or All Fools' Day as it is sometimes known. Possibly evolving from the pagan festival of Saturnalia and its subsequent incarnation Festus Fatuorum (Feast of Fools), April Fools' Day has no readily identifiable cultural origin. The most popular theory is that it came from sixteenth-century France, when, in 1582, Charles IX decreed that the country would switch from the Julian to the Gregorian calendar. Among other changes, this meant that New Year's Day moved from April 1 to January 1. With no modes of mass communication, word of the new calendar spread slowly. After several years, small pockets of the population either hadn't heard about or refused to accept the new dates and continued to celebrate the New Year on April 1. The rest of the populace looked on these dissenters as backward rubes and referred to them as April Fools. Such people were often sent on fools' errands or made the butt of elaborate practical jokes.

Two famous April Fools' pranks:

🌿 On April 1, 1957, the distinguished BBC news program *Panorama* featured a segment on Swiss farmers who were enjoying a bumper spaghetti crop thanks to the combination of a mild winter and the elimination of the spaghetti weevil. The report was accompanied by footage of farmers harvesting spaghetti from among tree branches. Viewers were fooled, to the point that many called to inquire as to whether a spaghetti tree would grow in the English climate. The BBC replied that one should "place a sprig of spaghetti in a tin of tomato sauce and hope for the best."

🌿 On April 1, 1996, the Taco Bell Corporation issued a press release that it had bought the Liberty Bell from the federal government and the historic symbol should now be referred to as the Taco Liberty Bell. The National Historic Park in Philadelphia, where the Liberty Bell is housed, received thousands of angry calls, and Taco Bell issued a second release a few hours later revealing the joke. Not to be outdone, White House press secretary Mike McCurry, when asked about the sale, announced that the Lincoln Memorial had been auctioned off and would now be known as the Ford Lincoln Mercury Memorial.

In Scotland, April Fools' Day is forty-eight hours long with the second day devoted to pranks involving the human posterior. Called Taily Day, it may be the origin of the "Kick Me" sign.

When my friend Eric Kerns was a kid, breakfast on April 1 always featured scrambled eggs dyed a lurid color, and his school lunch would contain a strange component like a bag of uncooked pasta or a lime Jell-O sandwich. To this day his mother calls him at dawn from her home in California with some hoax: "We won the lottery!" "Your sister is moving to Sri Lanka!" Creative pranks can be a great tradition because children love to be complicit and secretive. Just be sure to steer your family in a direction that's playful and funny; you want to have everyone in stitches . . . but not literally.

Daylight Savings Time

A system for setting the clock ahead one hour for half the year was envisioned by Benjamin Franklin in 1794, but never seriously considered until 1907, when London builder William Willett noted the widespread movement away from an agrarian lifestyle, where people arose at sunrise. In his pamphlet *The Waste of Daylight* he wrote: "Everyone appreciates the long, light evenings. Everyone laments their shrinkage as Autumn approaches, and nearly everyone has given utterance to a regret that the clear bright light of an early morning, during Spring and Summer months, is so seldom seen or used."

Daylight Savings Time (DST) was adopted in Germany and Austria in 1916, and by 1918 most other European countries had followed suit. The United States left the decision to observe DST up to each individual state and county until 1966. In 2007, allegedly in response to America's energy woes, DST was extended by three weeks in the spring and one week in the fall. DST now starts on the second Sunday of March and ends on the first Sunday in November. Prior to 2007, Daylight Savings ended a week before Election Day (first Tuesday in November), and there was a vocal lobby pushing for an extension as a way to encourage greater voter participation. With the current schedule, DST ends after Election Day in some years, enabling researchers to gauge its effect on voter turnout.

A timely ritual, which is more widely practiced than I had imagined, involves testing the batteries in your household smoke alarms on the days you change your clocks. Little kids love being lifted up to the ceiling to press the test button and get a kick out of the piercing shriek.

Take Our Daughters and Sons to Work Day ✤ April

In 2003, the Ms. Foundation expanded the Take Our Daughters to Work Day to include boys, on the fourth Thursday in April. I'm fortunate that my job has no restrictions regarding visiting children, so both Trainer and Isabel come often to the museum where Joe and I work. But that's not the case everywhere, so be sure and take advantage of this opportunity to share your professional life with your kids.

May Day ✿ May 1

May Day is one of the few pagan holidays that the church never polished up and appropriated. Almost three hundred years before the birth of Christ, Romans welcomed the season with a bacchanal in honor of Flora, the goddess of spring and flowers. Called Floralia, the festival was six days' worth of singing, dancing, and stomping to awaken the earth.

As the Roman Empire spread into Britain and Western Europe, Julius Caesar reported that the Druids (in what is now the United Kingdom) had a similar spring rite, called Beltane, named for the Celtic sun god Bel. Believing that the fairy spirits were close at hand on Beltane, on the eve of May peasants and villagers lit huge bonfires, called Bel-fires, to protect their crops and livestock from sorcery. There was singing and dancing to arouse the earth's fertility, and even as late as the eighteenth century it was customary to offer a human sacrifice, for which men drew straws, while villagers drove livestock through the flames for purification.

New brides and childless women danced beside the blazing Bel-fires, couples went into the forests in search of privacy (these trysts were called greenwood marriages) and a maypole was cut down in the woods and raised on the village green to "bring on the May." The Celts always used a living tree for their maypoles, believing them to be sacred. The woods, after all, were where the gods and goddess dwelt, and each tree had its own spirit. The maypole was decorated with wildflowers and long ribbons. Celebrants each clasped a ribbon, then joined hands and danced around the pole in hopes that its spirit would make them and their lands fruitful, interweaving their ribbons with every step.

> When you knock on wood for luck, you are preserving a two-thousand-year-old Celtic tradition by asking the tree spirit to bring you luck.

As Europeans shifted from hunting to more agrarian societies and as the Celts felt the influence of Rome, the rituals associated with Beltane were in turn influenced by the Roman festival of Floralia. Thus Beltane came to be known as May Day and expanded to include the arrival of spring. In medieval England, May Day was one of the biggest celebrations in the year, starting before sunrise, when revelers went into the fields to gather flowers, and ending with singing, music and dancing. There was a Queen of the May (from which our modern-day beauty pageants probably evolved), a Green Man, and a Lord of Misrule, sometimes accompanied by the King of Unreason and the Abbot of Disobedience.

Although the Church never altered May Day for its own purposes, neither did it approve of the occasion. In 1555 Calvinist rulers in Scotland outlawed the festival, despite ensuing riots. Pious Puritans destroyed maypoles throughout England, calling them stinking idols. With growing pressure from the Church, Parliament outlawed May Day in 1644,

ON MAY 1, 1886, 350,000 laborers staged strikes across the United States and Canada in support of an eight-hour working day. The date was probably selected because, unlike Easter, May Day was the one holiday in the year many workers spent with their families, but didn't spend in church. Six men were killed in the Chicago strikes, which sent shockwaves across the world and led to the Haymarket Riot. In 1889 the Working Men's Association proclaimed May 1 to be International Workers' Day, also known as Labor Day. In 1894, U.S. politicians voted to set aside a day in September as Labor Day. In 1947, May 1 was designated as Loyalty Day, and the holiday flourished during the late 1940s and 1950s (the McCarthy era and Cold War years), but since the Vietnam War it has become a historical footnote. However, elsewhere in the world, May Day remains an important date on the Socialist calendar.

but the move was so unpopular that when Charles II was restored to the throne in 1660 he reinstated the holiday, and Samuel Pepys described the beginning of Charles' reign as "the happiest May Day that hath been many a year in England."

By the time the Victorians got hold of the festival in the 1800s, the freewheeling abandon of May Day had gone underground and it was transformed into a benign children's festival. In the United States, the holiday had all but disappeared by the 1970s, and the date was co-opted by labor groups who emphasized its historic political significance of May 1.

I remember leaving May Day baskets for neighbors when I was a girl, and many people have told me that they did this also as late as the 1960s. My mother-in-law fondly recalls working with her mother for weeks beforehand, baking and making construction-paper baskets which they'd fill with cakes and blooming spirea and leave anonymously on friends' doorsteps. This tradition stems from an ancient belief that the baskets could ward off evil spirits. With my kids, I've left May Day baskets for elderly friends at our local nursing home and often thought this would be a lovely tradition to revive in one's neighborhood.

The word May is a perfumed word.
It is an illuminated initial.
It means youth, love, song, and
all that is beautiful in life.
HENRY WADSWORTH LONGFELLOW,
JOURNAL ENTRY FOR MAY 1, 1861

Cinco de Mayo ❧ May 5

Contrary to popular assumption, Cinco de Mayo does not commemorate Mexico's independence from Spain (which is observed on September 16). Rather, it celebrates the David-versus-Goliath-like victory of the Mexicans over Napoleon's French army at the Battle of Puebla in 1862. It is a story of triumph over oppression when four-thousand Mexicans defeated eight-thousand French soldiers bent on conquest while the United States was preoccupied with the Civil War. A Mexican holiday that honors Hispanic culture as much as St Patrick's Day toasts Irish pride, Cinco de Mayo is celebrated more widely in the United States than in Mexico, where it is largely a regional holiday restricted to the state of Puebla.

Many American cities host spectacular Cinco de Mayo parades that feature prominent musicians and dance troupes. The largest Cinco de Mayo event in the world is held in Los Angeles, California, where more than 600,000 people celebrate with music and food. Festivals in San Francisco, San Jose, Minneapolis, and Denver draw hundreds of thousands of participants. Chandler, Arizona, has gone to the dogs with their Cinco de Mayo celebration by featuring chihuahua parades, chihuahua races, and a chihuahua pageant culminating in the coronation of a Cinco de Mayo chihuahua king and queen.

Celebrate the richness and variety of Mexican culture at home by setting aside part of the day or evening for the following:

❧ Learn how to make authentic enchiladas, tamales, menudo, and carnitas.

❧ Make a papier mâché piñata with your kids, and invite their friends over for a party that concludes with the demise of the piñata.

※ Teach your children the dance of La Cucaracha (the cockroach), also known as the Mexican Hat Dance. (It's a great way to get your boys to dance.)

Kentucky Derby Day ※ May

Held the first Saturday in May since 1875, the Kentucky Derby is the first jewel in the Triple Crown of American thoroughbred horse racing and the oldest continuously-held sporting event in the United States. Also called "The Run for the Roses" for the lush blanket of 554 roses that is draped over the winner, the Kentucky Derby also signals the official beginning of spring in Louisville. The adult beverage of choice is the mint julep, a frosty libation that can be made child friendly by serving straight sugar syrup and soda water in a frosted silver cup with a sprig of mint. A traditional meal might include burgoo, a thick stew of beef, pork, chicken, and vegetables that's been popular in the South since before the Civil War. In Louisville, the parties are as ramped up as Mardi Gras in New Orleans, and no gathering is complete without crooning "My Old Kentucky Home." On Derby Day, the grandstand at Churchill Downs becomes a sea of colorful hats. So if you're hosting a Derby day party, encourage your guests (of all ages) to wear them—the more outlandish the better—and award prizes for the most creative efforts.

Mother's Day ※ May

Since the 1500s, English churchgoers would worship at the nearest parish or "daughter" church, however, it was considered important to visit your region's anchor church or cathedral, the so-called "mother" church, at least once a year, and this annual pilgrimage was usually made in the middle of Lent. Concurrently, since the Middle Ages, it was also customary for children who were apprenticed to artisans or worked as servants in wealthy or noble households to live away from their families. The children were permitted perhaps onc visit homc per year, also during Lent. As this journey frequently coincided with the annual trip to the mother church, the tradition became known as going a-mothering.

> *I shall never forget my mother, for it was she who planted and nurtured the first seeds of good within me. She opened my heart to the impressions of nature; she awakened my understanding and extended my horizon, and her percepts exerted an everlasting influence upon the course of my life.*
>
> IMMANUEL KANT

Gathering flowers along the way, the children brought their mothers bouquets and sometimes small gifts. On the Sunday of their return, usually the fourth Sunday of Lent, the family would attend a church service and enjoy a day of feasting when the Lenten restrictions were lifted temporarily. This day became known as Mothering Sunday.

Mothering Day is celebrated on the fourth Sunday of Lent in England, and Mother's Day is celebrated on the second Sunday of May in the United States. American Mother's Day became official in 1870, when Boston suffragette Julia Ward Howe (author of the *Battle Hymn of the Republic*), issued a Mother's Day proclamation in the wake of the Civil and Franco-Prussian wars, calling on mothers to mobilize for peace and disarmament. A woman named Anna M. Jarvis dedicated her life to getting President Woodrow Wilson to recognize it as a national holiday, and in 1914, he did so. Because Ms. Jarvis' mother liked carnations, all mothers at her church in West Virginia received carnations on that Sunday. Funny how some traditions are born; carnations as a Mother's Day tradition—white for a deceased mother, pink or red for a living one—still endures.

In Mexico and other Latin American countries, Dia de las Madres became a national holiday on May 10 when an influential newspaper reporter in the 1920s proclaimed that to be the day and it stuck. Mothers are serenaded with "Las Mananitas" and often given roses.

While breakfast in bed or an elegant restaurant brunch are lovely acknowledgments, a few more ideas include:

※ Spend the day with the ladies in your life: daughters, mothers, in-laws, and sisters.

※ Give an annual manicure or massage to a special mother or group of mothers in your life. Or splurge on a whole day at a spa.

※ Over the course of the year, pay attention to your mom's new interests or activities, and give her a thoughtful gift that shows you've noticed. This is *not* the day for a new vacuum cleaner . . . unless of course she *really* loves to vacuum.

※ Send cards or notes to other mothers you admire. The first time I became a mother, I received cards and calls from several female friends welcoming me into the sisterhood.

※ On my first Mother's Day, my mother-in-law Mary Jane gave me an antique sterling napkin ring that was inscribed "Mom, 1998." She gave one to Joe on Father's Day, inscribed "Dad, 1998." To Isabel and Trainer, she also gave napkin rings inscribed with their names and the year of their births. We use them almost every night.

And what about stepmothers? Every year, my kids bring home marvelous handmade Mother's Day cards and gifts they've made at school. Until speaking with a stepmother recently, it never occurred to me to wonder what other children do when they have a mother *and* a stepmother. Make two cards? Leave one out? How confusing for them if they don't have a sensitive teacher. And how must a stepmother feel on this day? How would you feel watching a child who lives with you leave for the weekend, claimed by her real mother? United States census statistics show that approximately 1,300 new stepfamilies are formed every day, and it's predicted that by 2010, there will be more stepfamilies in the U. S. than any other type of family.

Some families observe Stepmother's Day on the Saturday before Mother's Day, when kids can acknowledge their stepmothers, without upsetting their moms. Another growing trend is sending cards to *all* the mothers we love—not just our own. In 1998, President Clinton's Mother's Day proclamation was amended to "On Mother's Day, let us honor all mothers—biological or adoptive, foster or stepmother—whose unconditional love has strengthened us."

Vesak ✿ May

Also known as Buddha Purinama, Wesak, and Visakha Puja, Vesak marks the most important events for the Buddhist community: the Buddha's birth, enlightenment, and final entrance into Nirvana. Held the last two weeks of May, all three occasions are celebrated on the day of the full moon of the fourth lunar month. This is a time to honor the life of the Buddha and his teachings of peace by performing acts of charity and gratitude. The lotus is a symbol of the Buddha and, temples are often adorned with folded paper lotus blossoms during Vesak. In 2006, the citizens of Singapore made 2,148,725 paper lotuses to symbolize of their desire for global religious harmony.

Memorial Day ✿ May

Originally called Decoration Day, Memorial Day is traditionally a remembrance day for those who have died in military service. Its actual origin is the subject of some debate; over two dozen cities and towns claim to have originated Memorial Day, but Waterloo, New York, was officially declared the birthplace of Memorial Day by President Lyndon Johnson in May 1966.

As early as the 1860s, communities began organizing events to honor the Civil War dead. The first official Memorial Day was proclaimed on May 5, 1868, by General John Logan, Commander of the Grand Army of the Republic. It was first observed on May 30, 1868, when volunteers placed flowers on the graves of both Union and Confederate soldiers at Arlington National Cemetery.

By 1890, May 30 had been recognized by the northern states as Memorial Day. The southern states continued to honor the Confederate dead on a separate day until after

World War I, when the occasion changed from exclusively a Civil War commemoration to one that included all American soldiers killed in battle. Since 1971, the holiday has been celebrated in almost every state on the last Monday in May, which was mandated by Congress with the National Holiday Act of 1971 to ensure a three-day weekend for federal holidays.

In 1918, inspired by the poem *In Flanders Fields*, Moina Michael penned *We Shall Keep the Faith*, which includes the lines:

We cherish, too, the poppy red
That grows on fields where valor led;
It seems to signal to the skies
That blood of heroes never dies,
But lends a lustre to the red
Of the flower that blooms above the dead
In Flanders Fields.

Moina Michael conceived the idea of wearing red poppies on Memorial Day and was the first to wear and sell them to her friends and co-workers to raise money for servicemen in need. On Memorial Day in 1922, the Veterans of Foreign Wars became the first organization to sell red paper poppies nationally. In 1948, a postage stamp with Moina Michaels' likeness was issued to honor her part in the creation of this tradition.

Solemn observance of Memorial Day has altered somewhat over the years, and some feel that the attachment to a three-day weekend in 1971 has distracted from the true meaning of the day. In a Memorial Day proclamation in 2002, the Veterans of Foreign Wars stated: "Changing the date merely to create three-day weekends has undermined the very meaning of the day. No doubt, this has contributed greatly to the general public's nonchalant observance of Memorial Day." Many Americans do think of Memorial Day as the official beginning of summer, signaling a time for backyard barbeques, fun at the beach, and lazy days at home, but many communities across the United States also continue to pay homage to those who have fallen in battle with parades, church services, and flag-draped cemeteries.

For many Americans, showing support and respect for the sacrifices and losses sustained by our military families is especially significant today. There are many ways your family can do this:

※ Spend a Saturday putting together care packages to send to troops overseas, including handmade cards from your kids that express support for those who will receive them. There is abundant information available on the Internet regarding specific items that are needed and how to pack and send them.

※ Deliver gift baskets to your local veterans' hospital with your children. Having the opportunity to thank some of our servicemen and women in person for their bravery is something neither you nor your kids will soon forget.

※ If a family in your community has a loved one serving overseas or lost a family member in the line of duty, make a point of remembering them on this day. A gift card for groceries, clothing, or toys, or a big bag of coffee beans and home-baked muffins with a handmade card from your kids is a simple way to show solidarity and support.

Acts of Remembrance

Throughout the world, there are poignant rituals associated with the remembrance of loved ones. Among these is the well-known Jewish tradition of leaving a stone at a gravesite rather than flowers, a reminder that, at the end, we all return to the earth. After Paulette Wein's mother died, a friend brought her a stone that had naturally assumed the shape of a heart, which Paulette placed on her mother's headstone.

According to Syrian custom, when someone dies he must be buried within twenty-four hours. The mourning period, however, continues for forty days. During that time, friends bring food to the bereaved household. On the fortieth day, there is a celebration called Arbaeen (which means fortieth).

Among the rich, shadowy traditions of rural Jamaica there is a ritual called Nine Night. Essentially a wake, friends and family of the deceased gather every night for nine nights after the death (or just on the ninth night if other evenings are omitted) to share food and songs. Why is it called Nine Night instead of Ninth Night? Because, as poet Everton Sylvester told me, Jamaicans don't pronounce "th."

> . . . the sense of smell, almost more than any other, has the power to recall memories and it's a pity that we use it so little.
>
> RACHEL CARSON

In China, Quing Ming is a day to honor departed ancestors and typically falls in the first half of May. Ancestor worship is an important ritual practice in China and to Chinese all over the world, and on April 5 people sweep the graves, bring fresh flowers, and make offerings of burnt joss paper, wine, and food. Kites are flown on this day, and a particular kind of sticky rice wrapped in a leaf is specially prepared.

Jewish families sit *shivah* (Hebrew for seven), usually in the home of the deceased, for seven days following the funeral. Guests comfort and look after the family and serve as hosts to other visitors. It is appropriate to bring food, especially round foods which symbolize the cyclical nature of life, and to help with the dishes and general cleanup afterwards.

In central Africa, a tree is planted on a deceased person's grave, because a tree symbolizes the soul with roots that travel down to the afterworld. Spiritual connections between trees and gravesites are also found in Haiti, as well as African American communities in the South, especially Mississippi and Texas.

Some customs lend themselves to being observed within a specific time frame, while others can be observed on Memorial Day or at any time throughout the year:

* My friend Sally Purcell always plants flowers at her late husband's grave on the Friday before Memorial Day, not because he served in a war, but because all her children tend to be home for the long weekend. Three generations visit Grampie, and while the adults plant flowers the kids play in the beautiful cemetery. Later, the family gathers for a lunch.

* A friend's sister passed away during childhood and was buried near the family's summer cottage on Lake Michigan, her favorite place. Every summer, her siblings collect shells from the shore and place them on her headstone.

When I visit my mother's grave and find small, smooth beach pebbles on her headstone, I know some of her friends have stopped by to visit, too. When I was growing up, my mother, grandmother, and I spent every Thursday afternoon at the public library. After my mother passed away, I set up a modest memorial fund at my local library from which

IN ADDITION to the more formal remembrances, there are also highly personal moments that, in their own ways, become private memorials. The sense of taste or smell can transport us like laser beams to the past and connect us powerfully and profoundly to our lost loved ones.

My grandmother lived with us, and her specialty was making brownies for her grandchildren. Today, whenever I make her recipe for my own children, I tell Trainer and Isabel about how their great grandmother made brownies for me whenever I needed comforting, mixing the batter in her big earthenware bowl and serving them on a green Fiesta plate, and how she felt sort of squishy and smelled of baby powder when she hugged me. The combination of a warm oven, fragrant chocolate, and the act of recreating her recipe while recounting stories about her not only brings her vibrantly back to me but also makes her come alive for my children. (I recently made a batch of brownies from a mix, and then a batch from her recipe, and asked the family to vote. Of course, hers won hands down.)

My mother wasn't much for wearing makeup, but one Christmas her mother-in-law sent her a box of perfume samples from Paris. On lazy afternoons I'd enjoy looking at them in their fancy cardboard box on her dresser, each one tucked snugly into the silk liners, smelling them, touching them, and enjoying the feel of their petite weight. She wore perfume on rare occasions, but I still remember the fragrance of one in particular when I'd hugged her in her brown taffeta party dress. After she died, I found one of the samples in her bathroom—forty years and five houses later! It was almost empty, but she'd saved it. I keep it in my bathroom and open it up every once in a while and take a whiff (there isn't even enough left to dab behind my ears) whenever I need a mom fix.

several books each year are purchased that are age appropriate for her grandchildren. A bookplate is inserted that reads "In Memory of Grandmother Ellie." For me, borrowing these books keeps her memory alive while my children receive a legacy of reading and literature. I've noticed that several other families have done the same in remembrance of their relatives.

During the eighteenth and nineteenth centuries, headstones and other grave markers were frequently inscribed with the deceased's name, dates of birth and death, and an epitaph. Some people prepared their own inscriptions, while others, perhaps less confident in their writing skills, hired a monument poet. Not surprisingly, many epitaphs are sentimental tributes, however, some are funny or delightfully cryptic. Shorter and pithier than an obituary, a well-crafted epitaph often gives a spirited sense of the person long after they are gone. My father and I put one on my mother's headstone that was an inside joke and made everyone in my family chuckle (and would have delighted my mother), but my publishers thought it was a bit too R-rated to be reproduced here.

Here lies a poor woman who was always tired,
She lived in a house where help wasn't hired.

PEMBROKE, MASSACHUSETTS

Here lies
Ezekial Aikle
Age 102
The Good
Die Young

EAST DALHOUSIE,
NOVA SCOTIA

Julia Adams
Died of thin shoes.

APRIL 17TH 1839 AGED 19 YEARS

The pretty flowers
that blossom here
Are fertilized by
Gertie Greer
Now Ain't
That Too Bad

CHICAGO, ILLINOIS

Died April 3, 1882
Aged 34 years,
6 months,
28 days
Murdered by
a traitor
and a coward
whose name is not wor-
thy to appear here.

JESSE JAMES,
KEARNY, MISSOURI

Last Day of School ❧ June

Finishing a year of school is a big achievement, and many parents have created small rituals that make their kids feel special, and have become traditions over the years:

❧ With your children, invite their teacher(s) over for brunch, lunch, or dinner at the end of the year. Let the kids help plan the menu and prepare the meal.

❧ Make a sign for the front door: "Congratulations Mary! You're Going to Be a 5th Grader!" or whatever is appropriate. Jeannie Aplin did this a few years ago for her girls and didn't realize she'd created a tradition until one year she realized her daughters had come to expect it, asking in the morning, "What will my sign be tonight?" The signs hang in their rooms for months afterwards.

❧ Get together with your children's friends and their parents for an end-of-the-year potluck cookout.

❧ With the kids, make a list of what each person wants to do over the summer. Put the list up on a bulletin board or refrigerator and check off items as they are accomplished.

❧ Thank the school that has done so much for your children. Offer to buy library books, art supplies, musical instruments, or sports equipment for the coming year.

Father's Day ❧ June

Ironically, the inspiration for Father's Day came from a Mother's Day sermon. In 1909, Sonora Smart Dodd of Spokane, Washington, heard a minister extolling the virtues of motherhood and decided that her father, Henry Jackson Smart, a farmer and Civil War veteran (who had raised Sonora and her five young siblings after his wife's death in childbirth), deserved public recognition as well. So on June 19, 1910 (Henry's birthday), she declared the first Father's Day celebration in Spokane. In 1924, President Calvin Coolidge publicly supported a national Father's Day, and eventually, in 1966, President Lyndon Johnson proclaimed this day a national holiday. Six years later, President Richard Nixon signed into law the designation of the third Sunday in June as Father's Day. Today, Father's Day is the fourth largest card-sending occasion in the United States.

Don't be fooled—many men profess to not care about the day, but they secretly love the attention. Ideas for the fathers in your life:

❧ Are there any dads who don't love to eat? Wake yours up with his favorite breakfast. Ask your kids to assist, or if they're old enough let them prepare the whole meal.

❧ Many fathers are so busy it's hard for them to take the time to plan extra activities. Acquire tickets to a favorite sporting event or concert for Dad and a few of his male friends. Give them an annual "Dads' Night Out" and make sure they don't have to deal with any of the details.

❧ If the father in your life has a particular hobby, such as carpentry or gardening, dedicate the day to helping him launch or complete a project. If he needs specialized tools to accomplish the job, don't buy them for him; give him a hardware store gift card instead. Choosing from among the different makes and models is half the fun.

Many fathers would like to have a personal touch in their office, but are afraid that pinning up dog-eared construction paper drawings will make their workspace look unprofessional. Solve this by having several pieces of your child's artwork framed professionally. You'll be surprised how impressive a finger painting looks under glass.

Ask your children to write a poem for their father and then illustrate the page.

One of the more creative ideas I've heard for Father's Day comes from the Kerns family. A few years ago, Eric received a pair of apple tree saplings from his two young daughters. The trees are varietals that can cross-pollinate and eventually bear fruit. Last year one of the trees produced three small apples that he and the girls ceremoniously ate together one autumn afternoon.

Summer

*Deep summer is when laziness
finds respectability.*

SAM KEEN

❄ Welcoming Summer ❄

School's out, the lazy hazy days are here, the calendar's full of vacation and weekend plans, and it's hot, hot, hot. The joys of summer are many, and simple traditions abound in this sunny season:

❄ Usher in the Summer season with an old fashioned ballgame. Do it like we did as kids—no uniforms, all ages and abilities, and a parent at the pitcher's mound. Follow the game with a potluck cookout.

❄ Serve gloriously seasonal meals all summer long—corn on the cob, heirloom tomatoes, pesto, and peach cobbler. We eat corn only in August, and boy, do we eat a lot of it.

❄ Explore someplace new, for the weekend, a day, or an afternoon. Visit a water park. Go kayak fishing or horseback riding. See a travelling exhibition at a museum or historic home. Find a new pleasure the whole family can participate in and enjoy.

❄ Tackle an outdoor home project. Even fairly young kids can help put a fresh coat of paint on a fence, kitchen chair, or shed.

The Summer Solstice ❄ June 21

Although the solstice is known as midsummer, many believe summer begins on the longest day of the year. In pagan societies, it was thought the sun god was at the pinnacle of his power on the solstice, and immense torches were lit in his honor. Bonfires were kindled with the bones of dead animals (bone fires) and dancers would encircle the blaze while the more daring men leaped over the flames. Fairies and other spirits were thought to be most active on the solstice, especially on the eve. Indeed, Shakespeare's play *A Midsummer Night's Dream* features a host of enchanted happenings. The solstice is still a magical night, especially in northern Europe, and at Stonehenge in England, where thousands gather every year to witness the sun aligning with the monolithic standing stones on this day.

Independence Day ✸ July 4

This thoroughly American holiday commemorates the date when the thirteen colonies broke from British rule and signed the Declaration of Independence, establishing the philosophical foundation for a new nation. Time-honored traditions include Fourth of July parades, picnics, and concerts culminating in spectacular fireworks displays, and here are a few more ideas:

✳ Start the morning with a "patriotic" breakfast of waffles topped with red and blue berries and a dab of whipped cream. If you're hosting a family picnic, serve a red-white-and-blue cake (decorated with white icing, strawberries or raspberries, and blueberries).

✳ Is there no parade where you live? Jeannie and Richard Besser of suburban Atlanta invite their neighbors to join an annual street procession of kids, dogs, and decorated floats (wagons, bikes, and tricycles draped with crepe paper steamers). The march concludes at someone's house (preferably with a pool) for a cookout.

✳ At the Williamstown Theater Festival, the Declaration of Independence is read aloud on July Fourth. It may sound corny, but it's thrilling. The measured cadences and ringing phrases were authored by some of the greatest writers in the English language (Thomas Jefferson, among others) and were intended to be declared out loud. Start this stirring tradition at your annual picnic—you'll be glad you did.

✳ If rain or fog keeps you indoors (my editor lives in the San Francisco Bay Area where it's often too foggy to see fireworks), rent a copy of *1776*, the movie based on the Tony-award-winning Broadway musical. The second Continental Congress comes alive in this hilarious reconstruction of historical events; I can still hear my cousin Bradley singing every verse of "But, Mr. Adams" in his golden tenor.

✳ Eric Kerns fondly recalls visiting the temporary roadside fireworks stands in California with his dad and looking over the huge variety of fountains, pinwheels, ground-bloom flowers, and bottle rockets. After dark, they gathered with neighbors in a nearby cul-de-sac to ignite their purchases. Sadly, you can no longer legally buy or launch fireworks in many states, including California, so be sure to check local laws before creating a Big Bang.

Baseball Season ✳ April through September

You're probably wondering why I've placed baseball in the Summer section when opening day is in April. Well, despite its springtime launch, Americans have traditionally associated baseball with summertime, even affectionately referring to their favorite ballplayers as "the boys of summer." Indeed, it's such a popular pastime that you could write a book on the tradition and meaning of baseball in our culture, and many have. The Library of

Congress contains 4,176 works about basketball and 5,424 books on football, which seem like a lot, until you compare them with the whopping 9,626 books dedicated to baseball. This makes sense; baseball and America grew up together. The history of the game tells a broader tale of the history of immigration, industrialization, integration, and the commercialization of athletics. For many Americans, baseball is not only our national pastime, it is part of our national psyche, and even our language, with words such as home run, grand slam, and struck out (have I covered all the bases?) entering the lexicon of daily vocabulary.

Politicians have attached themselves to America's pastime as well. President William Howard Taft was the first commander in chief to throw out the first ball at a game between the Washington Senators and the Philadelphia Athletics on April 14, 1910. Every President since, with the exception of Jimmy Carter, has opened at least one baseball season during his tenure with this ritual.

There are thousands of rituals, traditions, and superstitions associated with various leagues, teams, players, and cities, from *perogi* races in Pittsburgh to Anaheim's rally monkey to the Yankees' dancing grounds crew. But many baseball rituals are personal, shared by family or friends. Eric Kerns was driving past a small cemetery in Massachusetts just a few days after the Red Sox broke the curse and won the World Series in 2004 for the first time in eighty-six years. He was both amazed and charmed to see that World Champion Red Sox pennants had been stuck into the ground or attached to headstones all over the cemetery (no doubt by die-hard fans).

Other personal rituals I'll throw out:

❋ Invite friends over for an opening day party to watch the season opener.

✳ Take your family to a major league game. Eat hotdogs, let the kids get sticky with ice cream and Cracker Jacks, and experience this time-honored summer pleasure. Or make it a special parent-child occasion; Steve Swoap, father of four, treats one kid a year to a Boston outing for a Red Sox game.

✳ Check out local minor league teams (you've always wanted a Toledo Mudhens cap anyway, right?) Our local club, the North Adams Steeplecats, has a huge following. It's just a few dollars to get in (so if the kids only sit through three innings it's not a big deal) and a fun way to spend a summer evening with friends.

✳ Computing baseball statistics can sharpen your kids' arithmetic skills without them realizing it. A few months spent figuring ERAs, batting averages, and on-base percentages, and they'll be primed for math in the fall.

Summer Vacation ✷

A few years ago, a friend of mine ruminated about the iconic family vacation, and the remarkable fact that every spring so many parents plan one, forgetting that the previous summer they vowed never to take one again. Even the word "vacation" may be a misnomer for parents with young kids, but as children get a bit older, vacationing with them can be great fun and the basis for wonderful memories.

Summer camping trips are at the top of many people's lists of favorite vacations. When I asked Jack Wadsworth about his family traditions, his eyes lit up as he described the canoe expeditions he took every year for five years with his wife, their four children, and two other families (totaling six adults and seven kids) to northern Saskatchewan, which they got to by floatplanes, with canoes lashed to pontoons. It was a rigorous two-week adventure that covered several hundred miles and ranged from Canada's Fond du Lac and Back Rivers, a treacherous route that dipped into the polar seas just above the Arctic Circle, to Alaska's Noatak River, where around the campfire they read aloud from the journal of David Thompson who explored the Noatak for the Hudson Bay Company in 1796.

Over the course of five summers, the families learned about themselves and about qualities that are important, such as the fact that in a pinch (negotiating rapids on a daily basis), a person's mental attitude is more important than physical strength or canoeing abilities. Jack Wadsworth grew up with a love for canoeing and inspired that love in his kids. He told me that, although they complained at the time about the lack of creature comforts, his now grown children look back on those trips as some of their fondest childhood memories. Today, several of them have re-launched the tradition with Jack and his grandchildren. (And Jack's wife Susy leaned over with a smile to tell me she's just as happy to have moved on to less strenuous outings.)

If you can't muster an overnight canoe trip, a hike and picnic are a good way to experience the outdoors. Audrey Werner's mother found an interesting meadow a short distance from her home. After checking with the farmer who owned the land, she took her kids there several times each summer for picnics. The farmer had pushed large "glacial deposits" (boulders) into the center of the field, which the kids dubbed Tree Point Rock. Some cedars along a fence, which they named the Little Green Forest, provided cover for bathroom breaks. The cow path and a distant hill also had names. Audrey and her siblings ran around chasing each other, making up stories, and avoiding the cow pies.

Others wrote to me about small family moments that, while not traditions per se, were repeated often enough that they came to represent the spirit of a tradition.

✳ When Diana Walczak and Jeff Kleiser leave for vacations, they load the car with their three kids, a nanny, and a drooling malamute. When I asked Diana about their particular rituals, she responded immediately: "Packed and ready in our car, we never, ever leave the driveway of our house before a family trip until each and every person lets out a high decibel 'Yee Hah!!!!!' Then we can go!"

✳ When her daughters' best friends take a trip, Jeannie Aplin prepares a small bag for the girls to give their friends on the eve of departure. After the girls decorate the bags with stickers and drawings, Jeannie fills them with healthy snacks, interesting magazines, and a clever time-occupying game. (The family reciprocates, though they give the Aplin girls junk food, cheesy teen magazines, and cheap toys that inevitably get more mileage.)

✳ One family maps out their route, assigning designated Whine Zones where the kids can be as obnoxious as they want. Mom makes it clear that bellyaching is not allowed in the No-Whine Zones and attaches a suitable penalty, such as denying a turn in a coveted seat for the rest of the trip.

✳ My college roommate's father insisted on reading aloud historic roadside markers on every trip. The kids would groan every time he pulled over, but darned if my roommate didn't know a lot of quirky American history. Those markers note interesting tidbits, like the one on the Mohawk Trail near my home that describes shunpiking. In the 1800s, travelers often took an alternate route to avoid paying tolls along the turnpikes, thus, shunning the turnpikes. Today, the term has come to mean traveling leisurely on a back road.

※ When we take a trip in our minivan, it's possible for Joe and me to be listening to a radio program, Trainer to be watching a DVD, and Isabel to be listening to a CD. This is liberating in a way, but thinking back to my own childhood, it was on the road that we sang songs, played word and alphabet games, and learned geography with the license plate game. So we make it a point to actually be together, both acoustically and mindfully, at least some of the drive.

※ When I was growing up, we moved a lot. New to each community, my parents and I didn't know many people, so on weekends we'd take off to historic and natural sites within a three-hour drive. I learned a lot on these trips, and years later I have distinct memories of how close the three of us felt on those adventures, and the treats that accompanied the travel, such as sleeping all together in one motel room and staying up late to go out for dinner. (In those days I defined a good restaurant as one that didn't have gum stuck under the table.)

Once in a Lifetime Trip ※

In America, a trip across the country is a rite of passage, and there are many ways to do it. When my friend Lincoln Russell drove cross-country with his teenage son Morgan, Morgan agreed to the trip as long as his dad abided by one rule: no museums and no vegetables. They had a blast. Carole Schultz set out with her two sons determined to bypass the obvious monuments and focus only on the quirky ones, such as visiting the nation's largest ball of twine in Cawker City, Kansas. The fun began the previous winter as they mapped out their route long before they left home.

Another friend, who lives near the Appalachian Trail in Massachusetts, intends to hike a portion of the Trail from Massachusetts to Virginia (where his parents live) when his kids are old enough, just so they have the satisfaction of saying they walked to Grandma and Grandpa's house. Personally, I am inspired by the idea of cross-country skiing the longitude of Vermont with my family. It can be done, through a combination of logging roads, hiking trails, and golf courses that cover the length of the state.

You might also take your children to the land of their ancestors. Maybe invite your sister or cousin to come along with her kids. I've floated the idea to my cousins of taking a bike trip together one summer along the southern coast of England to see where our grandmother's family hails from. And when Isabel gets older, we hope to return to Guatemala to explore the ancient Mayan culture and see the land of her birth.

Repeat Trips ❋

A number of people also told me about one-time excursions that evolved into annual events they wouldn't dream of missing.

❋ Every year in late summer or early autumn, Sarah Purcell and her closest girlfriends psyche themselves up for winter (they live in upstate New York where it's easy to feel snowbound) by traveling to Lake Placid for a weekend of hiking, relaxing, and eating well. Every spring, the same group thaws out in Manhattan for a weekend of shopping, eating out, and catching a Broadway show. Another friend spends Memorial Day weekend with her college roommates; they take turns choosing the destination, which has ranged from Charleston to Miami Beach. Many hotels and resorts have noticed this growing trend and offer special rates for women vacationing together.

FOR MANY OF US, a cherished memory is the end of summer trip, when dad takes off the last week of August, and the season culminates with Labor Day weekend. Pardon my rant, but the blissful end of summer is in danger of being sabotaged by youth sports programs. Even elementary school kids are called home for football and soccer practice in mid-August. One of my nephews, a fifth-grader, chose to miss a soccer game over Labor Day, asking his mother to explain to the coach about their family's decades-old Labor Day weekend tradition of staying at a mountain camp that's been in the family for three generations. The result? He was benched for the season, despite being a good player—a tacit punishment for missing that one game. Similarly, my nine-year-old nephew begged his father to cut short a fishing vacation on Cape Cod because he feared that if he missed football practice and a weigh-in during the third week in August he'd fall behind or be penalized. Nine . . . years . . . old.

It used to be that if you wanted to play sports, you grabbed a ball and found kids in the neighborhood. You didn't need a uniform, or fancy equipment, or an organization; if kids were on vacation, your team was a little smaller. Now, no one's playing in the backyard, and kids are on organized teams with demanding schedules, all too often run by coaches who care less about playing the game and having fun, and more about winning and getting ahead. It's part of a trend of burdening kids with an overabundance of lessons, sports, and enrichment programs that leave them breathless, all in an effort to prepare them for the future, which, let's face it, is a thinly veiled effort to give them a leg up so they can beat out the competition and get into a good college. I have nothing against good colleges (indeed, I went to one), but I don't think the life of a nine-year-old should be centered on building a resume. Holding onto traditions are a way to shift the center of gravity away from this mania, and bring the focus back to the point of summer when you're a kid: having fun.

✳ Robin Brickman has spent one weekend a year with her siblings and mother—no spouses, no kids—for many years. For convenience, it's often scheduled to precede or follow another family event, such as a wedding or bar mitzvah. (No need to go far afield; after a wedding in San Francisco, visit the Napa Valley; after a bar mitzvah in Boston, head out to Martha's Vineyard.) Although her mother is no longer able to travel due to failing health, Robin continues to make these annual trips with her siblings, all of whom are grateful the tradition was started while their mother was still able to participate. Another option is to gather at one sibling's home and send that person's children and spouse packing for the weekend. What's important is to reconnect, free of distractions.

✳ The weekend after Labor Day, my mother's family gathers for three days at a resort on Lake Winnisquam in New Hampshire. The place isn't fancy (in fact, it's falling apart), but it's at water's edge, and because we book our stay for the off season, the rates are even lower than they would be in the summer. We all pitch in on meals and cook together and bring canoes, kayaks, fishing gear, and bikes. Even those on a limited budget can afford the weekend.

✳ Although we don't adhere to a particular schedule, most years my cousins get together for a weekend or day trip. Sometimes these trips are loosely organized around a theme, such as skiing with our kids or exploring some aspect of our shared heritage. We are descended from the Coffin family, among the early settlers of Nantucket, and several summers ago we spent a day wandering through old cemeteries searching for Coffins. A highlight of the trip was photographing each other in front of the boardinghouse where three of our mothers had worked summers as waitresses in the 1940s. We'd grown up hearing the story of how my mother waited on a guy who was the spitting image of movie star Gene Kelly. When she summoned the nerve to ask him if he was, in fact, Mr. Kelly, he said no, but that he was often mistaken for the movie star. As he left the restaurant, she watched him walk away, trying to decide whether to believe him. Sensing her gaze, he turned and did a dance step right out of *Singing in the Rain.* It was such a hoot to visit fifty years later where this scene, which has been folded into family legend, took place.

✳ One family gathers all three generations—forty-plus people—for a family ski/skate Olympiad weekend in Vermont once a year in memory of grandparents who were very athletic and competitive.

✳ If actual travel isn't an option, try a no-cost version of virtual travel dreamt up by my friend Audrey's mother. Audrey and her three siblings would pile onto their mom's lap as she sat in a large wicker rocking chair and together they'd "go to Montreal." They'd imagine the destination, then sing and discuss the sights they were rocking past.

✳ Consider inviting a niece or nephew to stay with you for a week. You'll really get to know them when they're away from their parents, and lasting bonds can form between cousins. When I was eight, my aunt Phoebe invited me to spend a week with her family in Rhode Island. We'd been living in Indiana for a few years, and I hadn't seen her, my uncle, or my four cousins in quite a while. Sitting at breakfast the first morning, I turned to Aunt Phoebe, nodded towards my uncle, and said, "What did you say your husband's name was again?"

Every other summer, various members of my family gather at the HF Bar Ranch in Saddlestring, Wyoming; in 2007 there were nineteen of us. The tradition was started in the 1950s by my great aunt, and after a twenty-five-year hiatus her daughter Nancy Duble revived it in 1997. Each family has a cabin along a creek, and mornings and evenings are spent horseback riding in the foothills of the Big Horn Mountains. On the final night, we gather on the covered porch for an awards ceremony. The kids meet in secret beforehand to decide which award to give to each family member and make the corresponding drawings. The summer I was pregnant, I won the Best Napper award, which featured a sketch of me prone with feet sticking out from under a blanket. Another year, when I finally found the nerve to gallop on the last day, I received the Late Loper award. Our son got the award for Littlest Cowboy, Biggest Dude. I have them framed in a guest room, and they are among my favorite drawings.

Back Home ✻

When summer travels are over, there are creative ways to preserve your memories and reflect on your experiences:

✻ Hang a map of the United States or the world in your child's room, and after each trip find the place you've just visited and mark it with a sticker.

✻ Jeff Kleiser and Diana Walczak presented us with a great thank-you gift after our families spent a vacation together: the story of our trip told by their three kids, with every page illustrated with a photograph or drawing highlighting our experiences, annotated with quirky text. It read like a storyboard (Jeff and Diana are film animators), and was requested by our son as his bedtime book for months. Diana told me they always make a book after a trip, and send copies to grandparents and others who might be interested.

❋ Celebrating a Birth ❋

In ancient days, birth was a perilous time. Considering that only 50 percent of children lived to the age of five in the year 1800, it's not surprising that many customs and superstitions greeted an infant's arrival. Even today, a newborn is one of the most fragile, wondrous creatures imaginable, and throughout the world we still usher in birth with fanfare. While some superstitions are extinct (the belief, for example, that a hare crossing the road in front of a pregnant woman foreshadowed a baby with a harelip) others, such as the fear that setting up a crib before birth is bad luck, are still practiced in many places.

> *What is this talked-of mystery of birth,*
> *But being mounted bareback on the earth?*
>
> ROBERT FROST

In the Beginning ❋

Throughout the world, new life is welcomed in different ways:

❋ In China, for the first month after giving birth, a mother is not supposed to touch water or get out of bed. She cannot wash or be exposed to the wind, as Chinese-born artist Jennifer Ma explained; she is expected to stay in her room and nurse her baby for thirty days. Called Sitting Month, this custom is common all over China. When the month is over, the new mother's family hosts a party so she can receive guests and present the baby, and hard-boiled eggs, dyed red for luck, are given to the visitors. It's customary for every child born to get this treatment, but it's particularly important for the first grand-child of a family.

✳ In Scotland's Orkney Islands, parents *weet the heid o' the bairn* (wet the head of the baby) to bring the child luck. Then a celebratory bottle of whiskey is brought out for the baby's father and other men. Elsewhere in the British Isles, this custom is called "wet the baby's head," and is celebrated by male friends treating the new father to a few rounds at the local pub.

✳ The Ga people of Ghana wait a week after a baby is born, then carry the infant outside to see the sun. There the child is named, and several drops of water and liquor are placed in the infant's mouth to signify the difference between truth and lies. The hope is that the child will grow up to taste right from wrong. (Even Ghanaians living abroad do this, although salt is sometimes substituted for liquor.)

✳ In parts of rural Jamaica, islanders bury the placenta and umbilical cord with a sap-ling three days after a baby's birth. The tree becomes the baby's tree, sometimes known as a navel-string tree.

✳ In Cambridge, Massachusetts, shortly after his birth in 1910, Charles Addison Ditmas was placed in the case of an eighteenth-century grandfather clock that had been in the Ditmas family for four generations. It was simply something the family did and continues to do. Mr. Ditmas grew up to become the devoted clock keeper of Harvard University's two hundred clocks for sixty years, until his death at the age of ninety-one in 2001.

✳ In many parts of Africa, planting a tree is part of a child's naming ceremony, with a tree chosen that best represents the characteristics the parents wish for in their child.

May you be as strong as the oak, yet flexible as the birch;
may you stand tall as the redwood, live gracefully as the willow;
and may you always bear fruit all your days on this earth.
NATIVE AMERICAN PRAYER

✳ There are beautiful ways to honor the birth of a child into your family and your community. An adaptation of the African tree-planting custom (described above) is to give new parents a Colorado blue spruce seedling (a tree noted for its longevity) in a monogrammed baby cup.

✳ When our son was born, we were given a crab apple tree to plant in our yard. For Isabel, we planted a peach tree. The kids love watching their trees grow. You can highlight your child's tree on each birthday by decorating it with ornaments or strings of lights, hanging a birdfeeder or a swing from the branches, or (if it's a flowering tree) cutting blossoms from it and setting an arrangement of them on the dining room table. Particularly nice is selecting a tree that blooms in the month of your child's birth. According to the Talmud, in Biblical times a cypress (symbolizing gentleness and sweetness) was planted for a girl, a cedar (for strength and stature) for a boy. When the daughter or son grew up and married, a *chuppah* (a wedding canopy that symbolizes the Jewish home) was fashioned from the branches of her or his birth tree.

When her twins were born, an Australian friend who had settled in California planted two native trees to Australia in her Berkeley garden to symbolize the fact that her growing family was taking root in American soil.

Preserving Memories ✳

After our son was born, my best friend called me at the hospital and said, "Tell me your birth story!" I relived every detail, and over the next few weeks was amazed as girlfriends told me their own stories. You'll also want to share the details of the experience with the star of the show, so, while still in the moment, preserve the event for your newborn:

✳ Write your baby a letter within a week of his birth, while you still have the emotional intensity that you won't remember six months later. Or start a collection of letters, composing one on each birthday. Another variation is to write in a journal every day for the first year of your child's life, and give it to her when she's grown.

✳ Capture the story of your baby's birth on video. If there's time, you and your spouse might take a few minutes before going to the hospital to interview each other. Following the birth, take the time to record the story of how your child was born and what the day was like for you. You'll be glad you did.

✳ When we adopted Isabel, I fretted that I wouldn't have a birth story for her. But after we returned with her from Guatemala City, I made a book that captured the story of her birth into our family—our flight to Guatemala City, her first moments in our arms, Trainer giving Isabel her first bottle, and walking through the streets of Antigua with her. My favorite passage in the book was written by Trainer, who was five at the time: "When I first touched your skin, it made my belly shake." Mine too.

✳ Save your newborn's baby blanket or home-coming outfit. A few days before I was due to have Trainer, my mother-in-law gave me a baby blanket with satin trim and rosebuds that my husband Joe had been swaddled in on *his* trip home from the hospital. When we brought Isabel home, she was wrapped in the same blanket. If your parents (like mine) weren't sentimental about saving such things, choose a blanket or outfit for your child to wear home with an eye towards passing it down.

Ceremonies ✺

In the Christian tradition, a christening is a ceremony that welcomes a child into his or her parents' church. It can take place anytime, though in some cultures it is done sooner rather than later. (In the Dominican Republic, for example, infants are baptized within the first cycle of the moon after birth.) During the ceremony, it is appropriate to incorporate personal gestures into the centuries-old liturgy. I know of an Episcopalian minister in Norman, Oklahoma, for example, who asks if anyone in the congregation wishes to whisper something in the infant's ear; he then carries the baby to those who raise their hands. Each participant is expected to reiterate that thought to the child over the years as he or she grows. At St. John's Church in Williamstown, Massachusetts, the priest asks all the children in the congregation to gather around the baby for the christening.

✳ In the Jewish faith, a lovely tradition is the naming of the baby after a relative. This is done at the *bris* (covenant), when a baby boy is named and circumcised. Among the

Ashkenazim, it is customary to name the child after a deceased person while the Sephardim name a son or daughter after someone living. The ceremony occurs when a boy is eight days old; for girls, the ceremony (called *brit habat*) is not always performed on the eighth day, though in recent years it has become more standard.

✳ When Jonquil Wolfson and her husband had their daughter, they washed her feet, and brought her under the same chuppah that was used at their wedding. They also explained why they chose her name Talia, which means the dew of God; Israel is a desert country and for six months out of the year, dew was all that kept the crops alive in biblical times. A less literal translation is water of life.

✳ In South Korea, on a child's hundredth day of life (*baek-il*), families thank the gods for taking care of the baby, pray for wealth, longevity, and good fortune, and serve an elaborate banquet to ensure the success of these requests. This tradition dates back to a time when infant mortality was high, and having a child survive one hundred days was cause for celebration. With today's much lower mortality rates, it has become simply an occasion to congratulate a baby's family; far more important has become the celebration of a first birthday, or *tol*.

✳ In Iceland, a child isn't named until the christening, which is usually held two to three months after the birth. It's not uncommon to name children after their grandparents, and most Icelanders are aware of what their names mean; many are associated with nature or animals. Our friend Magnus, for example, knows that his name means magnificent one, and that his brother's name, Sigurbjorn, means one who conquers a bear. Magnus's son Benni, who is eight, loves that his last name means tougher than a bear. As in many Muslim and Native American cultures, there is the hope that a child will take on the characteristics of his or her name.

Godparents ❋

In the traditions of the Catholic and Anglican churches, godparents were originally responsible for a baby's welfare and spiritual development should anything happen to the parents; today, the godparents' role has come to mean many things. Some parents interpret the role literally, and choose someone from their church. Others consider it a secular obligation, picking a friend or relative who will take a particular interest in a child's life. I never had godparents growing up and was envious of those who did as they seemed to have a special relationship. But what if godparents don't live up to their duties or do not stay in touch with the godchild? I know children who have been disappointed when a sibling has an involved godparent and theirs is a no-show. My sister-in-law Sarah found herself thinking about a family friend, "He would have made a great godfather." So she made him a "Fairy Godfather" to her youngest child.

Unusual Baby Gifts ❋

While most baby gifts are appreciated, some are particularly memorable:

❋ When Sarah Purcell brought home her new baby in October, her sister-in-law left a glowing pumpkin on the kitchen counter with Welcome Willie carved into it. For a Christmas baby, leave a tiny tree (suitable for replanting), or for twins born in the summertime, a pair of blueberry bushes on the porch, with a note that you'll return to plant them.

✳ If you have a party to celebrate your baby's christening or birth, in lieu of conventional baby gifts, ask each guest to bring a small item that can be collected and stored in a box that your son or daughter will open on his or her twenty-first birthday. The items could connect him to his beginnings (a leaf from the woods behind his home, a copy of a newspaper with his birth date, or a photograph of the neighborhood) or it could be something that would contribute to her life (a poem or song you've written, a favorite book, or a complete CD set of the Beatles).

✳ When a Muslim baby is born, the parents customarily make a donation to a charity to thank God for the gift of their new child. In India, Hindu parents shave their infant's head on the seventh day after birth (if the baby has enough hair, otherwise they wait), measure the weight of the hair, and give that weight in silver to a charity. Soon after Katherine Myers' daughter was born, little Tenley underwent surgery at Boston Children's Hospital. Today, when Katherine and her husband Jerry receive a birth announcement from friends, they honor the birth and remember the exceptional care Children's Hospital gave their daughter by sending a donation in the baby's name. A British friend, whose infant daughter was hospitalized at Christmastime in 1986, still brings champagne on Christmas Eve to the nurses on that ward, and a cuddly toy for the sick child in the bed where his daughter stayed.

✳ On their first night home, take the parents a hot meal. We received this from thoughtful friends and, boy, did we appreciate it. The two women who delivered dinner didn't just make a casserole: they brought wine, salad, chicken smothered in apricots and orange sauce, rice . . . and there was enough for two days! I was so grateful. Snow shoveling, lawnmowing, and car washing also make great gifts.

✳ When your best friend or sister has a baby, take the bridesmaid dress that you wore at her wedding (which you've never worn since, right?) and use the fabric to make a baby quilt. If you're feeling ambitious, ask other bridesmaids to donate their dresses and make a quilt for the parents, too. Have a sewing bee with the bridesmaids, and turn it into a group project.

✳ I come from a long line of coastal Yankees, and when my son was born, my father made a beautiful wooden cradle in the shape of a small boat (with seagulls for the rockers). Inside he placed a small brass plaque:

For James Trainer Thompson
Born March 3, 1998
Crafted by his grandfather
H. Potter Trainer, Jr.

Each time it has been used since—from Isabel to the babies of friends and relatives— my father has added an additional plaque to the bow, inscribed with the name and birth date of each child who has been lulled to sleep in this cradle of love.

✳ When my sister-in-law Sarah was ready to have children she worried that it was taking too long to get pregnant. Her wise girlfriend Wendy (who had had three kids) told her, "You need to have faith," and sent her a pair of baby booties. Sarah was instructed to keep the booties tucked away in a drawer and, whenever she felt anxious, to take them out and hold them, smell them, gently caress the fabric, and feel the baby-ness of them. Sarah got pregnant, and those booties next went to work on friends who adopted or gave birth to babies in Boston, New York, Wyoming, Vermont, and Houston. The chain got so long, as friends gave them to other friends who gave them to friends, that Sarah lost track of them, though she isn't surprised to hear that they've kept on working. Just a simple pair of white infant socks, they encouraged a powerful chain of faith, hope, and support.

❋ Happy Birthdays ❋

Centuries ago, only kings, saints, and heroes were allowed to celebrate birthdays. Over time, however, parties for children became more common, probably as a way to protect little ones from the wicked spirits and fairies that were thought to cause mischief and possess a child's soul on the anniversary of their birth. Other children were invited to the party to serve as decoys and befuddle the spirits as to whose birthday it was. Music and dancing also helped fend off the fairies, and gifts (considered a positive force) were given to frighten away the malevolent forces. Even the birthday cake with its candles (a protective circle of fire) offered a measure of protection, and cards were delivered several days before the birthday, never after, to keep marauding spirits at bay. (Interestingly, to this day, we apologize if we send a belated birthday card.) We are left with the essence of these beliefs, with birthdays being among the most anticipated—or dreaded—events in people's lives.

Most people I spoke to had strong opinions about birthdays. Many go to great lengths to make a birthday person feel special from start to finish. If you grew up with a big to-do made of your birthday, you may want this treatment your entire life. (This can be a problem with spouses who may not necessarily remember the day, let alone the importance of it. You might as well make it clear early in the relationship that this day means a lot to you.) And for those of you who never felt sufficiently fêted on your birthday, it's never too late!

To many people, starting the day by having "Happy Birthday" sung to them—even after they are grown up and no matter where they are in the world—is important. "In my family," said one mother, "kids who have left home get a midnight phone call and are serenaded . . . no matter their age." Wrote another: "My mom is still the first person to call me on my birthday, playing the piano and singing away. I've got to say, writing about this particular tradition brings tears to my eyes! I can't imagine a birthday without a serenade from my mother."

Recording the Years ✺

Many people wrote to me about the little birthday rituals that eventually grow into annual traditions. Here are a few you can adapt for your family:

✺ Every year, mark your child's height on a door molding of a closet, bedroom, or the kitchen.

✺ Take a photo of your child in the same location on each birthday. You can display these in a row (or hide them and surprise someone on his fiftieth birthday) so you can see the changes over time at a glance. One woman took a photo of her one-year-old daughter in her mother's purple Emilio Pucci dress from the 1960s. She did the same for every birthday thereafter (using similar backdrops). As her daughter grew into the dress, the photographs became an amusing montage.

✺ It's also fun to recreate old photos of parents, grandparents, or siblings utilizing similar clothing and backgrounds.

※ On your child's first birthday, buy a tablecloth that can be used year after year. Have him leave a hand print along the cloth's edge (and every year thereafter), thereby creating a handmade palm-print border. Ask party guests to sign the cloth or add little drawings with a permanent marker.

Other Birthday Rituals ❀

※ Some families honor a person's half birthday, which falls six months after the actual birth date, and they celebrate by doing everything half way. The idea's a little half-baked, but kids will love it. Serve half a cake with half the appropriate number of candles, pour the drinks half full, and serve half a plate of food. Sing half the birthday song, and give a gift that's half of something.

※ My friend Paulette gets a call from her twin brother every year at 10:05 P.M., the precise time she was born which, incidentally, is forty minutes after he was born (and he, of course, never fails to remind her who's older).

※ For her twins, Diane Porter makes a layer cake, cuts it in half, frosts it, and gives one half to each child. (Inside the layers she tucks little surprises, Mardi Gras King Cake-style that they find when they cut into the cake.) I also know a woman who, when her twins grew up and moved away from home, bought a birthday card, cut it in half, and sent each twin half of the card on their birthday.

※ Consider celebrating a golden birthday (when your age matches your date of birth, for example you turn twenty-one on October 21) in a special way. The party might have an astronomy theme, with sparkler candles on a star-shaped cake and a telescope set up for your guests to enjoy the celestial phenomena in the night sky.

✳ Give the birthday child a crown to wear all day, and let her choose all manner of things: the menu for the day's meals, who sits where in the car, and which songs are played on the radio. Plus, the birthday child doesn't have to do chores.

✳ In one family, everyone dabs butter on the nose of the birthday child, and it's become something of a challenge to be the first one to sneak up from behind and butter the honoree's nose. A shiny nose, which smoothes the way for the coming year, foretells good fortune. (When these kids grew up and got engaged, they ruthlessly judged whether a sibling's fiancé would fit into the family by how he or she responded to the buttering up.)

✳ While driving with my three-year-old son one day, we were listening to NPR when they announced it was naturalist John James Audubon's birthday. When we got home, I pulled out a book on Audubon's bird paintings and later that evening we toasted him at dinner. A month later, my son and I were talking about remembering someone who had died, and Trainer made a reference to "the bird man." I didn't understand him at first, and he said, exasperated, "You know, the artist." Similarly, Laurie Werner, the daughter of classical

BIRTH FLOWERS

JANUARY carnation or snowdrop
FEBRUARY violet or primrose
MARCH jonquil or violet
APRIL sweet pea or daisy
MAY lily of the valley
JUNE rose or honeysuckle
JULY delphinium or larkspur
AUGUST gladiola or poppy
SEPTEMBER aster or morning glory
OCTOBER marigold
NOVEMBER chrysanthemum
DECEMBER holly

musicians, always knew the date of Beethoven's birthday because they toasted him and played his music during dinner every December 16. You needn't make a big fuss—it's just an incidental way to share a little history. On Mozart's birthday, you could rent *Amadeus*, listen to his music during dinner, or ask everyone to bring one fact about Mozart to the table. You can do this with Einstein, Dr. Seuss, Picasso . . . the list goes on.

The Party ✸

When planning a party, it's good to keep in mind that the spirit of the party is more important than any fabricated grandeur. I'll never forget a party that well-intentioned friends threw for their four-year-old daughter soon after arriving in the Berkshires from a large city. Being in the fashion industry, they were used to extravagant special effects and loved to host big parties. (Halloween at their grand Victorian house was legendary.) On this perfect June afternoon, their vast lawn was covered with an enormous bouncy house in the shape of a giraffe, a makeshift corral with pony rides, and a magician performing tricks. The guests were enjoying (and clucking about) the upscale carnival atmosphere, but the birthday girl was nowhere to be found. I spied her later on the porch, cowering between the pant legs of her nanny. It's an image that has stuck with me.

Don't get me wrong they are terrific parents, and carry the same gusto and think-big mentality to other family activities, be it camping, making a video for a class assignment, or driving cross-country in a motor home. But, for a young child's birthday party, more is not necessarily better. Nor is it what your kids will take away from an event. Do you remember the presents you received as a child or how lavish the parties were? I don't. I remember who came and what we did and how much fun it was trying to win at musical chairs.

※ If grandparents and relatives live far away, you might consider separate friends and family parties. The grandparents, aunts, uncles, and cousins gather on the actual birth date for dinner and cake, while the friends party can take place on the weekend. Jeannie Aplin has a Christmas baby and solved the problem by having the family dinner on her daughter Annalie's actual birth date and the friends party later. Jonathan Secor takes it a step further, preferring to celebrate the birthday month. He and his kids will have a party at home on the actual day, go to New York and visit grandparents on a weekend near the date, and then see other relatives on another weekend during the month. Birthday lights and decorations are kept up the entire month.

※ For older kids, you might consider a creative or unusual theme and involve them in the planning and decorating. One family's son chose an ancient Greece theme and wrote his guests' names in Greek on the invitation. They created a game that featured drawings of the Olympian gods hanging on the wall and cards containing descriptions of each of the deities' feats. The children had to match the name and description with the picture, and whoever got the most right won a prize. Afterward, the kids played charades with the descriptions.

Milestone Birthdays ※

※ My father has always written me a letter on important birthdays—twenty-one, thirty, forty—in which he tells me stories about me through the years, about our family, and what he loves about me. I treasure each one and look forward to them.

✳ As one man's fiftieth birthday approached, his wife asked each of his friends and relatives to do something special on one of the fifty days leading up to the big day: one person sent fifty jokes, another made a $49 donation to a favorite charity, someone else left forty-eight balloons in his backyard, and so on.

✳ When Eyal Rimmon turned fifty, his wife rented out the local cinema, and when he and she (arriving late) took their seats in the dark theater and the film began to roll, he was startled to see that it was a movie about his life. Moments later everyone in the theater—filled with a hundred friends—erupted and yelled "Surprise!"

Your Own Birthday ✳

You know best how you'd like to celebrate your birthday, and it can be different from year to year since, after all, turning thirty-two is quite different from turning fifty-four.

✳ My girlfriend Jeannie always takes the day off if her birthday falls on a weekday. With three daughters and a husband, she has a busy life, but she reserves that 9 to 3 slot on March 23 for herself and plans a day that satisfies what she desires at that particular point in her life—whether it's going to a Pilates class followed by lunch with a friend (as she did when her girls were young) or going into the city to the New York Botanical Garden and, at the end of the day, buying an orchid plant for herself. Her choices are always deeply personal and satisfying, and she doesn't feel the need to spend a lot of money to make herself happy. She's always been that way. I remember calling her on her twenty-second birthday (she was living in the Berkshires while I was in Manhattan) and finding her on her porch on that rare warm afternoon, sitting in a rocker, sipping coffee, listening to

Joni Mitchell, and reading a seed catalog as she contemplated her summer garden. It was exactly what she wanted to do that day.

✳ Another woman I know organizes an overnight trip with her best friends every year for her birthday. The first year they stayed at a hotel, went hiking, then painted ceramic plates (sounds juvenile but was fun, she reported), had dinner, and went out dancing. The following year they rented a beach house for the weekend, and another year they chartered a sailboat. When men come into a room, she notes, they take up a lot of oxygen, and every once in a while its nice to be with just girlfriends in a place uninterrupted by children, chores, making meals, or the myriad details that comprise our lives.

IN CHINA, symbolic foods are served on special occasions to invoke specific wishes, and birthdays are no exception. Throughout China, and among Chinese Americans, it is customary to serve "long life" noodles on birthdays to ensure a long life. If you're serious about the custom, or if an important birthday is being celebrated, the bowl is filled with one long continuous noodle to symbolize longevity.

Making Your Child Feel Special ✳

People told me of small gestures they revive year after year, or perhaps every few years, to make their kids feel special on their birthdays. Some of my favorites:

✳ In one household, little wrapped gifts appear throughout the day—a present on the child's chair at lunch or in the bathroom by his toothbrush. He's told that a birthday elf has come. A scavenger hunt later ensues to find the next gift and to look, in vain, for the elf.

✳ When kids seize on a topic (be it trains, trucks, ballet, or dinosaurs) they can't seem to get enough of it. One mother gives her kids a birthday certificate dedicating the month to their favorite subject. Dinosaur Month, for example, might include a trip to a natural history museum, renting *Ice Age*, hunting for dinosaur books at the library, and making dinosaur cookies.

✳ Former Montessori teacher Gertrud Mueller Olson gives her children two envelopes on each birthday, one marked New Privilege and the other New Responsibility. She found that her kids enjoyed the new responsibilities every bit as much as the privileges, because the responsibilities marked their growth and maturity. Privileges might include a later bedtime, a larger allowance, an extra video night (or being able to watch PG-13 videos), while responsibilities could include feeding the dog, setting the table, or emptying the dishwasher. You could even tie them together: the privilege of having a new puppy entails the responsibility of feeding and walking it.

✳ A screenwriter received a birthday letter from her father every year until he died when she was fourteen. It's one of her cherished memories. "When I was two," Chris Levinson said, "he could peg how I was going to be at age thirty."

✳ In one family, everyone takes turns during the birthday dinner telling the birthday honoree what they appreciate most about her. My son's second-grade teacher did something similar: on each child's birthday, the other kids in the class each wrote a page about the birthday person and included a drawing. These were stapled together into a book that

IN MANY PARTS OF THE WORLD, a first birthday is highly significant. To South Koreans, a child's first birthday, called a *tol* (see page 100), is enormously important. The child wears a *hanbok* (traditionally a brightly colored silk outfit complete with booties, hat, and a purse for both boys and girls) and is seated before a heavily decorated table with embroidered silk screens as a backdrop. The table is set with symbolic foods (steamed rice cakes for a pure spirit and longevity, rice cakes coated with red bean powder to ward off disease, sticky rice cakes to make the child tenacious) as well as objects (a bow and arrow to symbolize a warrior, a knife for a good cook, a needle and thread for longevity). The child picks the objects and foods that appeal to him, thereby predicting the life he will lead. Our nephew Gus chose a ruler and the jujube (a type of fruit), signs that he'll be talented with his hands and have many descendants.

the birthday child (blushing furiously but secretly loving it) read to the class while sitting on a specially designated birthday chair.

☀ If the climate where you live favors this idea, consider planting flowers either that bloom around the time of your child's birthday or have meaning to your child. As they get older, children can help care for their flower beds, and you can decorate the table with the blooms. Born in May, I always associate my birthday with lilies of the valley, lilacs, and peonies, and to this day they remain my favorite blossoms. Isabel, who was born in December and whose middle name is Rose, has four rosebushes, so far, in our yard.

☀ Larry Arab's daughter Jenny was born on the first day of spring, and every year he and his wife give her a bouquet of spring flowers and serve pasta primavera for the birthday meal.

❋ Discover which famous person in history shares your child's birthday, and talk about that person. "Being born on the birthday of Columbus," Louisa May Alcott wrote in *Collections from My Childhood:* "I seem to have something of my patron saint's spirit of adventure." This is a great idea for nieces and nephews too: you might research who shares their birth date, and send them something related to their predecessor—a biography or a guest pass to a museum that features them.

❋ On the birth date of the daughter she gave up for adoption, Jody Fijal always lit a candle for the child she'd never known, and Jody's mother gave her a single red rose in honor of the granddaughter. Jody remained hopeful that one day she would receive a call and it would be her daughter. (As this book went to press, she did get the call and now has dinner every Wednesday with her daughter, who, it turns out, lives only thirteen miles away.)

❋ There is a lovely Thai tradition where parents buy birds or fish (one for each year of their child's life, plus one to grow on), sprinkle them with holy water, then release the animals to the sky and rivers for good luck.

As They Grow

As clichéd as it sounds, it's true that if I had a dollar for every time an older person told me "enjoy their childhood; it goes by in a wink," I'd be rich. Each season is filled with occasions that take note of a child's development—which can slip through our fingers unnoticed, if not recorded—and there are many everyday rituals that mark the passage through childhood.

Perhaps the best advice my cousin Sue gave me when Trainer was born was to keep a notebook and when he did something wonderful or said something funny, to write it down that same evening. (You think you'll remember it later, but you won't.) Other ways to record a child's growth:

✳ Write a letter to each of your children once a year, perhaps on their birthday. In it you can include anything from what you love about being their mother to what they've done that you'd like to remember. Tuck away the letters and give them to your children when they are grown. There are many variations on this theme; once a year you might also sit down with your kids and write down each child's favorites: food, books, movies, toys, activities, teachers. Over the years you'll see how they change.

✳ My mother-in-law Mary Jane was so excited the first year her first grandson spent Christmas with her that she decorated the house to the hilt, put a sleigh in the yard (that magically had a present in it every morning from Santa's elves), and planned all sorts of outings for Trainer. It was a wonderful visit, and the next month she surprised us with a book she'd created, entitled "Trainer's First Christmas in Oklahoma," filled with photos, mementos, and decorative borders she'd made from cut up Christmas cards. Best of all was her annotated story of the visit, from when our plane touched down to when she took us to the airport for our departure. It was one of Trainer's favorite bedtime books for years.

✳ When Joe earned his pilot's license, his father gave him an aviator's watch with the date inscribed on the back. My mother-in-law recently gave Isabel the Willow Ware tea set that her great aunt had given to her at the age of four. If you don't have any heirlooms from your family, the tradition can begin with you: give each grandchild a watch or a set of pearls when they turn eighteen.

Family Communication ✳

It's natural for siblings to bicker and fight, and rituals can help turn little niggling conflicts into constructive change or growth.

✳ Hold a family conference. Make it official—take turns being the moderator, and post an agenda on the refrigerator the week beforehand so people can add to the list. Sample topics can include chores, homework, allowances, curfews, television restrictions, requests, upcoming vacations, or whether to take in a Fresh Air Fund kid next summer. The family conference encourages group participation and negotiation. Establish rules of order such as no criticizing or fighting. This is a time and place to demonstrate problem solving and peaceful conflict resolution.

✳ Talk, talk, and talk some more. Make a point of discussing current events at dinner. Your children will learn about the issues of the day, and how to respond, through conversations with you. If it doesn't come naturally, try this: one night a week, ask each child to pick a news article that interests them and lead a discussion of it at the dinner table.

✳ Take a night off from the kids to discuss the kids. Many couples, when they have the rare opportunity to go out without the kids, don't want to spend the evening talking about them, but Linda and Richard Eyre have a monthly dinner on their own that's dedicated to discussing all their children, one at a time. They call it the "Five-Facet Review" because they cover five topics: how each one is doing physically, socially, mentally, emotionally, and spiritually. They are convinced it helps them nip problems in the bud and appreciate their children more.

Kids Rule ✻

Giving children a little authority and autonomy empowers them:

✻ Paulette Wein's mother would declare a Children's Day once every summer. The kids were allowed to eat anything they wanted, go to bed anytime, and do whatever they wanted within reason. Moreover, they could ask their mother to do crazy things, like turn somersaults and stand on her head. (Note: this is from a mother who had two kids; when she later had twins, she abolished Children's Day.)

✻ Once a year, Jeff Strait lets his kids play hooky from school and go skiing after a particularly great snowfall. If you live in the city, you could go skating or head for a museum instead. Each child gets to pick a hooky day and go on their own with mom or dad. There's something wonderfully conspiratorial for both parent and child when they play hooky together. (And you may be surprised who you see on the slopes.)

Bedtime ✻

Kids crave ritual at night if they aren't exhausted. When they're relaxed and fresh from their baths, there can be a fluid moment between the excitement of the day and the dreaminess

After a few stories, a lullaby is comforting. Inspirations include: "Stay Awake" (from *Mary Poppins*) • "Rainbow Connection" (from *The Muppet Movie*) • "Edelweiss" (from *The Sound of Music*) • "House at Pooh Corner" (by Loggins and Messina) • "Good Night" (by the Beatles) • "Dream a Little Dream" (made famous by the Mamas and Papas) of sleep, and it is a perfect time to heighten the spiritual dimension of your child's life. If you feel indifferent about prayer, consider reading a book of poems or songs. Read aloud with them, even as they get older; it will inspire you all in the same direction.

In India, children often sing hymns before going to bed. To this day, when I hear "An Irish Lullaby," I hear my mother's husky alto singing to me in the dark before I dozed off to sleep. When I needed comforting, I requested that song, and she sang it to me for years.

When Trainer was a preschooler, he'd crawl into bed and say, "So tell me about my Big Day." Isabel does the same (though she says, "Let me tell you about my day" and therein lies the difference between my two). Tucking in your child, reflect on the things that happened that day. I've also found that, if you turn out the light and stay with them, you will sometimes hear their deepest thoughts and concerns.

So many people told me a beloved tradition was reading chapter books aloud before bed with their parents long after they'd learned to read. There are so many great ones (in addition to the *Harry Potter* series):

Dr. Doolittle • *The Adventures of Tom Sawyer* • *The Wolves of Willoughby Chase* • *Just So Stories* • *A Thousand and One Nights* • *The Matchlock Gun* • *Island of the Blue Dolphins* • *From the Mixed Up Files of Mrs. Basil E. Frankweiler*

❊ Coming of Age ❊

This book was inspired in part by a coming-of-age story. Spending Christmas in Oklahoma with Joe's family, my mother-in-law gave me the gift of a massage at a local spa. While I usually avoid talkative masseuses (my theory being that, if I am going to hear their life story, perhaps they should be paying me), I enjoyed this woman a lot, and as we talked about children and holidays, she told me about her one revered tradition: when each grandchild turns thirteen, she gives the child an envelope at her annual Fourth of July barbeque. In it is an itinerary of a trip that the child will take in August with her and her husband. She said she wasn't sure who looked forward to it more—her husband or the child. The trips have been rather grand—England, France, the Canadian Rockies, and Mexico. The grandparents select the location based on the child's interests. I thought it was such a great idea that I was prompted to ask other people about their traditions.

❊ Take a parent-and-child trip. A son's trip with his father can be a profound experience for both parent and child, especially since in our culture more often than not it is the father who is home fewer hours than the mother. With either parent, an outdoor expedition allows a child to test his physical prowess and enjoy the one-to-one quality time, which lends itself naturally to conversation, be it a canoe expedition, river rafting, or a bike trip. The trip might be tied to a theme—following the journey of Lewis and Clark, or hiking part of the Appalachian Trail—which can be researched and planned over the winter months. But don't wait until your son is a teenager to propose a father-son outing. Since Trainer was five, he and Joe have flown most summers to Oshkosh, where they meet up with Joe's father. The trip includes a few days of bad road food, stopping along the way to see Niagara Falls, kicking the tires of planes they covet at Oshkosh, and three generations of Thompsons yukking it up together. It's never been dubbed a tradition, and I've never been excluded—and indeed my mother-in-law Mary Jane joins them for the adventure—but I've been busy or at home with young Isabel, and it has evolved into a near-annual adventure for father and son.

✳ Take a grandparent-and-grandchild trip. A generational trip without the parents is becoming increasingly popular; according to a 2006 poll of American Express travel agents, 70 percent of their bookings were for grandparents taking their grandchildren on trips. The benefits are many: the connection between generations, the opportunity to pass on stories and values, the fun of planning, the chance to share a hobby or passion, and the closeness that results from parents not being around. Some people travel individually with grandchildren, while others invite cousins of the same ages as companions. Travel pros suggest the best ages are between eleven and fourteen—old enough that the kids can physically take care of themselves but not too old to find the trip uncool. (Although my father, at the tender age of six, took a cruise from Boston to Florida with his grandmother in 1927 and still remembers seeing Charles Lindbergh fly overhead on his record-setting transatlantic flight.) For more information, there are several organizations to contact: Generations Touring Company, Elderhostel, or Grandtravel.

✳ Let them travel on their own. Several organizations specialize in wilderness experiences for young adults. Perhaps the best known is Outward Bound, which focuses on growth through a nature challenge that is unfamiliar, physically demanding, and adventurous. There is also the School of Lost Borders in Big Pine, California, which specializes in wilderness rites-of-passage experiences for young people. Located in the country of lost borders (the old Paiute Indian name for the spectacular Owens Valley), the school teaches pan-cultural ways of helping youths cross the borders into new adult lives. (You'll want to research any organization before you send your kid into the wilderness to survive on berries and twigs for three days, though.)

❋ Take a trip to explore their heritage. Chris Oliveri and her husband Steve adopted two children, a son from Ecuador and a daughter from Guatemala. When their son turned thirteen, the family traveled to Ecuador to see where he was born and experience his cultural heritage, and when their daughter turns thirteen, they will visit Guatemala. "Some people have bar mitzvahs—we visit birth countries," Chris quipped.

Bar Mitzvah and Bat Mitzvah ✺

Speaking of bar mitzvahs, this ceremony marking when a boy becomes an adult in the Jewish community is a coming-of-age ritual that dates back to the fifteenth century. The words mean son of the commandment in Hebrew (bat mitzvah means daughter of the commandment), although *mitzvah* can also be translated as a good deed. Children are given responsibility for their actions and expected to observe the commandments of the Torah at this age, and the ceremony marks acceptance of that obligation. Celebrated on the Sabbath (which begins at sundown on Friday evening and ends at sundown on Saturday), it is an important rite of passage in the Jewish faith.

The ritual is also timely; at precisely the point when a child is on the cusp of adulthood—searching for meaning, experimenting with trouble, a jumble of emotions, energy, and curiosity—the Jewish faith encourages a child to spend up to a year studying the moral laws governing their people and preparing for this momentous occasion. The ceremony involves prayers, recitations, and songs in which the child participates. It is the first time the child reads aloud to the congregation from the Torah, and often he or she gives the lesson. (One friend, at her baby's brit habat ceremony, asked guests to each fill out a card and write a wish, poem, or idea for her daughter. Then she put away the cards, saving them until her daughter prepares for her bat mitzvah.) A more contemporary mitzvah is for the child to perform a social action; the person receiving the bar mitzvah might ask those attending to bring a book that he'll donate to a homeless shelter, or he might collect used cell phones and bring them to an outreach center.

Turning Thirteen ❋

When Meg Cox's niece turned thirteen, Meg happened to be renting a beachside condominium with her sister. They threw a pizza party for their niece, then later that night the sisters made a circle with candles and sparklers on the beach, had their niece step inside the circle, and described the kind of amazing woman they knew she would become.

Another woman put together a birthday book to present to her daughter when she turned thirteen. For several months before, the mother wrote to family, friends, and people her daughter admired: artists, leaders, teachers, even famous authors. She explained that she wanted to give her daughter a special keepsake—a book of thoughts and ideas to live by—and she asked each person to write something to her daughter and, if inspired, also to send a small item, such as a photograph, drawing, recipe, cartoon, Bible verse, or song lyric.

Another friend with three daughters has chosen a private activity with each girl that's suited to their interests: a day-long hike in the mountains worked for one whereas a day trip to New York museums was more appropriate for another.

Both Hopi and Apache women are given baskets during a special ceremony that marks the transition from adolescence to adulthood. You might consider giving your daughter a basket—maybe a Hopi or a Nantucket basket—when she turns thirteen. It could be small enough to hold her earrings (maybe she also gets her ears pierced on this day) with a note inside explaining the inspiration for your idea.

Native American Rites of Passage ✺

I discovered that many women are thinking about how they might commemorate their daughter's important transition into womanhood. A good place to look for spiritual inspiration is among Native American tribes.

When a Navajo girl comes of age, the tribe stages a ceremony that lasts five days. During this time she is called Changing Woman (a legendary creation goddess) and wears what Changing Woman wore: a sash and jewelry of white shells and turquoise. An older woman in the tribe whom the girl has chosen as her mentor washes the girl's hair and adorns her with the jewelry while singing chants. She then gives the girl a vigorous massage to mold the child's body into that of a woman. Her only tasks are to run several times each day from west to east (in pursuit of the sun) and to grind corn for the enormous cake that the tribe will eat at the end of the ceremony.

The Apaches have a four-day sunrise ceremony for girls that includes dancing and running to meet the rising sun at dawn, singing sixty-three songs, and reenacting the

Apache creation myth, during which the girls attain the physical and spiritual power of White Painted Woman (also known as Changing Woman). During the ceremony, each girl gives gifts, healings, and blessings to her people and in return receives prayers and good wishes for prosperity, a long life, and fertility. Her fortitude during the activities, which are physically and intellectually exhausting, is considered a good indicator of her temperament later in life.

In the early 1900s, when the U.S. government banned Native Americans from performing their spiritual rituals, these ceremonies were conducted in secret, and over the years the practice nearly disappeared. It was not until the American Indian Religious Freedom Act in 1978 that the Sunrise Ceremony was re-established openly on many reservations. Today many tribes conduct an abbreviated two-day ceremony. An exhibition at the Peabody Museum at Harvard offered a touching account of Mandy Begay's participation in the Sunrise Ceremony:

Today, approximately 30 percent of Apache girls participate in this ceremony. You might consider attending one of these ceremonies on the Fort Apache Indian Reservation in Arizona or at the Mescalero Apache Indian Reservation in New Mexico over the Fourth of July weekend.

Ever since I was old enough to understand the meaning of the Sunrise Dance, I was told that it was essential for me as a growing woman to have one. I hated the idea and couldn't understand why dancing at sunrise for two days, and singing sixty-three songs would make a difference in my life. I felt it was only some stupid ritual. I didn't want to make a fool of myself by dancing in front of the community, and what would I get out of it anyway? Therefore, it came to me as a surprise when I had strong feelings while I participated in one as an assistant for my friend Laura's Sunrise Dance. . . . There we were, the two of us, dancing in front of the entire community. I was embarrassed in the beginning. Everyone was staring. . . . The songs came one after another and the summer sun rose higher and higher. . . . I let my body dance to the music, and once that happened, I was gone. . . . Everything that was in front of me, I didn't see. . . . I was taken by the meaning of the Sunrise Dance. This dance was to help build my endurance, and it would symbolize my womanhood. I started this dance as a child, but I would end it as a woman. . . . The singers sang louder and louder of our Apache ways, love, and friendship. They were telling me to be strong in life and to live life to its fullest. The louder they sang, the harder I danced. . . .

—MANDY BEGAY

La Quinceañera ✽

When a Latina girl turns fifteen (*quince*) the passage is marked by a religious ceremony that signifies she has become a woman and, historically, was considered ready for marriage. The ceremony is followed by a party to introduce her into adult society. La quinceañera refers both to the fifteen-year-old and the celebration held in her honor.

As Latin communities have flourished in the United States, the quinceañera has become an increasingly grand affair. (Event planners in San Antonio estimate that quinceañeras comprise up to 25 percent of their annual business). Like a wedding or debutante ball, these parties can escalate financially. Responding to the increasingly ruinous costs associated with some of the more elaborate parties, in the 1980s a group of Catholic priests in Texas issued a resolution discouraging lavish quinceañera parties, encouraging parishioners instead to return to a simpler, more spiritual approach whereby a grandmother cooks the tamales, an aunt makes the dress, and the party venue is the family's backyard. In San Antonio, the archdiocese performs a quinceañera mass in May, but in order for a girl to participate, she must study at the church for a year.

The quinceañera also includes a thanksgiving mass for the girl, called a *misa de accion de gracias*, to which she wears a white dress to signify her purity and carries a floral bouquet. Seated at the altar, she is flanked by parents and grandparents, and up to fourteen escorts (one for each year of her life) called maids of honor and chamberlains. These attendants are usually a combination of male and female cousins, siblings, and close friends. Additionally, a young boy carries a pillow to the altar with the girl's first pair of high heels, and a little girl carries a pillow bearing a tiara or crown. During the service, the girl's father switches her shoes from flats to heels. The girl is given a ring or bracelet (to represent the circle of life and her unending responsibilities to society), a pair of earrings (to listen better to the word of God), a cross or religious medallion (symbolizing her faith in God and herself), a Bible or prayer book, and a rosary. At the end of mass, she leaves her bouquet at the altar for the Virgin Mary, and young children pass out *bolos* (party favors) to those who have attended the service.

A fiesta follows, where the *festejada* (the girl being feted) and her father dance the first dance together. Then there is a choreographed waltz with the girl and her court of fourteen young people. Her mother or grandmother crowns her with the tiara, and there is also a toast and ceremonious cutting of a large birthday cake (for sweet dreams). The girl may give a doll to a younger sister or cousin as a symbol of her passage from childhood.

Male Rites of Passage ✺

When you ask people today about male rites of passage, they might recall something they've seen in *National Geographic* or on the Discovery Channel about tribal or aboriginal customs in which a boy survives in the wilderness for a week, returning as a man. If asked for an equivalent ceremonial event in the United States or Europe, you will probably draw a blank, or you may get a list of milestone events such as getting a driver's license, graduating from high school, joining the military, voting for the first time, pledging a fraternity, or landing a first job. However, none of these is an actual rite of passage.

In Western culture, there is no widely practiced ritual that defines the moment when a boy becomes a man and that prepares him for the responsibility of manhood. (The Jewish bar mitzvah is the only ritual that comes close, but a thirteen-year-old boy returns to junior high—not exactly the domain of men.) With nearly 50 percent of American marriages ending in divorce, the father and mother may prepare a son for manhood in two different homes and perhaps with contradicting values. Positive opportunities for male development, such as the Boy Scouts and YMCA programs, have declined in recent years, and there has been an over reliance on professional sports and the entertainment industry to provide male role models.

Since the 1980s, there has been a movement afoot to develop a new model for a male rite of passage, ignited by the writings of Robert Bly (*Iron John*) and Sam Keen (*Fire in the Belly*). However, both authors emphasize that any modern, codified rite-of-passage ceremony won't contain much social force until our culture values such rites and that today's youth do not grow up knowing that they are preparing for their rite of passage into manhood. If you have a son, you might want to read these books, not necessarily for specific suggestions, but simply to consider a dialogue that concerns itself with what it means to grow up as a young man in the twenty-first century.

Autumn

The year's last, loveliest smile.

WILLIAM CULLEN BRYANT

Welcoming Autumn

Delicious autumn! My very soul is wedded to it,
and if I were a bird I would fly about the earth
seeking the successive autumns.

GEORGE ELIOT

New England in the autumn lives up to the postcard: dry sunny days yield to cool nights, there's a curl of wood smoke in the air, the Canada Geese head south in perfect "V" formations, and the woods begin dipping into spectacular golds, crimsons, and umbers. Fall is a time of harvesting, and people today still honor the bounty with small but poetic gestures: hanging dried Indian corn on front doors (an ancient sign of giving thanks), placing pumpkins on the stoop, and leaving a bushel basket of apples on the porch for passersby.

And don't forget the scarecrows; many ancient cultures believed that plants housed spirits with supernatural powers and that when the crops were harvested, these dangerous spirits would be released. For protection, the Druids would burn a large effigy that represented the vegetation spirit. (Indeed, Julius Caesar mistakenly thought that Druids sacrificed humans when he saw these effigies from a distance and wrote of them in *Gallic Wars*.) To this day, tens of thousands of people of all ages and backgrounds gather in the

Nevada desert every September for a week-long festival called Burning Man. On the final night, an enormous effigy of a man is ceremoniously set ablaze. Decorating our yards with a "farmer," dressed in dad's plaid shirt and jeans and stuffed with newspapers, recalls this thousand-year-old Druid tradition.

Along with the Druids, agrarian societies from the Greeks to the Mayans realized that the cycle of growth, death, and renewal was necessary for survival, and so as winter approached, they set aside time and developed festivals to give thanks for the harvest, the dates historically revolving around the fall equinox. The season is still filled with events that make the most of the bounty of the harvest and that encourage us to savor the last vestiges of warmth and sunlight.

Lammas 🌿 August 1

The idea of a harvest celebration at the beginning of August is at least a thousand years old. As summer peaked, it was time for the ancients to take in their first major crops. It was an occasion for joy (larders full with the bountiful products of their labor) and also sadness as the days grew shorter and the growing season wound down. The Celts celebrated with a festival from sunset August 1 until sunset August 2 and called it Lughnasad after the sun god Lugh, whose light began to dwindle after the summer solstice. The Anglo Saxons called the day Lammas (or loaf-mass) to commemorate the harvesting of the grain. The first sheaf of wheat was ceremoniously reaped, milled, and baked into a loaf, and in England, the custom of baking a loaf of bread for Lammas, leaving it on the windowsill, and decorating the house with sheaves of wheat, continues today.

Sukkoth

This lovely Jewish holiday spans eight days and celebrates nature whether you're in the city or the country. Celebrated a week after Yom Kippur (usually in late September or October), this three-thousand-year-old festival was born of necessity, when farmers lived in settlements that were often far from their fields. At harvest time, it was impractical to travel back and forth nightly to their homes, so a temporary hut, called a *sukkot*, was built beside their crops. The focus of this holiday is to leave behind the warmth and comfort of your home and stay in an outdoor shelter that is open to the sky to experience the vagaries of weather and prepare for the holiday of Sukkoth. As you might imagine, kids love to get involved in building the sukkot.

In New York City, Rachel Chanoff's orthodox relatives build huts of sticks on their porches, fire escapes, and rooftops, and it's worth a drive through the Williamsburg section of Brooklyn to see all the variations of the sukkot hut. While many Jewish families eat their meals in the sukkot hut, some actually turn it into their home for eight days, sleeping in it as well. According to Jewish law, the hut must be handmade from materials found in nature and have no more than three walls, or at least be open to the outdoors so that the stars and moon can be seen through the roof. Our local rabbi serves all meals in his family's sukkot in the backyard, and his wife also hangs out there after school, playing checkers or reading with the kids.

There are strong food traditions associated with sukkoth, especially among Brooklyn's tightly knit communities of Jews who trace their roots to Syria, Lebanon, Iraq, and Egypt. Linked by food, family, and religion, the women cook all day together—chopping, stuffing, and folding—and mothers pass recipes down to daughters for the savory dishes, ranging from little meat pies to stuffed eggplant and veal stew.

Autumnal Equinox 🍂 September 22 or 23

The first day of fall, the autumnal equinox is one of two days out of the year when night and day are of equal length. In the ancient annual cycle, this was actually the second harvest; as methods of agriculture became more uniform and sophisticated the fall harvest was moved back as late as possible to maximize crop yields. As such, the autumnal equinox became synonymous not only with the completion of the harvest, but also the end of summer. This final gathering of crops and the beginning of preparations for the long winter ahead marked a time of thanksgiving for all that nature had provided. Although the autumnal equinox falls in September and not November, the connection to the harvest has many parallels to our modern Thanksgiving.

🍃 You can celebrate this time of year with a comfort dinner—a rich stew with seasonal root vegetables, home-baked bread, the last of the greens for a salad, and apple pie. Or serve fidget pie, a traditional English dish made with bacon, onions, potatoes, and apples that was served to farmworkers during the harvest.

🍃 Cut and dry herbs. Tie them with a ribbon and hang from a pothook, to be enjoyed while cooking. You can also crush the leaves for sachets that you can make for the holidays with your children.

Go to a farmers' market with the kids and pick out gourds and pumpkins for a seasonal centerpiece. The gourds are so oddly shaped that the kids will get a kick out of arranging them (and painting them too).

Make a corn dolly using dried cornhusks. This is an ancient tradition to assure a good growing season for the following year. The doll would be made from the last husk or sheaf of the season and saved until spring. It was believed that the doll held the spirit of the grain, and she would be plowed into the first furrow of spring to bless the new planting.

Back to School 🌿 August or September

My mother loved to tell the story of my first day of preschool. Stepping on the bus, I turned to her, blew a kiss, and said, "Don't look back, Mummy." Of course I meant that *I* shouldn't look back, but the symbolism wasn't wasted on my mother, who recounted the story for years with a chuckle about her only child, it's a new chapter in the life of all involved. People sent me numerous reminiscences about their first day:

Serve a big breakfast that will symbolically fortify the kids for ten months of scholarship.

Bring out a special plate that is used when your child starts school, earns a good grade, or achieves a particular academic or extracurricular goal. When your child arrives home that first day, make his snack more festive: serve it with a pitcher of milk and a vase of flowers or turn it into a tea party. Let's face it—most days our lives are nothing like *Leave It to Beaver*. After-school snacks might usually consist of string cheese and juice in the car while on the way to soccer practice or ballet. But on this day, make it something to look forward to. In the years to come, you can wrap the special plate and give it to your child when he or she marries or has a child.

🍂 Start tucking notes into your child's lunch box. So many women wrote that they did this all through their children's school years, especially on days when their child had a big test or was troubled by something. "I remember on my last day of high school," wrote Kaarin Lenstrom-Sheedy. "Mom put in a note that said how sad she was that this was the last lunch note she'd be writing me."

> They always looked back before turning the corner,
> for their mother was always at the window to nod and smile,
> and wave her hand at them. Somehow it seemed as if they
> couldnt have got through the day without that, for whatever
> their mood might be, the last glimpse of that motherly face
> was sure to affect them like sunshine.
>
> LOUISA MAY ALCOTT, FROM *LITTLE WOMEN*

Earth's Bounty 🌱

In today's world, where supermarkets offer tomatoes in January and acorn squash in June, there's a disconnect between our daily sustenance and the natural cycles of growth and harvest. But harvest festivals—perhaps the first of humankind's important collective celebrations—are still found in every culture around the globe. Some mark the beginning of the harvest and the anticipated bounty, while others commemorate the end of the harvest, with a focus on reflection and giving thanks.

Blessing of the Animals 🌿

A tradition started by St. Francis of Assisi in the thirteenth century (whose feast day is October 4), this service was brought to California centuries later by Franciscan padres. It's probably derived from a Roman custom of paying homage to Venus, the goddess of love, by blessing animals to inspire fertility. A number of cities, including San Francisco and Santa Fe, designate a Blessing of the Animals day. A favorite event with kids, check to see if there is a service in your community.

Oktoberfest 🌿 September or October

This German festival originated in Munich in 1810, when King Maximilian hosted a reception for the October 17 wedding of his son Prince Ludwig, the future King of Bavaria. With parades, horse racing, and loads of beer, the reception was such a hit that the king established a yearly festival that would last sixteen days. Chilly winds from the Alps can bring early snow to Munich, so, in 1880, the festival was moved to late September. Today Oktoberfest runs from a Saturday in September until the first Sunday in October. With the great influx of German settlers to the United States in the mid-1800s, there are many Oktoberfests celebrated in the United States, most notably the German Fest in Milwaukee that draws over 100,000 people.

TAILGATE PARTIES Every autumn weekend, hundreds of thousands of college and professional football fans around the nation look forward to the big game and the social celebration that accompanies it: the tailgate party. For some, tailgating is a tradition that's as important as the sport, and a reasonable percentage of tailgaters don't actually attend the game.

Food, and lots of it, is the center of any good tailgate party, but it's not just burgers and dogs on all those grills. Menus for tailgating seem to follow strict regional and traditional rules, often featuring dishes that emphasize pride of place and history. You won't find Philly cheesesteaks in Texas or barbecued short ribs at Yale. Cooking is often done on a grand scale, with massive custom grills equipped to prepare food for hundreds of fans. There's a spirit of competition and one-upmanship, to see who can put out the most impressive spread and elaborate decorations. Tailgating has a particular history in the South, and it's not uncommon at universities like Auburn, Vanderbilt, or Ole Miss to see women in semiformal attire sipping cocktails from crystal goblets and serving their grandmothers' cherished recipes on vintage china.

Moon Festivals

While the sun is revered in many European and Middle Eastern cultures, in the Far East the moon is honored, and throughout Asia there are fall moon festivals (also called harvest festivals or mid-autumn festivals), which historically were a time to give thanks for the rice harvest. In China, the Harvest Moon Festival is called Zhongqiu Jie and is as important a family holiday as our American Thanksgiving. According to Chinese legend, the moon is at its biggest and fullest on this day; it appears larger than other full moons, probably because of the dry fall air. There is even a custom of acknowledging the moon's birthday during the harvest moon. Lasting three days, the festival is held near the time that the full moon appears on the fifteenth day of the eighth month in the lunar calendar, usually mid-September.

Food is central to this festival. Much as we have a tradition of turkey at Thanksgiving, the Chinese roast a pig and serve mooncakes and other foods that are made into round shapes to symbolize familial unity and harmony. Zhongqiu Jie is a beloved holiday, with many poems written about it. A Chinese American friend living in New York told me she always has a Harvest Moon party, even if it's simply sitting on the fire escape with friends to catch a peek at the moon and read poetry.

In South Korea, the moon festival is called Chuseok and is celebrated with ancestral memorial services, rituals associated with dress and food, and traditional games. *Song-pyon* (rice cakes made with bean paste) are eaten, and there is a mass exodus from cities on Chuseok as Koreans return to their home villages (Korean papers even run articles

CHINESE MOONCAKES If the opportunity presents itself, introduce your children to Chinese mooncakes. Legend holds that mooncakes date back to the late Yuan dynasty (AD 1279–1368), when the Han people plotted to overthrow the conquering Mongols. The peasants spread a rumor that the plague was spreading and that the cure was to eat a special mooncake. The peasants gave the mooncakes only to friends and allies, who broke open the pastry and found a note inside that read "Revolt on the fifteenth of the eighth moon." It was in this way that the Han gathered their forces and overthrew the Yuan. To this day, mooncakes are eaten to remember how their ancestors outsmarted the invaders. At Chinese harvest moon festivals you'll find children munching on these round, yellow cakes, which are typically sweet but can also be savory. Famous for their love of puns, the Chinese stamp each mooncake with a word—prosperity, luck, and so on—that not only promises good fortune, but also gives a clue to the ingredient inside.

about how to combat loneliness if you have to stay in Seoul). Contemporary life is changing this home-coming ritual, however, as younger generations of Koreans increasingly hire strangers to sweep their ancestors' graves and transmit real-time photographs of their deceased relatives' tombs via the Internet so they can conduct their ceremonies at home in front of the computer screen.

Feast Days

Festivals honoring a particular saint's feast day have long been symbols of cultural identity for European immigrant populations in the United States. Many of these feast days are celebrated during the autumn and originated as fundraisers for local Catholic parishes. Such events have become more secular in recent years, and if you see them advertised, by all means, go—they are a terrific way to share in and learn about the cuisine, music, and ethnic identity of different American cultures.

Growing up in southeastern Massachusetts, I was most familiar with the Feast of the Blessed Sacrament. The largest Portuguese festival in the United States, it's held the first weekend in August in the fishing port of New Bedford with a special mass, a parade, carnival rides, concerts, dance performances, and lots of food. The smells are intoxicating—skewered *carne d'espeto* barbecuing over enormous outdoor pits, steaming kale soup, grilling linquica sausage, and baking Portuguese sweet bread. Thought to have originated in 1915 with four immigrants from Madeira who promised to create a special day to honor God if they survived the ocean voyage, the Feast of the Blessed Sacrament is also celebrated in neighboring towns with large Portuguese and Cape Verdean populations, such as Fall River and Onset.

APPLE HARVEST Since the 1960s, a visiting-worker program has been in place for Jamaicans to come north to work the Vermont apple harvest. Sanctioned by the U.S. and Jamaican governments, it's a coveted, if back-breaking, job as it pays handsomely over a short period of time with more than one thousand Jamaicans participating in the program. A good number of them are Christian, and halfway through the harvest, usually the last Sunday in September, they organize a Jamaican "hymn sing" at the Shoreham Congregational Church. Everyone's invited to this gospel concert, where an offering is taken to benefit a Jamaican church back home.

Perhaps the best known Saint's day is the Feast of San Gennaro, held in Little Italy in New York each September and attended by over a million people. Originally a religious celebration for the patron saint of Naples, whose feast day is September 19, the Feast has grown from a one-day affair organized by Italian immigrants in 1926 to a ten-day celebration of Italian and Italian American culture with parades, free entertainment, a dizzying array of food stands, cannoli-eating contests, and a candlelit procession starting at the Most Precious Blood Church on Mulberry Street with the priest carrying the statue of St. Gennaro through the streets. When I first moved to New York after college, I took an apartment on Prince Street in SoHo in early September and was pleasantly shocked when I went out to wander the streets after dinner and bumped into New York's oldest, biggest street festival. It's fun for all ages and a great opportunity to introduce your kids to Italian American music, cuisine, and culture. Other cities have followed suit with ethnic festivals and fairs.

National Hunting and Fishing Day 🐾 end of September

While not a hunter myself, I do fish and have lived much of my adult life in rural areas of New England where hunting is a time-honored ritual to many. Though hunting and fishing are now largely recreational activities in the United States, every hunter I know still hunts for sustenance and has a freezer full of game meat at the end of the season.

The moral debate over hunting notwithstanding, the legacy of the American sportsman in the last hundred or so years is significant: not only were hunters and anglers the earliest and most vocal supporters of conservation and scientific wildlife management, they were also the first to recognize that suburban development and unregulated hunting and fishing were threatening the future of many species. President Theodore Roosevelt, an avid outdoorsman, led the charge, and the first laws governing the sustainable use of fish and game, the issuing of hunting and fishing licenses, and taxes on sporting equipment to fund state conservation agencies all appeared during his presidency. Today, hunters and anglers are major contributors to both national and state conservation programs and are currently responsible for more than 75 percent of the annual funding for wildlife programs. In 1972, President Nixon made the fourth Sunday of September National Hunting and Fishing Day, writing, "I urge all citizens to join with outdoor sportsmen in the wise use of our natural resources and in insuring their proper management for the benefit of future generations."

Each year on this day, national, regional, state, and local organizations stage some three-thousand, open house hunting-and-fishing-related events, featuring everything from shooting ranges to suburban frog ponds, providing millions of Americans with a chance to experience and appreciate traditional outdoor activities. Last September, my father called on a Saturday night and asked if we'd read the latest issue of *Massachusetts Wildlife* magazine that he had given Trainer for Christmas (we hadn't yet). The next day the Hamilton Rod and Gun Club would be putting on a free event that he thought we might enjoy, so Joe and Trainer drove to Sturbridge, Massachusetts, to discover a terrific annual outdoor expo then in its ninth year. They attended workshops on fly casting, fly tying, birdhouse construction, skeet shooting (which included a gun-safety course), archery, and rock climbing. All events were outdoors and free of charge. Run by volunteers, the expo is just one among thousands across the country.

Rosh Hashanah

Also called the Jewish New Year (or the days of awe), this ten-day period begins with Rosh Hashanah and ends with Yom Kippur. The most important of all Jewish High Holy days, Rosh Hashanah and Yom Kippur are purely religious, not related to any historical or natural event.

Rosh Hashanah (head of the year) is a festive, family event that lasts two days, beginning on a Friday at sundown, to celebrate the beginning of a new year and mark the anniversary of the world's creation. The holiday involves a number of symbolic foods, and both the Ashkenazi, whose ancestors emigrated principally from Eastern Europe, and the Sephardim, whose ancestors came primarily from the Mediterranean region and North Africa, say a blessing over apple slices dipped in honey to signify a sweet year to come. Chicken soup and dumplings might be served, followed by fish, and always the sweet egg-based challah bread, baked into a round loaf to represent the year's wholeness. A traditional menu always includes dishes prepared with fruits—chicken with apricots and marmalade, for example, or lamb with prunes and dates. Seasonal fruit is at the table and is part of the New Year prayer: "May your seeds be as many as the pomegranate." Whatever the menu, sweetness is the prevailing theme.

Yom Kippur

The culmination of the New Year is Yom Kippur, the most sacred day on the Jewish calendar. It is the time when Jews face God's judgment for their actions over the past year and when atonement for the previous year's sins is performed. Centuries ago, it was believed that one's sins could be transferred to animals, especially goats, which were driven into the wilderness and sacrificed (the origin of the word scapegoat). Today, those over the age of thirteen typically spend the day fasting, repenting, praying, and giving thanks to God. People sit down to a large meal before sundown, then spend much of the next twenty-four hours at the synagogue. In the ten days leading up to Yom Kippur, Jews are responsible for contacting those they feel they have wronged and apologizing or making amends for those transgressions. It's common to connect with spouses, family members, friends, and colleagues during this time of contemplation and atonement. Then, on Yom Kippur, it is time to ask God for forgiveness.

When I asked Steve Greenberg about his family's traditions, I got a sly smile and the following story about his father. In September 1934, the Detroit Tigers were four games ahead of the Yankees, with an eye on the pennant. The next game was on September 10, Rosh Hashanah. The Tigers' baseball legend Hammerin' Hank Greenberg agonized over whether to play on a High Holy Day. Reporters queried Detroit's top rabbi, who said it was okay to play, since Rosh Hashanah was the beginning of the new year and a festive

Speaking of Greenberg

The Irish didn't like it when they
    heard of Greenberg's fame
For they thought a good first baseman
    should possess an Irish name;
And the Murphys and Mulrooneys said
    they never dreamed they'd see
A Jewish boy from Bronxville out
    where Casey used to be.
In the early days of April not a
    Dugan tipped his hat
Or prayed to see a "double" when
    Hank Greenberg came to bat.
In July the Irish wondered where
    he'd ever learned to play.
"He makes me think of Casey!" Old
    Man Murphy dared to say;
And with fifty-seven doubles and
    a score of homers made

The respect they had for Greenberg
    was being openly displayed.
But on the Jewish New Year when
    Hank Greenberg came to bat
And made two home runs off
    Pitcher Rhodes—they cheered
    like mad for that.
Came Yom Kippur—holy fast day
    world wide over to the Jew—
And Hank Greenberg to his teaching
    and the old tradition true
Spent the day among his people
    and he didn't come to play.
Said Murphy to Mulrooney, "We
    shall lose the game today!
We shall miss him on the infield
    and shall miss him at the bat,
But he's true to his religion—and
    I honor him for that!"

—EDGAR A. GUEST

occasion. The news made the front page of the *Detroit Free Press*. This was a time when many Americans were prejudiced or ignorant about Jewish ways. Detroit pitcher Elden Aukcr was quoted as saying: "I came from Kansas and I never knew what a Jew was. . . . The Jewish people in those days weren't in Kansas."

Hank pounded the ball over the scoreboard in the seventh, sending the Tigers closer to the American League pennant. The next day, Hank was vilified by New York Jews and rabbis (Yankees fans all) for playing ball on a holy day. Meanwhile, Yom Kippur was looming nine days away. Greenberg (batting .338 with twenty-five home runs) was the Tigers' most feared batter, facing one of the most important games of the season in the midst of pennant fever. What would he do? Would this son of an Orthodox Jew play ball?

On Yom Kippur, Hank Greenberg went to synagogue rather than the ballpark. Walking into the room, in the midst of the rabbi's prayer, Greenberg got a thunderous ovation. Edgar Guest, a syndicated newspaper poet of the 1930s, ran the poem on page 144 nationwide, which to this day, Hank's son Steve Greenberg and his family read aloud every Yom Kippur.

Other Rosh Hashanah customs include:

There is a lovely practice dating back to the fourteenth century called *tashlich* (to cast away), whereby people visit a flowing body of water on the first day of Rosh Hashanah and symbolically cast away their sins into the current.

The *shofar*, a trumpet made from a ram's horn, is blown one hundred times during the two days of Rosh Hashanah and again to herald the end of Yom Kippur.

While certain foods are sought out at this time, nuts are avoided because it was believed they could lodge in the throat, making prayer difficult.

There are five prohibitions for the sunset-to-sunset period of Yom Kippur: no eating or drinking; no bathing; no using of creams or oils; no wearing of leather shoes; and no sexual relations. Many people also wear white clothing to symbolize purification.

Halloween ✿ October 31

Candy bars and cartoon character costumes notwithstanding, most of our contemporary Halloween activities and icons are derived from ancient Celtic rituals from Northern France and the British Isles. The Celts believed that when important natural transitions occurred—when day turned to night or where earth met sky or the ocean met the shore—a thin membrane separated the land of the living from the spirits of the dead, and it was possible for the dead to slip back into the mortal world at that intersection of time and space. October 31 was just such an important natural transition point. In 50 BC, only two seasons were recognized, summer and winter, and the end of October was the conclusion of the harvest, the moment when summer ended and winter began and time transitioned from one year to the next.

The beginning of the Celtic year was November 1, and the end-of-harvest—Samhain, or summer-end—celebration was held on that date. A festival for the dead was celebrated on Samhain Eve, when the souls of the departed were thought to walk among the living, perhaps even possessing the body of an animal (particularly a black cat, which remains an enduring symbol). Burial mounds were opened to release the deceased ancestors, and roaring bonfires were ignited on the hillsides to guide the wandering souls toward home for the winter. People dressed in scary costumes to keep evil spirits from recognizing them and trying to possess their bodies. Roving gangs would sing and ask for food donations to placate the spirits—possibly the origin of trick-or-treating—and families would set a place at the table for any recently deceased family members. Candlelit gourds, grotesquely carved to scare off malevolent spirits, were placed beside doorways. (Pumpkins were adopted by early American settlers as superior replacements to the gourds.) Samhaim Eve was a night on which fairies, cats, witches, and bats were thought to roam the countryside.

In eighth-century Ireland, the Church tried to replace Halloween, by then a 1,300-year-old tradition, with a Feast for the Blessed Dead and October 31 became All Hallows' Eve, hallow being Old English for saint, which was eventually shortened to Hallowe'en. In the ninth century, Pope Gregory II declared November 1 to be All Saints' Day, to honor the minor saints who lacked their own feast day. But the Church couldn't squelch the pagan traditions and Halloween flourished, especially in Ireland where celebrants accosted wealthy landowners for food and played tricks on them if the squires were foolish enough to decline, later blaming the tricks on the mischievous spirits wandering the countryside.

Halloween came to the United States in the 1840s with the great wave of Irish immigrants. Today, children keep this holiday alive, swarming the streets after dark dressed as ghosts, goblins, and princesses. You might consider making your kids' costumes (many people recall their mother's homemade costumes as a favorite childhood memory). Enlist their help and chat about Halloween's history as you sew and glue together. I have an Australian friend who insists her kids dress up as dead spirits—"Otherwise they miss the whole point!" No superheroes or television characters for her children. She also insists that they make their own costumes, in an effort to escape the commercialism that threatens to suffocate what is now America's number two holiday in retail sales, behind only Christmas.

Halloween is a holiday where small personal rituals make the event special, and often the events leading up to Halloween are half the fun:

Make rubbings of historic tombstones with butcher paper and charcoal pencils. Hang them throughout the house as decorations. The kids learn something about history and work on a craft project while having fun with ghoulish humor.

When my kids were preschoolers, I made a haunted maze at home by taping together discarded refrigerator boxes. You can paint Day-Glo eyes on the walls and hang plastic spiders and webs. Older kids will enjoy sticking their hands into bowls of jello, cooked spaghetti, hard-boiled eggs, or cold beans while blindfolded and trying to guess what they are touching. You can easily organize a potluck dinner around this theme for friends with young kids, and give the little ones a big activity while you're socializing with the other adults.

My sister-in-law invites friends to her house for a light supper before trick-or-treating with her kids. The children get a kick out of her witches' stew (black bean soup).

Samhain was one of the most important fire festivals in ancient Europe; light was thought to have power over darkness, and even to this day when you walk the streets on Halloween, the lights from pumpkins on stoops and in windows is comforting. If local laws permit, you might have a bonfire in your yard. It's warming, mysterious, inviting, and a wee bit threatening all at the same time.

When my uncle Joe moved out of the home he'd lived in since 1947, my cousin went to check the house before putting it on the market. While he was there, a neighbor came over with a letter. It turns out that for twenty-four years, Uncle Joe—who loved to take photographs of people wherever he went (and made my aunt Janet cringe when he'd ask strangers for their addresses so he could mail any good pictures to them)—took snapshots of the neighbor's kids in costume whenever they stopped by his house trick-or-treating. A few days into November the photos would arrive in the neighbor's mailbox. Wrote the neighbor: "My wife and I would just like to thank him and let him and his wife know that they made a fondly remembered difference in the lives of my three kids with these snapshots. I'm sorry they won't be here any longer a part of Halloween, and while everyone realizes change, I just want them to know that through that single thread of kindness, they will be in my kids' and their kids' memories as they knock on that particular door on Whortleberry Lane. It's amazing that such small gestures can become so meaningful, and I just have to let him know."

Try a game of pumpkin-hopping: scatter pumpkins on the floor, far enough apart but close enough together so that kids have to hop over each pumpkin. Align the pumpkins so they are progressively bigger and harder to hurdle—anyone who touches a pumpkin is eliminated.

Hold a pumpkin-carving contest. The carving is preceded by a trip to the local pumpkin patch where everyone gets to select their own artistic canvas. You can assign an aesthetic theme or let the carvers' creativity run riot. And don't forget prizes for the winners. (I've done this with my kids and their cousins and later used their pumpkins as table decorations at a family party.)

Or consider incorporating some Irish Halloween traditions into your holiday:

🍂 Colcannon is an Irish dish of cabbage (or kale) and mashed potatoes that's served year round but especially at Halloween, when coins wrapped in foil are buried in the potato for children to find. For dessert, serve barmbrack (fruit bread) with fortune-telling charms baked into each slice: a ring for marriage, a pea for poverty, a button for a bachelor, a rag if you're in trouble, and coins for luck.

🍂 A fun family activity: everyone finds a perfect ivy leaf and floats it in a bowl of water that's placed beside their beds overnight; if the leaf isn't spotty in the morning, you'll have good health until next year's Halloween.

🍂 An Irish Halloween always includes a bonfire. For luck, unmarried girls each cut a lock of their hair and toss it into the flames with the hopes that they'll dream that night of their future husband.

🍂 To play snap apple, thread an apple with string and hang it from a door frame or tree. The first to bite the apple without using their hands wins.

Dia de los Muertos 🍂 November 1 and 2

While Latin Americans don't observe Halloween, every November 1 and 2, across Mexico and throughout Mexican American communities, the dead are remembered in a celebration that is one of the most hallowed traditions in Mexican culture. Dia de los Muertos (Day of the Dead), with its mix of pre-Hispanic and Roman Catholic rituals, is a perfect illustration of the synthesis of indigenous Mexican and Spanish cultures that has come to define the country and its people.

Death held a particular significance in the belief systems of Mexico's ancient civilizations. Among the Aztecs, it was considered a great honor to die in childbirth or in battle or as a human sacrifice, as these endings assured a luxurious afterlife. In the middle of each year, the Aztecs celebrated two festivals—Miccailhuitontli honored dead children and Miccailhuitl honored the adult dead. The Spanish colonials reframed these celebrations to coincide with the Catholic holidays of All Saints' Day and All Souls' Day, and the success of the Church's conversion of Mexico is due in part to its willingness to incorporate certain pre-Hispanic customs with Christian rituals.

From mid-October through the first week of November, merchants all over Mexico fill their shops with the special accoutrements of Dia de los Muertos. Customers clamor to purchase papier-mâché skeletons and other macabre decorations; intricate tissue paper cutouts called *papel picado*; elaborate wreaths and crosses decorated with paper or silk flowers; candles and votive lights; and fresh seasonal flowers, especially *cempazuchiles* (marigolds) and *barro de obispo* (cockscomb). Bakeries offer sugary skulls, coffins, and grave markers along with special sweet rolls called *pan de muerto* (bread of the dead) that are topped with pieces of dough shaped like bones. In some regions, dark breads are molded into human figures called *animas* (souls). All of these goods are destined for the buyer's *ofrenda de muertos* (offering to the dead).

> *The Mexican is familiar with death, jokes about it, caresses it, sleeps with it, celebrates it; it is one of his toys and his most steadfast love.*
>
> OCTAVIO PAZ

In Mexican homes, elaborate altars are erected to honor deceased relatives, incorporating papel picado, candles, flowers, and photographs of the departed, and candy skulls inscribed with their names. Legend has it that the spirits of the dead pay a visit to their earthly homes on Dia de los Muertos, and living relatives and friends go all out to prepare for their guests. An elaborate feast is prepared incorporating the deceased's favorite food and drink. A washbasin and towel are provided so that visiting souls can freshen up before the meal, and the altar may be set with a pack of cigarettes for the after-dinner enjoyment of former smokers, or a selection of toys and extra sweets for deceased children.

It is also customary for relatives and friends to visit the local cemetery to maintain the graves of the deceased. Weeds are removed and headstones may get a fresh coat of paint, then the tomb is decorated with a cross of marigold petals and colorful wreaths of fresh or artificial flowers. Children's graves are adorned with brightly colored paper streamers and toys.

Hardly a somber occasion, family members gather at the cemetery on All Souls' Day for festive gravesite reunions. Some bring along picnic baskets, beverages for toasting the departed, and even musical instruments to accompany impromptu sing-alongs. Vendors set up stands outside the cemetery gates to sell food and refreshments, and the open-air memorial mass may open with fireworks.

By October, stores across Mexico are stocked with plastic pumpkins, witches' hats, and rubber masks, and many government agencies and private institutions are advocating the display of more traditional, hand-crafted and symbolic items in museums, schools, and other public venues. Conversely, many U.S. cities with sizeable Mexican American communities, especially in the Southwest, have become home to lavish Dia de los Muertos celebrations. Featuring concerts, craft fairs, and culinary festivals, these fiestas welcome participants from all cultural backgrounds.

Election Day   first Tuesday in November

Of all the days that should be federal holidays but are not, Election Day tops the list in the minds of many. In any case, it's an opportunity to teach kids about the importance of voting and being a participatory citizen. If parents vote regularly, their children are far more likely to vote when they become adults. In fact, in other democratic nations, where there is an established tradition of children accompanying parents to the polls, voter turnout is significantly higher than in the United States. There's a movement afoot to make this practice flourish here as evidenced by the abundance of related websites and magazine articles that have appeared during the last two presidential elections.

I'm more drawn to the personal nature of this basic, family civics lesson. People who remember going to vote with their parents have commented on the fact that it made a lasting impression. You can further elaborate on the electoral process by engaging in some family activities leading up to the big Tuesday:

Encourage your kids to talk to other adult family members and friends about their voting experiences. Who was the first presidential candidate they voted for? Who were their all-time favorite candidates, and did they win or lose?

Choose an issue to follow that affects your kids directly, such as the environment or education, then follow it through the campaign, noting what each candidate has to say. Talk with your kids about which candidate best reflects their views.

Weddings and Anniversaries

Many readers of this book may already be married, so why include a chapter on weddings? Well, you may have gotten a call from your best friend asking your daughter to be her flower girl and are wondering about familiar and not-so-familiar wedding traditions. Or perhaps your wedding is coming after the kids have arrived, in which case there are a number of beautiful rituals that you can adapt and use. Or perhaps, as Delia Ephron wrote in *Funny Sauce*: "Your basic extended family today includes your ex-husband or ex-wife, your ex's new mate, your new mate, possibly your new mate's ex, and any new mate that your new mate's ex has acquired."—in which case, you might need help with some creative party ideas. And then there are always anniversaries. . . .

> *Now you will feel no rain,*
> *For each of you will be*
> *   shelter to the other.*
> *Now you will feel no cold,*
> *For each of you will be*
> *   warmth to the other.*
> *Now there is no more loneliness,*
> *For each of you will be*
> *   companion to the other.*
> *Now you are two bodies,*
> *But there is only one*
> *   life before you.*
> *Go now to your dwelling place*
> *To enter into the days of*
> *   your togetherness*
> *And may your days be good*
> *   and long upon the earth.*
>
> **APACHE WEDDING PRAYER**

Were you to travel back in time and attend a fifth-century European wedding, you'd be amazed at how little has changed. Nearly all the accoutrements of the contemporary wedding—dress, veil, rings, flowers, toasts, and wearing a touch of blue—date back to ancient times. That said, verifying the historical accuracy of these rites, where little written record survives, isn't always easy. We do know that for thousands of years there has been some sort of ceremony marking the act of a man and woman coming together in a lifelong partnership. The word "bridal" comes from the

Teutonic words *bryd ealu* (bride-ale), referring to the ale that the man and woman shared to seal the union—a tradition that is incorporated into Greek Orthodox ceremonies to this day. The Anglo-Saxon word *wedd* referred to a man's commitment to marry a woman to perpetuate his lineage and also referred to the dowry he paid to her father.

By the early Renaissance, the ceremony was a handshake: The couple joined hands at the wrists (handfasting was the Celtic term or tying the knot) in a tavern or castle, and pledged their troth. The vows lasted thirteen moon cycles (a little over a year—the honeymoon), at which point they had the option of relinquishing their vows or renewing them for life. There was no government sanction or papal intervention until the fifteenth century when the Council of Trent declared that a priest must be present to declare the union official. By the early 1500s, the Church was trying to outlaw all weddings without a papal decree, and the ceremony moved into the church.

In other parts of Europe, different rules applied; in fifteenth-century Finland, for example, engagements were considered legally binding, and some couples (especially those living in rural areas, where travel was difficult) began cohabitating once they were engaged. It wasn't until 1988, believe it or not, when Finland's Marriage Act was reformed, and engagements were no longer considered legally binding.

The Date

Once upon a time, people married on the day they didn't work: Sunday. However, believing it a sacrilege to marry on the Sabbath, seventeenth-century Puritans squelched the idea of a Sunday wedding. For many centuries it was popular to marry when the moon was waxing (when a woman was considered most fertile) and at a time of day when the clock's hands were rising. The Chinese prefer to marry on May 18 because five-one-eight (*wu yao ba*) sounds like *wu yao fa* or "I shall get rich." Placing great importance on numbers, they also like to marry on the eighth of the month, because in Chinese the word for eight sounds like the word for luck. Malaysians prefer not to marry in July (the seventh month), believing, like the Chinese, that during July the dead wander the earth. The Irish prefer the last day of the year, thinking it will bring good luck. If you are contemplating setting a date, you might consider this traditional English rhyme:

Married when the year is new, he'll be loving, kind and true.
When February birds do mate, you wed nor dread your fate.
If you wed when March winds blow, joy and sorrow both you'll know.
Marry in April when you can, joy for maiden and for man.
Marry in the month of May, and you'll surely rue the day.
Marry when June roses grow, over land and sea you'll go.
Those who in July do wed, must labour for their daily bread.
Whoever wed in August be, many a change is sure to see
Marry in September's shrine, your living will be rich and fine.
If in October you do marry, love will come but riches tarry.
If you wed in bleak November, only joys will come, remember.
When December snows fall fast, marry and true love will last.

The Dress 🌿

Especially if you've been married before, choosing what to wear can be challenging. Do you wear white? A formal gown? With a train? What about a veil? For my first wedding, I chose a frothy white concoction that would have been right at home on top of a three-tiered wedding cake, and I loved every inch of it. But for my second marriage, I opted for a creamy-lace tea dress that had been my great aunt Edith's in the 1920s. (Last year I brought it out after fifteen years and wore it to a museum benefit. My husband looked at me and said, "Haven't I seen that dress before?" Oh well. . . .)

For a repeat performance, there are many traditional choices other than white. In biblical times blue symbolized purity, while in ancient Rome brides wore yellow. In Japan to this day, wedding kimonos can be any color except white. (White is reserved for mourning in most Asian cultures.) The Hindu bride wears two saris: the first one is given to her by her parents, and at the end of the ceremony she switches to a sari from her husband. Pakistani brides wear red to symbolize happiness, and the Chinese have worn red (the color of love and important for happiness) since the Ming Dynasty, embroidering peonies and chrysanthemums into their robes for wealth and luck. Indeed, red and yellow are often worn in Asia as well as in Egypt. In Europe, the clergy discouraged brides from wearing white; they thought it was in poor taste to advertise one's virginity, but it was better than wearing green—in England if you remarked that a girl "had a green gown" it meant she had been "rolling in the grass" with someone. Wearing white wasn't popularized until Anne of Brittany wore a white gown at her wedding to Louis XII of France in 1499.

By the late 1700s, white was the preferred color in Europe. In America, brides simply wore their best clothes. (Throughout the Revolutionary War, colonial brides wore a red satin ribbon to protest the British occupation—a precursor to the colored ribbons worn today for causes ranging from breast cancer to AIDS awareness.) White gowns were popularized by Martha Washington's daughter Nellie, who was married at Mount Vernon in 1799. Native Americans in California wove their wedding dresses with symbolic colors: blue for the south, white for the east, yellow or orange for the west, and black for the north. Both bride and groom wore silver and turquoise jewelry to ward off poverty and bad luck.

While the "something old, something new" rhyme is still slavishly followed by many modern brides, who hunt for an article of clothing that corresponds to each category, the original intent was: "something old" represented the bride's friends standing by her as she wed; "something new" symbolized her future; "something borrowed" was an item given by her family; and "something blue" was an article worn to signify her faithfulness to her new husband (harkening back to ancient Israel when brides wore a blue ribbon to indicate their fidelity).

Tossing the Bouquet

The custom of brides tossing their bouquets dates back to the 1300s and has its roots in the garter. In fourteenth-century Europe, good luck would come to the person who snatched something from the bride (fabric from her dress was especially prized) before she left the wedding feast. When guests started tearing the bride's dress to shreds, brides got smart and took charge of what they gave their guests, and so evolved the tradition of tossing the bride's garter. Interesting, eh? It gets better. The bride would take off her garter and throw it to the crowd to distract them and make her quick escape before they got her dress. By the 1400s, men had cottoned onto the trick and tried to tear off her garter before she left the party. When a gallant groom intervened and removed the garter himself, tossing it to the crowd, and the wily bride flung her bouquet as further distraction, two new traditions were born.

Bridesmaids

In ancient Rome, the law required ten witnesses be present at a wedding ceremony to confound the ever-lurking evil spirits—which, interestingly, is also the reason why bridesmaids used to dress identically, in long gowns similar to the bride's. While the maid of honor today is mostly an honorary title—she assists the bride in dressing and sometimes hosts a bridal shower—in Saxon times she helped the bride with all the wedding preparations, including the making of bridal wreaths and the wedding feast.

The Best Man

This role dates back to the Germanic Goths of northern Europe around AD 200. If a man couldn't find a girl from his own village to marry, he'd look for one in a nearby village, bringing along his best friend to assist. There was always the possibility that the bride's family would try to take her back, so the best man attended the ceremony armed and stood guard by the door while the bride and groom enjoyed their wedding night.

The Cake

The bridal cake originated with the Romans who thought that if they broke a cake (more like a biscuit) over the bride's head at the end of the wedding ceremony, she'd be more likely to have children. The guests then gathered up the crumbs for luck. By the Middle Ages, young girls would throw grains of wheat over the bride's head, and wedding guests brought small cakes. During Elizabeth I's reign, it was customary for each guest to receive a small cake, which they'd throw at the bride as she departed. (Good aim helped; if the cake touched her head or shoulders and you ate the crumbs, it meant you'd have good luck.) By the time of Charles II, the small cakes had become one large cake, and the three-tiered confection we know today was based on the spire at St. Bride's church in London.

Bermudans top their wedding cakes with a tiny cedar seedling; after the reception, the bride and groom plant the tree outside their home.

In Peru, tiny charms (including a ring) attached to ribbons are placed between cake layers. Each unmarried female guest pulls a ribbon, removing a charm, before the cake is cut. Whoever gets the ribbon with a ring attached will be the next to marry. A version of this tradition from the American South is realized at a bridal shower or tea: four silver charms attached to satin ribbons are baked into a cake. Each charm has a symbolic meaning; a silver coin for wealth, a ring or bell for the next to marry, a four-leaf clover for luck, and a thimble for spinsterhood.

Another custom from the South is the groom's cake, baked in a shape that's meaningful to the groom, such as a football for an athlete or a house for an architect. Often, it is the groom's cake that is sliced and sent home with departing guests.

THEY'RE PLAYING OUR SONG It's only a song, but it's one that you'll own your entire life. I remember my grandmother, years after my grandfather died, tearing up and leaving the room when a particular song came on the radio and I was quite mystified by the seeming power of that melody. Though bittersweet, what a lovely thing that a song has the immediacy to transport you back to a time, a place, a love. A couple I know argued about the song for their first dance—she wanted "In My Life" by the Beatles, and he argued that at age twenty-six, they didn't have the history suggested by the lyrics. Just last Christmas I heard someone sing it to her husband of thirty years, and indeed, they were old enough. It was beautiful, and reminded me that your song needn't be first played at your wedding—it can be on your anniversary, in your living room . . . A few ideas:

"You Send Me" by Sam Cooke

"At Last" by Etta James

"Crazy Love" by Van Morrison

"Dream a Little Dream" by Ella Fitzgerald

"You Are So Beautiful" by Joe Cocker

"How Sweet it Is to Be Loved by You" by James Taylor

"Love is Here to Stay" by Frank Sinatra

"When a Man Loves a Woman" by Percy Sledge

Throwing Rice

In virtually every culture and historic period, newly married couples have been showered with various grains, nuts, seeds, and flowers to ensure a fruitful partnership. Ancient Assyrians and Egyptians threw rice while the ancient Romans tossed flower petals. In later centuries, candy and coins were thrown at Italian newlyweds, while in Sicily guests aimed sugar coated almonds at the groom's friends while they kidnapped the bride. German brides kept a bit of salt and bread in their pockets to ensure that they never went hungry, while their grooms carried a few grains to guarantee a successful union. In North Africa, figs and dates were tossed to encourage a large family, while in Korea, the mother of the groom threw dates and chestnuts to her new daughter-in-law; how many the bride caught in her skirt was seen as a portent of how many children the couple would have. In China, lotus seeds are still offered to the bridal couple; in Chinese the words for lotus seed sound like continuously having children. If a bride refuses to eat the seeds, she makes her new mother-in-law very unhappy.

The Rings

Precious stones have been associated with mystical powers since ancient times, and the wearing of certain gems has long been seen as a potent talisman for romance. Babylonian astronomers assigned a stone, loaded with meaning, to each of the twelve signs of the zodiac, and men would wear the appropriate jewel each month. Over time, these birth stones came to be associated with particular human characteristics. By the Middle Ages, wearing a gem was a way to indicate a particular quality about yourself or perhaps your aspirations. Today, many people still identify with their birthstone (or their child's birthstone), and the ancient symbolism continues to resonate:

JANUARY Prized by the ancient Egyptians who believed they represented the blood of the goddess Isis, garnets were also extremely popular in Victorian times; the dark red variety was thought to flatter a woman's preferably pale complexion.

FEBRUARY In ancient times, dark purple amethysts were valued more highly than diamonds. The preferred choice of European emperors and kings, purple remains the color associated with the highest ranks of royalty.

MARCH It was once believed that an aquamarine would endow the wearer with fore-sight, courage, and happiness. Legend has it that sailors wore the pale blue-green stone to keep them safe from drowning and prevent seasickness.

APRIL Symbolizing innocence and purity, diamonds were thought by ancients to be sparks of lightning or splinters from the stars.

MAY Associated with the goddess Venus, the emerald symbolized fertility, romance, and verdant spring.

JUNE Coming from the sea and not a stone at all, the pearl was a symbol of purity. To the Chinese, the lustrous pearl still symbolizes power, wealth, and longevity.

JULY Hindus believed the ruby was the king of stones, while Marco Polo called it the most precious object in the world. Centuries ago, people who owned rubies touched the corners of their properties with the gem, believing it had the power to protect their homes from lightning.

AUGUST Sometimes called an evening emerald, peridot is one of the earliest trea-sured gemstones, found in Egyptian jewelry from the second millennium BC.

SEPTEMBER The color of the sky, blue sapphires were intended to remind humans of heaven, according to early theologians. Sapphires were often worn by clergymen to guard against temptation.

OCTOBER The multicolored opal represented magic, hope, and love.

NOVEMBER Golden topaz was prized as a symbol of fidelity and good cheer.

DECEMBER Treasured by Native Americans as a symbol of prosperity and harmony, blue skies and green earth, turquoise has been used as a talisman against the evil eye throughout the Middle East and North Africa.

There are several theories as to why wedding bands are worn on the third finger of the left hand. One is that the Greeks and Romans thought the vein in this finger ran directly to the heart—the *vena amoris* (vein of love). Another theory dates back to the 1600s, when a priest would bless the bride's first three fingers ("in the name of the father, the son, and the holy ghost"), dropping the ring onto each finger as he said the words, arriving last at the third finger. Anglo-Saxon brides wore the ring on the right hand until the ceremony, then switched it to the left hand. Double-ring ceremonies were popularized after World War II in the United States.

Wedding Customs Around the World

CHINESE A bride will bathe in water scented with pomelo (related to grapefruit) on the eve of her wedding to ward off evil spirits. The next morning she dresses and waits for a "good luck" woman to arrive to arrange her hair and cover her face with a red veil. The bride serves tea to her parents as a gesture of respect and thanks, and then her groom arrives accompanied by friends and musicians and takes her in a single-person carriage to his parents' home. As she leaves her home, the bride drops a fan, to represent her departure from childhood. Married friends shield her from the sun with an umbrella (to symbolize her vulnerable prenuptial state) and accompany her in a procession, all the while giving advice on how a married woman should behave. As she is paraded through the streets, the bride tosses melon candies to the crowd (signifying the tossing away of bad habits), and brings an apple to the ceremony, to represent the peace and tranquility she brings to the union. When the procession arrives at the groom's house, firecrackers are lit to scare away mischievous spirits, and the bride takes care to step over the threshold to ensure a successful entry into her new family.

KOREAN Korean weddings symbolically incorporate a pair of birds that mate for life: geese and ducks. The groom and his best man bring a carved representation of a goose (for fidelity) to the bride's mother, and the bride and groom are each given a carved wooden duck (one representing the husband, one the wife). After the ceremony, the ducks are displayed in the couple's home and are placed facing each other beak-to-beak as a sign of love. If an argument erupts, the person turns his or her duck away from the other to show anger.

JEWISH The bride and groom drink consecrated wine under a canopy, or chuppah, that represents both the homes of their ancestors and also the new home the couple will occupy together. The rabbi reads seven blessings (or seven guests will be called upon to each read a blessing), the bride and groom sip the wine, and the groom stomps on the wine glass. Breaking the wineglass symbolizes several things: the destruction of the Second Temple in Jerusalem, the fact that in the midst of joy there is sorrow in life, and that marriage is fragile and that one hopes the glass breaks instead of the marriage. The couple also signs a *ketubah*, or marriage contract, often artistically rendered so that it can be displayed.

EASTERN ORTHODOX Traditions abound here, from the blessing of the rings outside the church, to the multitude of threes throughout the service (the priest blesses the rings three times in the name of the Father, the Son, and the Holy Ghost, three prayers are said, and the priest leads the couple around the altar three times). Both bride and groom wear crowns attached to each other by ribbons. The crowns are exchanged during the service, and the couple drinks from a common cup to signify their new life together.

MUSLIM The groom leads a procession to the bride's home, stopping along the way at a mosque to pray and seek Allah's blessing. The groom is attended by a *serbala* (the youngest boy in his family, often a young nephew), and when the party arrives at the bride's home, her brother serves the groom sweetened milk (for a sweet start to married life). During the ceremony, the bride (who is heavily veiled) and groom are separated, even during the feast that follows. After the meal, the bride withdraws to put on the gifts of jewelry she has received, then returns and is seated beside her husband, and her veil is lifted.

HINDU A Hindu ceremony can last all day and, at minimum, a few hours during which the bride and groom are instructed about married life, receive blessings, chant mantras and complete the rite of Seven Steps (comprising health, strength, happiness, good fortune, children, longevity, and friendship) which concludes when the couple walk around a sacred fire seven times led by a priest. The bride usually wears a red sari with gold embroidery and gold jewelry given by the groom's family. The groom wears white trousers, a *kafni* (long shirt to the knees) and sometimes a turban.

SIKH The Sikh ceremony is called Anand Karaj (blissful union) and represents the uniting of the couple's souls. Weddings often take place in the morning, which is considered the best time of the day. The bride's parents place a garland around the groom and his parents, and then the bride and groom exchange garlands. The service is comprised of four verses from the Holy Book in which the obligations of married life are described. The groom leads his bride around the Holy Book as the verses are read and sung.

MEXICO In Mexican ceremonies, the rings and *arras* (a baker's dozen of coins representing a prosperous union) are blessed and exchanged after the vows. The bride and groom wear a *lazo*, a single garland that is draped around their shoulders.

Encore Weddings 🌿

When you marry someone with children, you acquire a stepfamily, also referred to as a blended family. An "encore wedding," as Peggy Post calls it, can be a joyous occasion and sets the tone for the joining of two (or more) families, but it can also be challenging. Children of divorce can lose a home and a parent and at the same time be expected to take on a new parent, perhaps new siblings, and maybe a new home. By the time the knot has been tied, a bride may feel she's been put through a blender. It's important to be flexible and not expect too much too soon—from anyone.

One idea is to incorporate the children into the service if they are willing and if it seems to be in their best interests. As families blend, new traditions can help the bride establish the bonds that will help everyone get through the challenges and complications that will, no doubt, arise. If it's the second time around for you, here are some suggestions from those who have been down that aisle before:

🍃 Each family member (children and the marrying couple) wears a piece of jewelry that is similar, such as a bracelet for the females and cufflinks or watches for the groom and the boys. Or perhaps the jewelry consists of several parts that make a whole. One woman and her two new stepdaughters wore charm bracelets—each started with a charm they had selected together and they plan to add to the bracelet as time and their interests dictate. A piece of jewelry given on one's wedding day is particularly memorable; I remember dearly the pearl and diamond earrings my mother-in-law gave to me the morning I married her son, and I look forward to passing them on to our daughter.

🍃 During the service, each family member carries a candle to a large, central candle, which is lit by all family participants. Or ask the children to join in the vows, which become

"We do" rather than "I do." Or ask a son or daughter to walk his or her mother down the aisle, with contemporary text that doesn't refer to giving away the bride.

🌿 Suggest to your new family that everyone takes a "family-moon" together, rather than the parents taking a honeymoon alone. What your family may need right now is to know that they are included in this brave new world.

> You never know what might be a fun gift. At my sister-in-law Sarah's rehearsal dinner, her maid of honor Meg McDowell brought out a linen napkin for the bridal toast. Meg told a story dating back to Sarah's high school days: One evening while Sarah's parents were out, Meg and Sarah had a dinner party. They used the best monogrammed linen napkins, and—serving the most elegant of meals (at age sixteen), pasta with tomato sauce—one napkin got ruined. Meg took it home to launder it but couldn't get rid of the stains. She kept it all those years, and when she brought it out and gave it back, I don't know who was laughing and crying harder—Sarah or Sarah's mother Nancy.

Wedding and Anniversary Gifts 🌿

While scrolling through the wedding registry for a young couple starting out offers a lot of options, what do you get for someone who's older or has been married before and is probably consolidating homes and possessions? For that matter, what do you give to your husband on your seventh, twelfth, or twenty-third anniversary? I've always disliked the traditional anniversary gift list. Who wants paper for their first anniversary, let alone cotton for their second? You reach five years, and get—surprise, dear!—wood. The crowning glory is ten, when you get—lucky you—tin. Now that's something to look forward to. While my knee-jerk reaction is to dislike conventional anniversary gifts, they can be recast in a way that makes you think differently about them. Take paper, for example. On my editor's first anniversary, she and her significant other took a trip to Istanbul. When they returned, she gave him a map of North America that had come from an Ottoman atlas, while he surprised her with an antique print of Constantinople. Other alternative ideas for weddings or anniversaries:

When Mary Steenburgen and Ted Danson married on Martha's Vineyard, they asked guests to each bring, in lieu of gifts, a hand-decorated paper lantern to the reception. (This works well for a one-year anniversary party, too.)

Create an anniversary quilt by asking friends to decorate a single square in any way they like, with their names embroidered or appliquéd someplace on the square. I put together a quilt for my parents' twenty-fifth wedding anniversary; friends and family members embellished their squares with memorable sayings and delightful embroidered scenes. (This would also make a lovely five-year cotton gift.)

When Shana Goldberg-Meehan and Scott Silveri married, they shared a glass of 1972 Chateau Lafite-Rothschild that Scott's grandfather had put away when Scott was born, with the intent of opening it on his wedding day. A similar idea is to give a case of wine that will mature on a couple's tenth anniversary.

On your fifth anniversary, give your husband five books that you think are important to read. On your tenth anniversary, give him ten CDs by artists he may not have discovered. On your fifteenth, give your husband a list of fifteen reasons why you love him.

On your twentieth, treat him to a twenty-day trip. You get the picture. He'll look forward to what you're going to cook up for the twenty-fifth.

🍃 One of the greatest ideas I've seen comes from a family that can afford a retreat for all generations; how wonderful to be part of a family compound that welcomes everyone for lazy days filled with decisions no bigger than shall we swim, canoe, or sail, followed by evenings of kick ball, s'mores, and chasing fireflies. One New Hampshire family that has a large Adirondack-style lodge and boathouse, fixed up one of the small ramshackle cabins on the property and gave it to their daughter as a wedding present, calling it Augusto Uno after her wedding date. When their second daughter married a trout fisherman, they built a second cottage, naming it Chasing Rainbows.

Happy Anniversaries 🍃

While many anniversary rituals fall into the rather boring dinner-and-a-movie category, a few break the mold:

🍃 Many African Americans still "jump the broom" at weddings or anniversaries, weaving their heritage into contemporary services. In colonial times, it was illegal for slaves to marry, so they would formalize their unions by jumping over a broom (a symbol of hearth and domesticity) into marriage, to the beat of ceremonial drums.

🍃 Let's face it—we all loved those big white gowns when we first wed, but when can you wear them again? On your tenth anniversary, invite your friends to a party, perhaps even at the venue where you were married, and ask your girlfriends to wear their wedding gowns.

A wedding is more than just the ceremony, and the events surrounding it are often a time when new friendships are made and old acquaintances are renewed. Eric and Molly Kerns married at a lakeside resort in Wisconsin and are planning a tenth-anniversary reunion there.

Senator John Edwards takes his wife to Wendy's on their anniversary. It turns out that on their first anniversary, they were in the middle of moving and found themselves tired and grungy at the end of the day, so they ate at the fast-food restaurant. The next year they found themselves at Wendy's again, and so it's become their tradition.

Anniversaries of the Heart

We all have them, and every day we create them. It's not your wedding anniversary; it's the day your partner first told you he loved you, or when you saw your mother for the last time, or when your son smiled for the first time. Sometimes it's even a season, not a day. When I see kids waterskiing, I think back on the summers I lived with my aunt Peggy at the beach and how she'd take us kids waterskiing every single day that the tide was up and the sun was out. (Two years ago I told her how much those summers meant to me, and she asked me to write her a letter about it as her memory was failing and she wanted to savor those times with me.) As Henry Wadsworth Longfellow wrote,

> *The holiest of all holidays are those*
> *Kept by ourselves in silence and apart;*
> *The secret anniversaries of the heart.*

Home and Hearth

Ah! There's nothing like staying home for real comfort.

JANE AUSTEN

A dozen years ago, *USA Today* conducted a survey as to what makes some adolescents more well-adjusted and high achieving than others. What did they have in their lives that other kids didn't? Sports? Church? After-school programs? Nope. Their families ate together on a regular basis. In numerous studies and interviews, eating dinner as a family as often as possible was judged to be one of the most important ways to solidify family bonds and promote closeness. Several townships in New Jersey have gone so far as to establish one Monday a month when no activities are scheduled—no sports, no school events, no town meetings—just to encourage families to eat together.

You wouldn't think you'd need civic intervention for this, but the family meal is being sabotaged by sports practice, extra tutoring, and parents working late. I know a banker who works full time, as does her husband, and takes great pride that every weeknight she gets one home-cooked meal on the table, no matter what, for her family (which includes a four-year-old and a seven-year old), even if dinner has to wait until 7 P.M. Of course, if I fed my four-year-old at 7 P.M., she would have a meltdown and ruin the meal for every-one. What works for one family may not work for another, but if it is a priority, do what you have to do to make it work: sometimes it means eating late, or shifting priorities, or limiting your child's extracurricular activities to one to two per season.

Or try other tactics. I was so tired of soccer practice being held at 5:30 on weeknights that I called our local youth center and mentioned how difficult is was to have a family meal with practice at this hour. The director polled other parents, who, it turned out, felt similarly, and the practice was moved to 4 o'clock in the afternoon.

Family dinners are also critical for blended families where kids may be commuting between two homes and aren't with you and your spouse on a regular basis. Thursday through Sunday they might be with their dad, or perhaps you have them during the week but your ex-spouse gets them on weekends. You might also have new stepchildren whose schedules don't regularly overlap with those of your own kids. How do you create a new family identity if kids are grabbing a slice of pizza from the oven and heading to their rooms or out the door not to be seen again until the following weekend? At least one night a week, carve out time for a family dinner.

The family meal . . . is a custom that can enrich our knowledge of our historic roots by carefully preparing food from our own ethnic tradition, that can enlarge our love of literature by readings of poetry easily adaptable to the beginning or the end of a meal.

FRANCINE DU PLESSIX GRAY

"Eating together matters," notes Dawn Miller, a columnist who writes frequently about blended families. "It matters much more than the quality of the food I have set out on the table. It communicates that we value spending time together, even in the midst of chaotic days. It's one of the small but significant ways we reaffirm our linkages as a family."

Family meals are also a time to teach values, whether it's an appreciation of your family's culinary heritage (serving the Italian carbonara sauce that your grandmother made), understanding the importance of nutrition and eating wholesome foods, or simply being together instead of ships passing in the night. A family meal also offers opportunities to instill manners, not just napkins in the lap and refraining from belching the ABCs, but being patient, courteous, and participating in the volley of conversation.

In my first job at Simon & Schuster, my boss cancelled a lunch date with a disagreeable author and rescheduled the meeting for 3 o'clock. Her words—"I just don't want to break bread with her"—still ring in my ears. How symbolic a meal is, where we do indeed break bread and engage with each other in a ritual that is tens of thousands of years old.

On days when warmth is the most important need of the human heart, the kitchen is the place you can find it; it dries the wet sock, it cools the hot little brain.

E.B. WHITE

And what important ceremony or celebration doesn't include food? Many people begin a meal with a prayer of thanks or a moment of silence. At our house, we clink our glasses in a toast. At Jeff Kleiser and Diana Walczak's dinner table, everyone holds hands and Jeff asks one of the children, "Do you want to start the squeeze?" She squeezes the hand of whoever is sitting to her left, who squeezes the hand of the person sitting to his left, and so on. The squeeze goes around the table several times, until Jeff says something to break it up (usually, "Let's eat!"). And instead of saying grace, I fondly remember the Weston family always sang grace. They had lovely voices and would sing "Oh the Lord is Good to Me" (the ultimate camp song) either in harmony or as a round.

Guess Who's Coming to Dinner?

Take a visiting professor, foreign exchange student, or new person in the community under your wing. In our town, government officials from Third World countries spend a year studying for graduate degrees at Williams College, and most of them come without their families. The college has a program that encourages residents to befriend these newcomers, inviting them to monthly dinners and holiday get-togethers during the academic year.

When Reverend Carrie Bail was growing up in Massachusetts, her parents had Sunday dinner after church, and they always made it a place of hospitality for visitors. The guests she remembers best were the international students from a local seminary who came to their church. "By the time I was five or six," she recounts, "I'd met people from Africa, Australia, and India. I grew up with the idea that all these people belonged around my table."

Initiate a coursing dinner with your neighbors. Each course is served at a different house or apartment. If you have only one course to think about, you can really make it impressive.

Launch a melting pot dinner. Everyone among your extended family or friends brings a dish that represents his or her culinary heritage.

Eric and Molly Kerns had a hankering for Prince Edward Island oysters and discovered it was actually affordable to FedEx two hundred of them to Vermont. So they gathered a gang of friends, who all chipped in, and for $40 per person, they enjoyed a feast of oysters, shrimp, and other savories.

Symbols of the Hearth

The kitchen is the heart of the home. It's where you help your children with their homework, linger over coffee with a girlfriend or wine with your husband, read the paper, and where countless conversations take place. There are several items in our home that have grown in significance to me and my family over the years:

THE KITCHEN TABLE Think of the memories associated with your kitchen table: rolling out pie dough with your mother, doing school projects with your kids on winter afternoons, sharing a cup of tea with your grandmother or new neighbor, laying out warm tomatoes from the fall harvest. The kitchen table carries as many memories as a photo album. When purchasing or making a table, choose one that can be passed down through generations, one made from real wood that will become lovingly worn and grooved after years of math homework, pumpkin carving, and family meals. Joe made our kitchen table from nineteenth-century beams recycled from a demolished building that had great meaning to us. Along with our living room fireplace, the table is a focal point of our home. Everyone gathers there, and I love how it reflects our history, as well as Joe's artistry and craftsmanship.

A RECIPE BOX My great-grandmother started a wooden recipe box that I discovered last year in my mother's attic, filled with handwritten recipes from three generations of women. I was amazed to find my grandmother's brownie recipe, which my cousins and I had thought was long gone. Annotate your favorite recipes for your children: "Your father and I first had this dish on our honeymoon in Honolulu." "This was served at my brother's bar mitzvah." "My mother-in-law (your grandmother) made this coffeecake for every family holiday."

A COOKIE CUTTER My sister-in-law gave me an unusual gift from the Chinaberry catalog: a cookie cutter made from the outline of my four-year-old son's hand. Among many creative ideas, the catalog suggested making hand-sandwiches on thinly sliced bread, spreading ice cream between two handprint cookies to build ice cream-handwiches for a summer party, or for Halloween, adding fingernails to handprint cookies out of sliced almonds. And why stop there? Use the cookie cutter as a pattern for making paper or fabric patches—sew a hand-shaped patch on your child's overalls, or trace the hand on colored paper for an unusual birthday invitation. For Mother's Day, I traced it with indelible ink onto a linen dishtowel that I gave to my mother-in-law. You can also make a border of hand prints on a sheet or pillowcase.

Shabbat

Imagine a time carved out weekly for self-reflection, spiritual renewal, eating well, spending time with those you love, and following intellectual pursuits. A dream in our busy world? In the Jewish faith, this ancient ritual, called the Sabbath (Shabbat in Hebrew), is considered perhaps the most important of Jewish traditions because it's the only one mentioned in the Ten Commandments.

Beginning at sundown on Friday and ending after sundown on Saturday, people are encouraged to set aside daily concerns and spend twenty-four hours engaged in rest and spiritual reflection. It might mean preparing a special meal with other family members or simply serving pizza with candles, going to synagogue service Friday evening or Saturday morning, or using the time to rest and study. It's all about making space and time for a break from the week's activities.

Havdalah, which means separation in Hebrew, is the end of Shabbat—the moment that separates the sacred space of Shabbat from the secular week. Havdalah occurs when you can see three stars in the sky (about forty-five minutes after sundown) on Saturday evening. There is a brief, lovely ceremony that welcomes the new week. It requires a twisted or braided candle with multiple wicks, a spice box, and a cup of wine. The candle is lit, and blessings are said over the wine (a symbol of joy), the spice box (representing the sweetness of Shabbat), and the flame (which helps us distinguish between light and darkness). At the end, you "catch" the light on your finger and reflect it back on yourself to hold the light of Shabbat in your heart until the following week. Then you wish others a good week and welcome the coming week with the words *Shavua tov* (a good week).

Other Shabbat traditions:

🍃 Light a candle for each parent and each child.

🍃 Light the candles at sunset or up to eighteen minutes beforehand.

🍃 Sing "Shabbat Shalom" or "Shalom Aleichem."

Sunday Nights 🍃

My sister-in-law Sarah reflected the sentiments of several people I interviewed when she said that when she was single and in her twenties Sunday nights were the loneliest of the week. Now, with a family and a pot of soup on the stove, Sunday suppers at home are a favorite. Other rituals:

🍃 During the school year, my cousin Doug's family had pizza, soda, and ice cream with three other families on Sunday nights after church. The kids all looked forward to it, and had fun going to each other's houses.

For Hans Morris, Sunday nights were made special with hors d'oeuvres and cocktails, then a nice dinner. He has continued the Sunday evening tradition with his wife and kids and added Poet's Corner: after dinner, everyone chooses a favorite poem and reads it aloud to the group.

One woman wrote to me that at her house, each family member draws another family member's name from a box on Sundays. Over the course of the week, they then anonymously do a good deed for that person. At the end of the week, trying to guess the person and the deed has become a Sunday night standard.

We create our own traditions for the same reason we create our own families. To know where we belong.

ELLEN GOODMAN

In my family, we always had our big Sunday meal at lunchtime. My grandmother and cousin Sue lived with us, and "the girls" went to church while Dad put in the roast. Walking in the door after church, we'd smell the roast cooking and sit down at the dining-room table for "dinner." The afternoon would be spent doing homework or working on a sewing project or raking leaves, and then after a light supper we'd all watch *The Ed Sullivan Show*, eating ice cream drizzled with chocolate syrup, tucked in on the couch. It was a ritual that ended one week, and began another.

I've tried to continue that tradition—we try to have no schedule, and we love quiet evenings . . . no phone calls if we can help it, just a nice dinner, and afterward, a cozy evening by the fire. In the winter, we cross-country ski or sled in the afternoon, and before I had kids I'd bake bread and let it rise while we were out. Now we make homemade pizza, letting the dough rise all afternoon and adding the toppings in the evening. There's something intoxicating about returning to a warm kitchen and the smell of rising bread. If you're tempted to spend too much time on emails or go to the office to get a jump on the week or go to the mall as if it were any other day, you might pause and think about the benefit and pleasure of reserving one day to rest, relax, and restore your vigor.

Home Nights

After the expansiveness of summer, fall brings a welcome coziness and a sense of tucking in at home, while still able to enjoy the invigorating air outdoors. When darkness starts to descend early and the temperature begins to drop, many of us feel like hibernating. Do it. Those times hunkered down at home with the family can be some of the most peaceful and rewarding of the year. Today's schedules are so full that you may have to schedule a "home night" in advance, but it's worth it.

Have a family slide show or video night. Digital photos can easily be compiled with a soundtrack, and who doesn't get a kick out of watching themselves on vacation, at weddings, or other family events? It still tickles me to go to my father's house and watch old home-movie reels of my great-grandfather touring the pyramids in Egypt in the 1920s.

Get out the guitar or sit at the piano and have a sing-along. When I was a kid we had hootenannies with Aunt Peggy on rainy Sunday afternoons in the summer, and we all loved it (and learned all those great show tunes).

🍃 Designate a cooking night with different themes, like making homemade pasta or tamales or an exotic foreign dish. I have delicious memories of helping my grandmother pick Concord grapes every fall from the vines on her veranda, then making grape jelly and sealing the Flintstones jars with wax (which she'd give to us months later as Christmas gifts).

🍃 Deborah Rothschild's family does the *New York Times* crossword puzzle together after dinner on Monday, Tuesday, and Wednesday nights. They are working up to tackling Sunday.

🍃 Movie night was suggested by friends who work in the film industry and make delightfully elaborate movies with their kids, but anyone can do it with a hand-held video camera. By the time our son Trainer was three he was already telling stories about dinosaurs, so one night Joe and he decided to make a movie. Joe filmed him telling his stories, shot close-ups of the plastic dinosaurs, and panned across the props and scenery Trainer had helped create. To this day, my son delights in watching his movie, and it was a great gift to send to Trainer's grandparents. As kids get older, they can work on more complicated projects that involve writing scripts, directing actors (you, siblings, friends), and postproduction (adding a sound track).

Family Homestead 🌿

This is a tough one as it requires money . . . a lot of money. It's a dream many people have: a piece of land, tranquility, continuity, family. So if you have money to invest, consider purchasing a retreat that can serve as a family homestead for generations. Dick

Sabot bought a rustic summer cabin on an island in Maine thirty years ago when he was an untenured professor with little money to spare. But Dick said buying that property was their single most important family act. Several of his children were born there, and when Dick passed away suddenly, his family buried him on the island. It will forever be their spiritual home.

Whether it's a cluster of cottages on the St. Lawrence, a rambling ranch house with room to expand in New Mexico, or a patch of beach on the Gulf Coast, a multigenerational homestead where cousins and aunts and uncles can mingle and share parental duties and pleasures is hard to beat. Informal, everyone barefoot, banging screen doors, an outdoor shower, and the thrill of the grill—these make for cherished memories.

My cousins have maintained a camp log at their place for almost a hundred years, and it's filled with the family's history: everyone who visits or stays there is expected to make a log entry, and its pages are pasted with telegrams, postcards, dried flowers, photographs, children's drawings, newspaper clippings, and sports ribbons.

Walk When the Moon Is Full

A favorite children's book of mine is *Walk When the Moon Is Full* by ornithologist Frances Hamerstrom. It's a true story about a child who never wanted to go to bed early, so during every full moon, her family would put coats on over their pajamas and walk in the moonlight. They saw stars and possum tracks and heard a woodcock's mating call. They went barefoot on a night in June, wondered if morning glories would open by the light of their flashlights (they didn't), and marveled that clover would fold its leaves in the dark. On one night, the family was staying in a hotel in the city, and although they didn't want to miss their nocturnal ramble, they couldn't see the moon in the glare of all the city lights. Undaunted, they went to a church, asked the nightwatchman if they could go into the steeple, where they found eight, fluffy, baby barn owls, their heart-shaped faces tipped toward the intruders.

Of course, this is an age-appropriate adventure; my first attempt at this, with my three-year-old and two cousins, was an utter failure. We began our moon walk just before bedtime on a crisp October night, well supplied with pumpkin cookies, glow sticks, and miniature flashlights. But by 8:30 P.M. in the mountains, the moon still hadn't risen yet. We hadn't even reached the driveway when one of the kids burst into tears, said he was scared, and begged to go home.

But at age eight it's a completely different story. Observing the moon can lead to discussions about astronomy, history, the space program, tides, nature, and mythology. On clear nights, the moon casts its silvery glow on meadows and forests, driveways and rooftops, bedposts and bedspreads, and it's magical. The ancient Greeks called the moon goddess Selene, and she crossed the sky in a silver chariot. The Romans called her Diana, and she hunted the nocturnal woods with a pack of silver-coated hounds. Teach your children about the waxing and waning moon and help them create a lunar calendar by watching moon phases. Have a Once in a Blue Moon party when there are two full moons in one month (note: the second full moon is the blue moon and happens every two or so years). Offer lunar treats: bring home mooncakes from a Chinese bakery, or bake moon-shaped sugar cookies. Or whatever you dream up. Maybe your kids get the treats as long as they keep track of when the moon is full and advise you a few days in advance.

❧ Thanksgiving ☙

Unlike most major holidays, this American day of thanks is secular in origin, centering around the gathering of friends and families to count our blessings. It is one of our nation's most beloved holidays for several reasons. There is no pressure to give gifts, and decorating is optional. Thanksgiving is for everyone—Christian, Jew, Muslim, Buddhist, atheist, and undecided. The date is always the fourth Thursday in November, which often guarantees a four-day weekend. And by many accounts, Thanksgiving is the holiday that draws the most people home or to wherever family is gathering.

Food is a centerpiece of the day, but family rituals are what give this holiday its power and make it among the most anticipated multigenerational days of the year. Thanksgiving is about the touch-football games and the walks in the woods or on the beach. It's about the board game by the fireplace or jigsaw puzzle in the den. It's about cousins racing through the halls and adults gossiping in the kitchen. It's a day of comfort, family stories, charity, gratitude, and rest (well, for everyone but the cook).

Thanksgiving was one of my favorite holidays as a child. In high school, I was in the bleachers in the morning, freezing with my father and Uncle Joe, cheering on our football team. My grandmother and mother were back home basting the bird, and when we opened the front door, we were greeted by the aromas of roasting turkey and baking pies that mingled with the smell of wood smoke from the crackling fire in the living room. Later in the day, aunts, uncles, and cousins would arrive bearing more food. We had our feast (for those who lingered, there were always leftovers), and we always included a neighbor, friend, or student at our table who, for one reason or another, would otherwise have been alone that day.

In recent years, there has been an effort to present a more complex and balanced view of the historical event this holiday commemorates. Displays at Plimoth Plantation include an Indian encampment enacted by Native Americans. Fortunately, while trying to portray history more accurately, one can also honor the inspiration of the holiday: to give thanks. What a wonderful concept: to set aside a day to gather with loved ones and be thankful for the bounty our land yields, for family and friends, and for the many things we often take for granted. Indeed, we can honor the diversity and struggle of an amazing nation that has yielded a holiday just to give thanks.

THREE KERNELS The first winter after the Pilgrims landed and established their colony, almost half of them died. Supply ships from England were delayed, and a strict rationing of their meager stores was imposed. The story goes that they were down to three kernels of corn per person when the first supply ship was sighted at last. There is a New England folk custom of placing three corn kernels beside each person's plate as a reminder of our blessings. Some people pass a basket around the table during the dessert course, and each person drops a kernel of corn into the basket as he or she recalls a blessing.

The First Thanksgiving

As every American child learns in grade school, Thanksgiving recognizes the first harvest that the Pilgrims reaped in 1621 after having landed at Plymouth on December 11, 1620. The conditions were brutal that first winter; their wheat wouldn't grow, and famine, disease, and harsh weather claimed the lives of 46 out of 102 *Mayflower* passengers. The following spring, with the help of the Wampanoag Indians, the Pilgrims planted corn, tapped maple trees, identified medicinal plants, and trapped local seafood.

That first harvest of 1621 allowed the Pilgrims to survive and inspired a three-day harvest party. Such harvest festivals weren't unfamiliar; English festivals called Harvest Homes were common, dating back to the Druids' autumnal feasts, and even as far back as the ancient Greeks, who celebrated the harvest by honoring Demeter, the goddess of agriculture. The Pilgrims invited the Wampanoag to share in their feast, and more than ninety attended—indeed, when the Pilgrims ran out of food, the Wampanoag gamely went into the woods and returned with five more deer.

Meals did not arrive at the colonial table in courses, rather, all the foods were served at the same time, including desserts. The Indians showed the English settlers how to make clam chowder, steamed lobster, popcorn, and cranberry sauce and introduced them to tomatoes, potatoes, sweet potatoes, pumpkins, squash, and corn.

WHAT THEY ATE IN 1621:
- Fowl (duck or goose, probably roasted)
- Fish (cod, bass, bluefish, clams, mussels)
- Berries and plums
- Boiled pumpkin, succotash, squash, beans
- Watercress
- Dried fruit
- Fried bread
- Nuts
- Corn soup
- Maple sugar candy

WHAT THEY DIDN'T EAT IN 1621:
- Pumpkin pie (flour supply was long exhausted)
- Milk or butter (no domestic cattle)
- Potatoes (thought to be poisonous)
- Ham (no domestic pigs)
- Sweet potatoes (not yet introduced)

A designated day of Thanksgiving didn't occur until 1623, when a drought caused the Pilgrims to gather in prayer for rain. When the heavens opened up the next day, Governor Bradford declared a day of Thanksgiving. (To the Pilgrims, a day of thanksgiving meant a day of worship, not a harvest feast.) Over the next century and a half, New England's colonial settlers periodically proclaimed special days of prayer and thanksgiving, mostly to commemorate military victories. But in 1789, George Washington established a National Day of Thanksgiving. Thomas Jefferson scoffed at the idea as too kingly, and belligerent citizens thought it ridiculous to honor the hardships of a few crusty Yankees from Massachusetts Bay.

Not until 1863, after a magazine editor led a forty-year crusade to honor the day, did President Lincoln, in the midst of the Civil War, proclaim the last Thursday of November as Thanksgiving. In 1939, President Franklin D. Roosevelt tried to

> The Wampanoag tribe celebrated six thanksgiving festivals annually: the Maple Moon Festival (to give thanks for the maple trees, the sap, and sweet syrup), the Planting Feast (to bless the seeds), the Strawberry Festival (for the first fruits of summer), the Green Corn Festival (to give thanks for ripening corn), the Harvest Festival, and a Mid-Winter Festival.

move the date up by a week to create a longer Christmas shopping season, which prompted a startled Congress to officially declare the fourth Thursday in November the legal holiday.

Giving Thanks

While Thanksgiving is a day to show gratitude for the blessings in our lives, some families find it awkward to lead guests in a prayer. Other rituals can give voice to our gratitude and are part of the many small details that make Thanksgiving a great American tradition.

On *A Prairie Home Companion*, Garrison Keillor once asked his studio audience to write down something for which they were thankful. He collected the responses and fashioned an amusing, touching song from them. You can do something similar (in our family, we made a poem instead of a song). Given the age of your audience, the responses can range from "I'm thankful for my new puppy" to "I'm thankful that I came out of the closet this year and you accepted me." If there are children at the table, give them the task of organizing the responses and reading the compilation aloud to the group as an improvised blessing before the meal.

My sister-in-law's church suggested that parishioners make a paper chain to symbolize their gratitude for the year's blessings. To do this, distribute strips of construction paper to family members on November 1. Ask each person to write on their strips what they are grateful for every day leading up to Thanksgiving. Before the meal, ask the kids to gather the strips and staple them together into a chain that can be used as a decoration in the dining room.

One family places an index card and pen at each place setting. Each person writes the name of the person to their left at the top of the card, then writes something about that person for which they are thankful. The card is passed to the right so the next person can add to the list. Eventually, each card will make its way around the table. Take turns reading the thank-you cards aloud after the meal.

At their first Thanksgiving, the Pilgrims bore the pain of having lost nearly half their friends, wives, husbands, and children. We all have empty places at our table and in our hearts, but we never forget those who are absent. My children don't remember their grandmother Ellie, but when they are served dinner on her china and sit below the portrait of *her* grandmother, they can recount stories about Grandma Ellie and how she served a particular stuffing every year. "We serve tradition," wrote *Boston Globe* columnist Ellen Goodman, "as proof of continuity in the midst of change, resilience in the midst of loss."

We return thanks to our mother, the earth,
* which sustains us.*
We return thanks to the rivers and streams,
* which supply us with water.*
We return thanks to all herbs, which furnish
* medicines for the cure of our diseases.*
We return thanks to the corn, and to her sisters,
* the beans and squash, which give us life.*
We return thanks to the bushes and trees,
* which provide us with fruit.*
We return thanks to the wind,
* which, moving the air, has*
* banished diseases.*

We return thanks to the moon and stars,
* which have given to us their light when*
* the sun was gone.*
We return thanks to our grandfather He-no, that
* he has protected his grandchildren from witches*
* and reptiles, and has given to us his rain.*
We return thanks to the sun, that he has looked
* upon the earth with a beneficent eye.*
Lastly, we return thanks to the Great Spirit, in
* whom is embodied all goodness, and who*
* directs all things for the good of his children.*

NINETEENTH-CENTURY IROQUOIS PRAYER

FOWL PLAY What would Thanksgiving be without turkey and cranberry sauce? A few years ago, Calvin Trillin lobbied hard to switch the national Thanksgiving dish from turkey to spaghetti carbonara, rationalizing that Columbus was from Genoa, but it didn't fly. It's interesting how food menus evolve, especially when reading what was served in 1621. Written records note that fowl was eaten but that doesn't mean turkey necessarily; turkey wasn't promoted until after World War II, when the poultry industry staged an aggressive publicity campaign.

As friends and family gather for dinner, ask each person to light a candle, toasting someone they would like to acknowledge—a new baby in the family, the scholar who has completed her dissertation, a loved one who has passed away, or a much-admired public figure. At one memorable Thanksgiving dinner, a five-year-old grandson raised his candle and said in a solemn tone that mimicked what he'd heard from the adults, "I raise this candle for my octopus Ophelia, who cannot be with us because she got torn, and Gamma is going to fix her. To Ophelia." As he raised his candle, the adults echoed, "To Ophelia."

What to Do with the Rest of the Day

Years ago, one friend bought a linen tablecloth especially for the holiday. As the dinner plates were cleared, she asked everyone to sign their names on the cloth. Later, she stitched over their signatures with embroidery thread. She changes the thread color each year, and has created a charming record of family at these gatherings along with their handwriting, especially cherished as children grow up and family members pass away.

Thanksgiving songs include "Bringing in the Sheaves," "Come, Ye Thankful People, Come" and "We Gather Together," which is actually a sixteenth-century folk hymn written to commemorate Dutch independence from Spanish domination—oh well. Moving from Boston to Santa Monica, what one friend missed most was listening to "Alice's Restaurant," Arlo Guthrie's Vietnam War-era saga of Thanksgiving revelry and civil disobedience, played in its entirety on Boston radio stations that day.

In one family, the youngest child is hoisted barefoot onto the end of the dining room table after dinner and, with loving hands to help, walks the length of the table.

Ode to a Turkey

For my own part I wish the Bald Eagle had not been chosen the Representative of our Country. He is a Bird of bad moral Character. He does not get his Living honestly. You may have seen him perched on some dead Tree near the River, where, too lazy to fish for himself, he watches the Labour of the Fishing Hawk; and when that diligent Bird has at length taken a Fish, and is bearing it to his Nest for the Support of his Mate and young Ones, the Bald Eagle pursues him and takes it from him. . . . For in Truth the Turkey is in Comparison a much more respectable Bird, and withal a true original Native of America. . . . He is besides, though a little vain & silly, a Bird of Courage, and would not hesitate to attack a Grenadier of the British Guards who should presume to invade his Farm Yard with a red Coat on.

BENJAMIN FRANKLIN,
IN A LETTER TO HIS DAUGHTER

Europeans had never seen corn before they met the Indians in Plymouth, yet today sixty-million acres of farmland in North America are devoted to corn. The Indians taught the Pilgrims how to grow, harvest, cook, and pop corn. Corn husks dolls were made by many Native American tribes and later adopted by the colonists. Engage the children in making corn husk dolls using dried corn husks, yarn or rubber bands, sticks for the arms and legs, paint (for the faces), and dolls' clothes if kids want to dress them up.

Minister Carrie Bail recounted an all-too familiar scene from her childhood: the women were busy cooking in the kitchen, the men were watching football on television, and restless kids were in the way. At this crucial moment, Carrie's mother pulled out a Jack Horner Pie—a metal pie plate, covered with brown paper, with ribbons protruding. Each child pulled a ribbon, at the end of which was a slip of paper with a clue written on it as to where a gift was hidden. The kids got busy searching for the gifts, which were usually games to play until the meal was ready.

Winter

What miracle of weird transforming
Is this wild work of frost and light,
This glimpse of glory infinite!

JOHN GREENLEAF WHITTIER

✳ Welcoming Winter ✳

Winter can be a magical time. Yet some people approach the season with a sense of dread. Even for those who enjoy it wholeheartedly, there is a lot of work involved in making merry. And for those whose spiritual beliefs don't fit into the Christmas/Hanukkah model, December can be a time of disconnectedness and loneliness.

In this chapter you'll find secular and sacred ideas that honor the winter season and allow you to welcome the "return of the light," whether you're religious or simply want to "throw off the toga," as Seneca the Younger did in AD 50 when he wrote: ". . . everywhere you may hear the sound of great preparations. . . . Were you here, I would willingly confer with you as to the plan of our conduct; whether we should eve in our usual way, or, to avoid singularity, both take a better supper and throw off the toga." Indeed, one family I know (he's Jewish and she's Christian) celebrate Hanukkah, the winter solstice, *and* Christmas. But, regardless of your religious persuasion and secular propensities, it's important not to feel pressured by all the choices that come with this time of year. Be generous with yourself, take a deep breath, and enjoy your own peace and spirituality in this exquisite season of light.

The Winter Solstice ✳ December 21 or 22

Increasingly, people who aren't religious but want to embrace the season have turned to solstice activities. As far back as we have records, there have been winter celebrations honoring the rebirth of the sun. This was true in ancient Babylon and Egypt, and even the origins of Christmas and, to a lesser extent, Hanukkah, go back to pagan rituals that encouraged the return of the light in the darkest days of winter.

Every December and June, for about six days, the sun seems to rise and set at roughly the same point on the horizon. This solstice (from the Latin *sol stetit* meaning sun stands still) had a profound effect on the ancients, who divided each year into two halves—the dark and the light—when the sun was either north or south of the equinox zenith.

Blustery midwinter festivities lasted from the solstice until early January. Before the year 1000, Scandinavians celebrated a pagan winter festival called Yule (or Jul, as the word first appeared in a Norwegian poem in 900). Celebrants gathered around large, slow-burning logs, drank mead, and listened to bards sing the great Norse legends. All quarrels were forgotten on the longest night of the year, and animals were thought to wait and watch for the sun's return.

The seven days preceding and following the winter solstice were a time of peace and stillness in nature when forest creatures seem to stay quietly in their dens. It was believed that during this time, a huge kingfisher bird (the halcyon) swooped down from the skies to calm the oceans and winds in order to build her nest on the waves and lay her eggs in peace (hence the phrase, halcyon days).

Occurring during the deepest, darkest phase of winter, the solstice was originally a fire festival to honor the sun and drive away winter demons; today it can simply be an occasion to embrace the changing seasons:

Every December, the Cathedral of St. John the Divine in New York City holds a special service that includes a performance by Grammy-winning musician Paul Winter. Called *Paul Winter's Winter Solstice Celebrations*, this wonderful event is broadcast annually on

National Public Radio. During the service, a giant, spinning globe ascends to the cathedral's vaulted ceiling, and one of the musicians plays a huge gong that rises like the sun.

✳ One winter solstice, Susie Tompkins Buell bundled up with friends, walked to the beach in front of her California home, and was amazed by the unusually low tide from the powerful pull of the new moon. It was so dramatic and invigorating, she checked the tidal chart and discovered that the summer solstice would cause a similarly low tide. Now every year on summer and winter solstices, she and her grandchildren greet the dawn on the beach with a picnic breakfast.

✳ Every winter, my friend Bill heads out into the California desert with some pals, lights a fire under the solstice moon, and sings Beatles and Dylan songs. My cousin Doug has a potluck, bonfire, and skating party at a pond across the street from his house. On the Canadian border, my sister-in-law Sarah and her husband Eric and ten other couples ski to a bonfire beside which a table has been set up with beverages and hors d'oeuvres, then ski a little further to someone's house for a potluck dinner. At our local community farm cooperative, members light a bonfire and host a potluck dinner to wrap up the harvest season.

"Doing the Winter" Around the World ✳

✳ In China, the solstice celebration Dong Zhi (the Arrival of Winter), also known as Ju Dong (or Doing the Winter), marks the turning point from dark to light, or when the *yin* qualities of the dark and cold give way to the balancing *yang* of light and warmth. It's still commemorated by dressing up, gathering with family, and serving a meal that includes rice balls to symbolize family harmony and togetherness.

✳ The Taiwanese serve twelve Mother Balls (representing the sun, one for each month of the year). Made by boiling rice dough in syrup and dying it red, the balls are laid out for the ancestors or placed over a doorway as a reminder of the sun's return.

✳ The Hopi tribe's Sun Chief observes the solstice by sitting on a rooftop for several days, watching the sun rise and set to determine the precise moment of the solstice. Then a prayer-offering ceremony called Sol-ya-lang-eu, begins, followed by a day of sacred activities and goodwill to honor the return of the sun.

✳ According to ancient Persian mythology, the sun god Mithra was born on the longest night of the year, and the Yalda (birth) festival was celebrated on the solstice to honor Mithra's victory over the darkness. Celebrants lit bonfires and kept vigil all night to make sure the fires didn't burn out, thus aiding the sun in its battle with the darkness.

✳ Las Posadas is a pilgrimage that begins on December 16 and reenacts Mary and Joseph's journey to Bethlehem. Mexican in origin—probably dating back to the time of the early

SANTA PIÑATA Some theorize that the piñata was brought to the New World by the Spanish, others believe it to be an ancient Aztec tradition. Originally a party game, piñatas were filled by the Spaniards with jewels, not candy. Today the piñata is used widely at children's birthdays, though in Mexico it's brought out at Christmastime. You can make a piñata by covering a balloon with papier-mâché. After it dries, paint on a Santa's face, cut open the top, and fill the piñata with small toys and treats, then place a Santa hat over the opening. Let the kids choose the recipient—a daycare center, a children's hospital, or Sunday school class.

Spanish missionaries—and widely celebated in Hispanic neighborhoods all over the U.S. today, participants are symbolically turned away at each house (like the holy family), until they reach the final house where they are welcomed with food and hospitality. One December evening while vacationing in Vieques, Puerto Rico, we saw a procession of costumed *peregrinos* (pilgrims) and *posaderos* (innkeepers) walking and riding horseback along the island's main street. In Guatemala, families in costume walk from house to house, partying as they are served chocolate, tamales, and breads.

Festivals of Light ✴

✴ For centuries, Swedes have observed the advent of the Christmas season with a festival of lights that incorporates both pagan and Christian symbols. On December 13, villages and rural communities throughout the country selected a local girl as their St. Lucia who, dressed in a white gown, red sash, and a crown of lingonberries and candles, went from farm to farm, house to house, lighting the way through the wintry darkness toward the manger of Jesus. Today, variations of this beloved festival still illuminate the year's darkest days all over Sweden.

✴ In Thailand, the Loi Krathong Festival of Light is held in November under a full moon. The word *loi* means float and a *krathong* is a boat made of banana leaves. Thais place a candle, three incense sticks, a flower, and coins into the krathong, take it to a river or canal, make a wish, and light the candle and incense before launching the boat, which will carry away bad luck.

✳ In India, Diwali is a five-day festival of lights held in October or November. While its specific origins differ from one region of the country to the next, Hindus of all sects celebrate Diwali with colorful lights and decorations, sweets and other delicacies, and fireworks.

Hanukkah ✳ November or December

Perhaps the best known Festival of Lights in the West is Hanukkah, which commemorates an historic event, but whose timing suggests a link to even more ancient light festivals. Two thousand years ago the Jews were ruled by a Hellenistic Syrian king, who took over their temples and threatened to kill them if they didn't give up the Torah and worship Greek gods. In 168 BC, the Maccabees (from the Hebrew word meaning "the hammerer") revolted and drove out the Syrians. In Jerusalem, the Maccabees discovered their temple had been desecrated with Greek statues and icons. After its restoration, they planned to rededicate the temple on the twenty-fifth day of Kislev, the ninth month in the Jewish calendar. But as the sacred menorah (a multistemmed candelabrum) was lit, they discovered the Syrians had contaminated most of the sanctified lamp oil, leaving only enough oil for a single day (with new oil a four-day ride away). Miraculously, the oil lasted for eight days, and Hanukkah, which means dedication, commemorates the rededication of the temple, freedom from persecution, and the miracle of the oil. To this day, food fried in oil, as a reminder of the temple oil, is a popular Hanukkah tradition.

Some rabbinical historians have suggested that the Syrian Greeks may have been performing pagan solstice rites in the temple on the twenty-fifth of Kislev, and that some of the Hellenized Jews may have enjoyed these events. The Maccabees might have chosen the twenty-fifth of Kislev as a day of rededication as a way to appropriate the most

THE FOUR-SIDED TOP called a dreidel (from the German word *drehen*, or "turn") is often given to children at Hanukkah. In times of persecution, sacred scriptures were hidden in a secret compartment in the dreidel. The five Hebrew letters on its exterior stand for AGMHH: A Great Miracle Happened Here. Or, if a dreidel is not made in Israel, it's AGMHT—A Great Miracle Happened There.

popular Greek rituals (including the lighting of candles) under the cloak of religious dogma, in much the same way that Christians repackaged December 25. Note that the eight-day Hanukkah festival is similar in length to Saturnalia, the Roman solstice festival (see page 203).

Regardless of the origins, the Jews transformed a dark time of year into a holy period of introspection and rededication of their faith. In the context of the Jewish calendar, Hanukkah is a relatively minor holiday, but since the 1960s it has been increasingly commercialized to correspond to the Christmas holiday season.

A TIME OF LIGHT

The eight branches of the menorah commemorate the days the oil in the temple lamp burned. (The ninth candle—the highest one—is called the *shamash*, or helper candle, and is used to light the others.) On the first night, two tapers are lit; the shamash is lit with a match, and the other is lit by the shamash. On the second night, an additional candle is lit, and so on, until the eighth night, when all are lit. The increasing light commemorates the growth of the miracle. (There is another tradition of keeping an unlit menorah next to the lit one, in observance of Jews who aren't free to light their own.)

A few years ago, Ben Binswanger's wife was a student working most evenings in the library. In Ben's family, it was important to light the menorah soon after sundown, so he'd sneak into the library each night with a menorah, which they'd furtively light in her cubby, and then he'd go home while she returned to studying.

Many people remember making menorahs as children. While there is an iconic shape, a menorah can be made out of virtually any materials. Help your children make one out of an outgrown toy like a train or blocks. You can even make one out of a flowerpot, with the candles planted in the earth. Menorahs come in all shapes and sizes; the only requirement is that the candles be spaced far enough apart that the flames don't touch each other. Lit menorahs are often placed in a window so they can be seen from outdoors.

A TIME OF GIVING

A traditional Hanukkah gift is *gelt* (German for money or gold) which can be real coins or those made of chocolate. The custom originated in Poland in the 1600s when parents gave their children money at this time of year to pay their teachers. Later, it was a reward for doing chores or other tasks. In the 1700s, poor children would knock on the doors of well-to-do households during Hanukkah and ask for gelt. Over the centuries, no doubt influenced by the Christmas tradition of gift-giving, more elaborate presents replaced gifts of money. There was a time when only the fifth night was dedicated to giving gifts, but the gift-giving eventually stretched over all eight days.

For those who wish to steer clear of the commercial holiday frenzy, suggestions from friends include the following:

✳ Devote one night to giving time or money (or both) to a charity of your choice. You might consider giving each child two bags of coins: one to keep for themselves and one to donate.

✳ Give one gift whose theme stretches over eight nights. My friend Jonquil reports that when she was a child a typical gift would be fun but practical. One year, Hanukkah gifts revolved around skiing: on the first night, she and her siblings each received new gloves; the next night, long underwear; the next night, ski poles, and so on.

✳ On the last night of Hanukkah, have a Gift-of-Self night, and ask each family member to give gifts that involve time, effort, and thought, but not money.

✳ Christmas: the Glitter and the Sacred ✳

May peace and plenty be the first
to lift the latch on your door, and happiness be guided
to your home by the candle of Christmas.
CELTIC BLESSING

Christmas is a wonderful time to create and sustain activities that center on family and an expansive spirit. Perhaps more than any other Christian holiday, Christmas is about generosity toward friends, family, and strangers, and, unlike most holidays, the spirit extends beyond a single day to embrace the entire season.

For those worn down by the commercialization of Christmas, it's also a felicitous opportunity to emphasize acts that are rooted in beauty, spirituality, and charity. For those forming new families, it's a time to compromise and introduce new ideas, incorporating customs from everyone's background while also creating some new ones.

The Birth of Christmas ✳

Imagine living before the invention of the lightbulb or even the gas lamp, and how good it must have felt to know that, after December 22, the days really would get longer. Four thousand years ago, Egyptians celebrated the "rebirth" of the sun in the dead of winter with a twelve-day party. Roman, Teutonic, and Celtic tribes, as well as Babylonians and Mesopotamians, also recognized the winter solstice in some fashion. In fact, the roots of Christmas are a mind-boggling blend of Nordic divination, Celtic fertility rites, and Roman holidays. That's why the Puritans hated it.

The Roman holiday was called Saturnalia to honor the agricultural god Saturn. From December 17 to 24, Saturnalia was, by all contemporary accounts, a pagan bacchanal. With the harvest complete and the light returning for another year, the empire put a lampshade on its collective head and proceeded to get squiffy. Masters waited on slaves. No fighting was allowed. No courts were in session. Merrymaking and masquerading in the streets were the order of the day. People decorated their homes with evergreen boughs, exchanged gifts, and were generally ancients-gone-wild. Indeed, Pliny built the first known sound-proof room so he could continue working during the noisy festivities. Saturnalia, and its related symbols and rituals, made such a lasting impression on European culture that many of our winter customs can trace their origins back to it.

The early church frowned on such behavior, but there was nothing comparable to divert people's attention from it; in those days, Christians didn't celebrate the birth of Jesus. A birthday was the day you ascended into heaven—no one cared about your entry into the mortal world—so only Easter was recognized. Yet something had to be done, so around AD 325 Pope Julius I proclaimed December 25 the day of Christ's birth to redirect the focus of this frenzied winter carnival. The date wasn't selected by chance: December 25 was the day that Roman Emperor Aurealian had, two hundred years before, claimed was the birthday of Sol Invictus (Invincible Sun). By the sixth century, the celebration of Christ's birth had spread to England (the Council of Trent declared the twelve days of Christmas to be sacred in AD 567), and by the 700s it had reached Scandinavia. Back in Rome, Charlemagne made Christmas an official holiday in the ninth century.

By the 1100s, Christianity had taken root in most of Europe. Many Christmas carols date from this period, and the colorful pagan ways were now firmly ensconced in Christian dogma; the Roman winter solstice—birthdate of the unconquered sun—became the birthday of Christ, and, over time, the wanton Saturnalia was stripped and repackaged as a ramp-up to "Christ's Mass."

The idea of Christmas being such a pivotal point on the Christian calendar is a relatively recent concept, perhaps spurred by St. Francis of Assisi, who in 1223 staged a play about Christ's birth that framed the story of the nativity as we know it today. Using Italian peasants and their livestock for his actors, he produced the first Christmas pageant. His intent was two-fold: The first was to entertain and educate the local populace. Books were not available (the Gutenberg printing press wouldn't be invented for another two hundred years), and literacy, except among the clergy and nobility, was rare. The second was to treat his animal actors to double rations. (St. Francis was a well-known animal lover.) It was quite a spectacle, and people came from miles away to see it. The pageant introduced stories about the birth of Jesus Christ that still are told—on Christmas Eve the birds came out to sing, the cattle spoke at midnight, the bees hummed in their hives, the animals knelt down, and the trees burst into bloom despite the winter cold.

By the 1600s, Calvinists were blasting Christmas pageantry, condemning its pagan influences, and on this side of the Atlantic, Puritans considered Christmas celebrations gaudy and immoral. In the fledgling Massachusetts Bay Colony, Governor Bradford fined colonists five shillings if they observed the holiday. Through the 1700s, pious Puritans—Quakers, Presbyterians, Methodists, Anabaptists, and Amish—would have nothing to do with it. But Dutch settlers along the Hudson River observed St. Nicholas Day on December 6 as well as Christmas, and holiday activities were alive in the South, especially in New Orleans and parts of Virginia, where caroling, hunting, and setting off firecrackers were part of the festivities. In Europe, despite the Reformation, Germans reveled in Christmas throughout the eighteenth century to the point that in 1775, the German government, worried about deforestation, banned the cutting down of small fir trees in Salzburg Forest. Wherever German immigrants settled in America, Christmas traditions flourished, especially those involving the tree.

In 1836, Alabama was the first U.S. state to declare December 25 a legal holiday. In 1843, English royalty tipped the balance when Queen Victoria's German husband Prince Albert introduced the Christmas tree to Britain by decorating one at Windsor for his infant son Edward, Prince of Wales. The British weren't wild about Prince Albert (or Germany, for that matter), but they were nuts about that baby, and the fact that Prince Albert had a decorated tree at Windsor Castle was recorded by the press in the most minute detail. Until then, Christmas trees had been snubbed by the English nobility and middle classes

> *It came as a surprising comfort to start this year's Christmas preparations. Each ornament, each recipe, was as soothing as the presence of an old friend.*
>
> ANNA METCALFE

as "too Prussian." The decorated tree was an overnight sensation in Britain and soon after in America. That same year, Charles Dickens wrote *A Christmas Carol*, and by 1856, President Franklin Pierce introduced the first White House Christmas tree. When *A Visit from St. Nicholas* (popularly known as *'Twas the Night Before Christmas*) was published in 1823, it did as much to etch the image of St. Nick into our collective imagination as St. Francis's pageant did for the nativity. The commercial image today of Christmas as a sugar-coated, child-oriented holiday is pure Victorian frosting.

Advent ✳

The Christmas season officially begins with Advent (Latin for *the coming*), a word the Church uses to denote the period of hope and preparation leading up to December 25. The idea of Advent most likely originated in Gaul in the fifth century as a way for Christians to prepare for the Epiphany on January 6 (when babies were often baptized and the birth of Jesus was celebrated) and later for Christmas. The length of Advent varied from twenty-one to forty days (beginning with the Sunday nearest the feast of St. Andrew on November 30), and is now considered to start four Sundays before Christmas. "Advent begins in a time of deep darkness—physical darkness—as the northern hemisphere slides inexorably to the moment of winter solstice," wrote Pastor Carrie Bail. "Part of the discipline of Advent is allowing ourselves to sink into that place of deep quiet, into the deep blue velvet stillness, to experience life at its most dormant, just like the bulb buried deep below the frozen soil."

ADVENT WREATH

The Advent wreath dates back to folk practices of Germanic and Eastern European tribes. During the December darkness, they would make evergreen wreaths and light bonfires to encourage an atmosphere of renewal. Christians, particularly German Lutherans in the 1500s, adopted the popular idea, and the wreath, brought to the United States by German immigrants, came to symbolize hope and everlasting light. Since the Middle Ages, four candles have been featured, often embedded in a circle of evergreens, though some churches place four candles on the perimeter and a fifth candle, to be lit on Christmas, in the center. The four candles each represent a Sunday before Christmas, the circular wreath suggests eternity, the greens suggest life in the darkest days, and the flames are a reminder of the return of the light.

ADVENT CALENDAR

In the early nineteenth century, literacy was still by no means the norm and few had access to printed calendars, so German Protestants would count the twenty-four days leading up to Christmas with chalk marks on their doors. In the late 1800s, one boy's mother hung twenty-four pieces of candy on a string, and allowed him to eat one piece each day in anticipation of Christmas. In 1908, remembering his mother's custom, Gerhard Lang, by now the owner of a printing shop, produced twenty-four small colored illustrations that could be displayed each day of Advent. It became so popular that soon he was printing a folding calendar with doors or windows that could be opened, and the "Munich Christmas Calendar" was a roaring success. After World War II, the unique calendar came to America.

One woman told me that her father made the family an Advent calendar every year, and the kids would take turns crossing off the days. Even after his children were grown, he continued to make one for each child and their families. He used the simplest materials—usually just crayons and white cardboard used to pack laundered shirts—and to this day, his daughter looks forward to opening the doors each night.

The Witherspoon Society (a group of progressive Presbyterians) recommends observing Advent in a holistic, global way that expands "our horizons of caring," and you can borrow ideas from their website or make up your own countdown—after a few days, my kids were adding their own suggestions. Here's the idea: take a coffee can and call it the "Advent of Caring" box. Each day, have kids put money into the box. The amount is determined by a simple thought about peace, the environment, or caring for others—starting local and going global. For example, on day 1 you put in a penny for every gift you received over the last year. On day 2 you donate a nickel for everyone in your household who took a shower or bath the day before, knowing that half the world's population doesn't have access to enough water to bathe regularly. On day 3 you contribute a dime for every girl in your family who goes to school, realizing that girls in many parts of the world don't have that option. On day 4 you give a quarter for everyone in your family who had enough to eat that day. On day 5, it's fifty cents for every family member who can drink the water from their faucets—acknowledging that millions of people the world over don't have potable water, or have to haul it over long distances. On day 6, put in seventy-five cents for every bottle you recycled that week. On day 7, donate a dollar for every time someone in your family walked or took public transport to school or work instead of driving or being driven that day. You get the picture. On Christmas day, determine as a family where to donate the money from your Advent box.

The Tree ✳

Even if you haven't strained the power grid with blinking, nodding reindeer on the lawn, winking lights draped across your shrubbery, or glowing icicles strung along your gutters, you probably have a Christmas tree. The tree can be procured many ways; you can buy one in town or go out into the woods and cut down your own. Julie Applegate grew up in rural Wisconsin, and every December, her dad would hitch up his team of horses to a sleigh, tuck the kids in under a woolly blanket, and head off for the local cemetery where they would cut down the loveliest big blue spruce tree that would fit through the French doors back home. Many years later she asked her father about the "cemetery thing," it having occurred to her that it was a bit unusual, and he explained that her grandfather had donated land to the cemetery and, as people kept dying, trees needed to be cleared away to make room for them.

PRESIDENT THEODORE ROOSEVELT was an ardent conservationist intent on protecting America's forests. While in office, he forbade his children from cutting down a tree for the White House Christmas, but the young Roosevelts disobeyed and hid the felled tree in a closet. When their father found out, he was furious and made the children visit Gifford Pinchot, a leading conservationist in the Roosevelt cabinet. Privately, Pinchot assured the president that careful culling of the forests was actually an asset to the natural landscape.

Ever since our children were babies, each December we've bundled up and headed for a tree farm with a thermos of hot chocolate, a sled, and a saw. We photograph ourselves in front of our selection, sip hot chocolate in the snow, and then cut the tree down. The U.S. Forest Service has a nationwide program whereby you can purchase a tree tag (usually for $5–$10) that allows you to harvest a "wild" tree from a National or State Forest. This actually contributes to the health of the forest, and the forest rangers are happy to direct you to good spots to find a tree.

As I enter the house of my youth, the familiar pine scent mingles with traces of clove and cinnamon, peppers and onions. I'm aware that I'm crossing a threshold into a haven of simple comforts and complex devotions, glimmering like shiny tree ornaments in the maze of my memory. For an instant, past and present collapse and I am no longer who I think I have become but who I have always been, defined by the events and attachments that transpired here, long ago, in this house.

DANA MICUCCI

ORNAMENTS

A surprising number of people expressed how important childhood ornaments were to them. Others described how they give their children a special ornament each year, choosing decorations that symbolize a personal milestone, a family trip, or a particular interest (a little stack of books tied with a book strap for first year of school, or a starfish to commemorate a beach vacation). Over the years, as each ornament is unwrapped and placed on the tree, it will evoke memories of places you've been, people you've known, and significant accomplishments. When your children are grown and leave home, give them each a box of their ornaments on a special occasion.

I particularly like to personalize ornaments for a baby's first Christmas. I find glass ball ornaments in antique and second-hand stores and personalize them with a glitter pen ("John Werner's First Christmas, 2002"), replacing the rusted hook with a satin ribbon. Another highly personalized ornament is to trace your child's hand on cardboard, cut out the shape, and decorate it on one side with paint, glitter, ribbon, and so on. On the other side, write a wish that your child has for that year. One woman found equally creative way to make her ornaments unique to her family. She found dozens of small identical wooden picture frames in a discount store. Though she had only one baby at the time, she hoped she'd have another, and so bought fifty (figuring it would cover two children through college). Each year she hangs new pictures of each of her two daughters, along with their names and the date, on the tree.

Decking the Halls *

A thousand years before the birth of Jesus, Egyptians decorated their temples with evergreens, pine cones, and herbs for the solstice. These plants were thought to be sacred, symbolizing eternal life in the dead of winter, and there are many such references in ancient Hebrew and Persian texts, Druid histories, and Oriental literature. The Romans and early Britons decorated with bay leaves, laurel, holly, ivy, mistletoe, and rosemary. Because they bore fruit in winter, ivy and mistletoe were considered so magical that the church banned them during the first centuries of Christianity. But after realizing how popular and deeply rooted these traditions were, church authorities recanted, and in the early seventh century, the Pope encouraged St. Augustine of Canterbury to use evergreens, fruits, and flowers. However, to this day you won't find mistletoe in a church.

MISTLETOE

In Greek mythology, mistletoe was the protective golden bough that Aeneas plucked from the live oak at the gates of the Underworld. A semi-parasitic plant that makes its home in trees, mistletoe was never allowed to touch the ground because the Druids thought it contained the life of the host tree. When Druid priests harvested mistletoe from sacred oaks on the sixth night after the new moon, the large clusters were caught in a cloth as they fell earthward. Small sprigs of mistletoe were distributed to ward off evil—it was hung over doorways to protect a home from lightning or on an infant's cradle to guard the child from fairies. It was believed that if a sprig was fed to the first cow to give birth after the new year the entire herd would be protected from disease. Kissing under the mistletoe dates to the pagan Saturnalia festival, and today one is supposed to pluck a berry and kiss under the sprig. When the berries are gone, so is the kissing.

HOLLY

Believing that Jesus' crown of thorns was made of holly, the French and English began to hang holly on their doors to indicate that they were Christians. According to legend, the holly berries on the crown were first white, but after it was pressed on his brow, the berries turned blood red.

POINSETTIA

The poinsettia was originally called *cuetlaxochitle* (flower that withers or mortal flower that perishes like all that is pure). Sacred to Aztecs, it was used in sacrificial rituals. After the Spanish Conquistadors invaded, Catholic missionaries arriving in Mexico were awed by the flower's beauty and, seeing the crucial role it played in Aztec rituals, spun a legend to attract the Indians to their newly constructed Christmas nativity scenes. Legend has it that a poor Mexican girl had no gift to offer the baby Jesus, so she picked a few scrawny weeds, and when she placed them at the feet of a statue of Mary, the weeds turned bright red. The legend spread throughout Mexico, Central America, and South America, and thus the poinsettia became the Flor de Nochebuena (Flower of the Blessed Night), a symbol of Christmas and conversion.

Kindle the Christmas brand, and then
Till sunne-set let it burn;
Which quencht, then lay it up agen
Till Christmas next returne.
Part must be kept wherewith to tend
The Christmas log next year;
And where 'tis safely kept, the Fiend
Can do no mischief there.

ROBERT HERRICK

In the early 1800s, a botanist named Joel Poinsett was appointed the U.S. ambassador to Mexico. An inveterate inventor and meddler, Poinsett was unpopular among the locals for his conviction that Mexico should be more like the United States, and locals coined a word to mean a pesky know-it-all: *poinsettismo*. In 1824, Poinsett went to a Christmas Eve mass at a small Catholic church and was bowled over by the nativity scene adorned with these exotic red flowers. Back home in South Carolina, he cultivated the species and gave the exotic plants as Christmas gifts. By the 1860s, the plant had been renamed *poinsettia* in the United States.

YULE LOG

The word Yule may derive from the Norman word for turning wheel, in reference to the cyclical rising of the sun after the winter solstice. Yule also means winter solstice celebration, referring to the annual tradition of dragging a great log from the forest into a village and setting it ablaze to drive away the evil spirits that lurked in the woods. Invading Britain in 1066, the Normans brought the Yule log custom with them, where it was adapted by Celtic Druids. Eventually, Celts and Gaelic Europeans brought the Yule log indoors and recast it as a Christian custom. After exchanging gifts on Christmas Eve, people would burn the log in defiance of the darkness, in honor of God's light, and as a symbol of the Christian prophecy of ashes to ashes.

The rules surrounding the Yule log gained in complexity over the centuries: it was only to be obtained from a tree on one's own property or a friend's property (it couldn't be received as a gift, for example, nor could it be purchased). It had to be large enough to burn twelve days with a bit left over to start next year's log, and was to be dragged inside by the entire family. It was usually cut in the spring and left outdoors where it was rubbed with cloves and other spices to make it aromatic by Christmastime. Once the log was lit on Christmas Eve, everyone threw holly branches into the fire to cast away that year's misfortune. A log that burned out in less than twelve days was a portent of bad luck.

The Yule log custom came to the American South in the 1800s. Slaves were responsible for hauling and tending it, which became of supreme importance, because agreements with their masters stipulated a period of rest in honor of the Christmas holiday, to be concluded when the Yule log ceased to burn. Slaves chose the toughest, greenest trees and would secretly douse the log with water to prolong the burning, prompting the folk-saying years later of something sodden having "as much water as a Christmas log."

CHRISTMAS STOCKINGS

I'm not much of a seamstress, but I made my children's stockings out of felt when they were infants, and am so glad I did. Every Christmas, I embroider the year and something memorable that has happened onto each stocking. The year our son was born, I stitched a simple rendering of the town where we live, with our house tucked against a mountain; another year I stitched a plane and the letters OK to represent our Christmas visit to grandparents in Oklahoma. The kids love reminiscing about past years—"Oh, that's the year we went to Oklahoma!" "That's the year Izzy was born!," "That's the year we started skiing!"—and they can use them for a lifetime. Now that knitting is fashionable again, there are many great Christmas stocking patterns available, too.

CHRISTMAS BY CANDLELIGHT

Early Christians were steeped in Judaic tradition, and during the Middle Ages a single large candle was lit at home as a reminder of the star of Bethlehem and of Jesus as the light of the world. Eventually, candles were transferred to the tree, and there are many associated legends. One has it that in the sixteenth-century Martin Luther took a walk under the stars on Christmas Eve and was so bedazzled that he wanted to share it with his family. He cut down a fir tree and brought it home to the nursery, lighting it with candles to brighten his children's Christmas. Some ideas:

* Illuminate your home with candles, and allow everyone to carry a candle to bed (under watchful eyes).

* Line your driveway or walkway with *luminarias*, as they do in Mexico and the Southwest, to symbolically light the way for the Christ child. They're easy to make: fill small brown paper bags with four inches of sand and wedge a votive candle into the sand inside each bag.

* There's an Irish tradition of placing a large candle in a front window on Christmas Eve to symbolically welcome the holy family.

✳ In Victorian England, people would place a candle in their front window during the Twelve Days of Christmas to let hungry strangers know that there was food and warmth within.

Holiday Performances ✳

Pick a holiday show, like *A Christmas Carol*, the *Radio City Christmas Spectacular*, *The Nutcracker*, *A Child's Christmas in Wales*, or *Amahl and the Night Visitors*, and take your children to see it in December. At New York's Trinity Church in lower Manhattan, the annual performance of Handel's *Messiah* was first performed in 1770. In 2001, the choir performed without their robes, which had been damaged on September 11, but, as the church was one of the few buildings in the immediate vicinity to remain standing, there were plenty of reasons to rejoice. Many churches throughout the country host *Messiah* sings; find one in your neighborhood—even if you're not much of a singer, it can be great fun.

THE NUTCRACKER In 1816, E. T. A. Hoffman wrote *The Nutcracker and the Mouse King*, a tale so dark that seventy-five years later, the publisher commissioned Alexander Dumas to write a frothier, friendlier version. The following year, in 1892, the story was presented by the Kirov Ballet in St. Petersburg, with a score by the ballet master's good friend, Pyotr I. Tchaikovsky. But there were complaints that the score was too hard to dance to, and though the ballet was performed elsewhere over the following decades, it wasn't until 1954, when George Balanchine restaged *The Nutcracker* at the New York City Ballet, that Tchaikovsky's *Nutcracker Suite* became perhaps the most popular ballet of all time. For those feeling a slight sugarplum overdose, Mark Morris's *The Hard Nut*, a wry send up created in 1991, is the perfect antidote.

Caroling ✳

Every year my cousins host the Foster Trainer Memorial Christmas Sing-Along in honor of our great uncle who loved Christmas carols. Three generations gather for a potluck dinner and caroling by the fire. We have established a consistent date so participants can schedule in advance. You can also find pubs and neighborhood watering holes that host public sing-alongs—such as the Kettle of Fish Tavern in Greenwich Village, where the owners bring in professional musicians to lead the singing; imagine two hundred people packed into the bar, playing marimbas, accordions, and guitars with everyone singing carols from photocopied sheets until the early hours of the morning.

Martin Luther loved carols; he sang to his children and his congregation and he inspired his countrymen to follow suit, which led to a profusion of great German carols beginning in the 1500s. In 1818, an Austrian priest and teacher wrote the exquisite "Stille Nacht" (Silent Night) and caroling continued to gather steam in Europe. In 1840, England's Queen Victoria married a German prince, Albert, also a lover of singing and caroling. Eventually, immigrants brought the custom to the United States, and, by the end of the Civil War, caroling became a way to minister to the elderly and sick who couldn't attend church services.

Of all the Christmas revelries, I encourage you to delight in singing, especially outdoors, for it fuels your soul, buoys your spirits, and promotes goodwill in a unique way. I even know some folks who sing to their animals. Sing with your children, and invite others to join you for a night of caroling around your neighborhood or to a hospital or nursing home (many churches organize such expeditions).

The Nativity Scene ✳

Every Christmas, Jim Govan of Arlington, Virginia, displays more than three hundred crèches that he and his late wife Emilia collected over many decades, beginning in 1962 when they were first married and bought a crèche for their first Christmas together. Other family crèche traditions:

✳ Each night during the week before Christmas, put out a new nativity figure. Talk about each character and how it fits into the story of Christmas.

✳ Place the figures of the Three Kings on the far side of the house or room and move them closer to the crèche each day, not landing them there until January 6, when, historically, they arrived in Bethlehem. Or hold back the manger until Christmas Eve, as they do in Puerto Rico.

✳ Display your nativity scene, but don't include Jesus (he doesn't arrive until December 25). Throughout the month, let children place a blade of straw in the manger every time they do a good deed. For very young children, this can be as simple as being polite, sharing toys, or accomplishing a task; the point is to encourage compassion and spiritual growth. (There's added incentive of giving the baby Jesus a soft, comfy bed.)

✳ If your child is adopted, a crèche from the land of her birth can be one way to incorporate her cultural heritage into your holidays. The nativity scene is revered in almost every culture, as people take the concept of Christ's birth with them and give expression to it during the Christmas season. We bought three tiny ceramic crèches (each is shaped like an egg) that we carried with us from Guatemala when we brought home our daughter.

We gave one to each set of the grandparents and kept one, which sits out on a bookshelf for the whole year.

Yours, Mine, and Ours: New Traditions for Stepfamilies ✳

Christmas can be especially hard for stepchildren. Not only do kids stand to lose the traditions they shared with their biological families, they may be shuffling between two households, neither of which necessarily feels like a safe, secure place they can call home. Throw in a potential income disparity between families, new stepsiblings, and possibly receiving modest gifts themselves while stepbrothers and stepsisters are showered with expensive gadgets from an absent parent—and you've got the makings for an emotional minefield. Blended families need new traditions to smooth the way:

✳ Make Christmas a season, not a day. If you focus traditions on that single twenty-four-hour period, and your children only see you every other year on Christmas Day, they'll feel they're missing something on the years they're with your ex. Create new traditions that aren't date specific such as picking out the tree, making wreaths, and shopping together.

✳ If you are with stepchildren on Christmas Day, don't push *all* your traditions on them at once; maybe this year you shouldn't visit your mother on Christmas morning—save that for a vacation day later in the week. Start traditions that will make new family members feel special—which may mean foregoing some favorite activities in favor of making time for new ones.

✳ Try not to force two celebrations on Christmas Day—"We'll be home in the morning, at noon you'll go to your father's house, then we'll pick you up at 4 P.M., with a quick stop for eggnog at Grandma Jane's on the way to Uncle Bill and Aunt Barbara's for their annual Christmas Day open house, then we'll end up at your Grandpa Jack's for supper because I know you wouldn't want to miss that."—unless of course you want the children's enduring holiday memory to be that of sitting in a car, racing against the clock.

✳ Be flexible. Be creative. Be generous. Ask them what *they* want to do to celebrate. Maybe they'd like to go ice skating on Christmas Eve or watch a holiday movie in the afternoon. Choose holiday activities that everyone can do together: skating, sledding, baking cookies. But don't be afraid to experiment with some separate activities that, while open to all the kids, don't require everyone to participate.

Christmas Music ✳

What would Christmas be without the music? A new crop of holiday albums is released every year in early to mid-November. I asked my friend Eric (who has collected close to two hundred holiday albums) to list his favorite under-celebrated recordings of all time:

"ALL ALONE ON CHRISTMAS" Darlene Love: This great rock 'n roll shuffle has jingling bells along with a great sax solo.

"SANTA CLAUS IS COMING TO TOWN" Bruce Springsteen and the E Street Band: Recorded live in 1975, this rarity captures the joy of the season.

"IN THE BLEAK MIDWINTER" Crash Test Dummies: This may be one of the most beautiful recordings of this song of all time.

"I PRAY ON CHRISTMAS" Harry Connick, Jr.: For a New Orleans-style Christmas, it's hard to beat Harry Connick.

"OI! TO THE WORLD" The Vandals/No Doubt: Both the original Vandals recording and the inspired No Doubt cover version are terrific. Ska-Punk for Christmas? You bet!

"LET IT SNOW! LET IT SNOW! LET IT SNOW!" Lena Horne: This is a classy, splashy big-band sound that transports you to the foot of the Rockefeller Center Christmas tree.

ANY TRACK OFF THE "CHRISTMAS SPIRIT" ALBUM Donna Summer: Whenever Eric has a Christmas party and this comes on the stereo, everyone asks who it is and where they can get it—no lie.

RUDOLPH THE RED-NOSED REINDEER was created by an ad writer for the Montgomery Ward department stores in 1939 as a Christmas coloring-book giveaway and by 1946, they'd given away six million booklets. The ad writer's brother wrote the song, which was recorded by Gene Autry in 1949 and sold two million records.

Christmas Movies ✳

Ugh, Christmas movies, you say. If I have to watch *It's a Wonderful Life* one more time, I'll slit my wrists with tinsel. I'm with you. But there are a few films that you may not have considered for your holiday viewing pleasure.

For Adults:

THREE GODFATHERS (1948): A classic John Ford western that stars John Wayne and Harry Carey, Jr. in a beautiful Christmas parable.

LOVE ACTUALLY (2003): An intertwining tale of eight couples dealing with life and love in the month leading up to Christmas. It's got a great soundtrack, too.

HOLIDAY INN (1942): Bing Crosby and Fred Astaire star in a holiday classic that features the debut of "White Christmas," one of the best-selling songs of all time.

THE THIN MAN (1934): Set during the holiday season, the dapper William Powell and the sassy Myrna Loy are dynamite in the first, and best, film in the *The Thin Man* series.

For Kids:

OLIVE, THE OTHER REINDEER (1999): An animated adaptation of Vivian Walsh and J. Otto Seibold's children's book which tells the hilarious story of a dog with reindeer aspirations.

RANKIN/BASS CHRISTMAS MOVIES (1970s): Most of these animated features, including *The Year Without a Santa Claus*, *Rudolph the Red-Nosed Reindeer*, and *Santa Claus is Comin' to Town*, have been released on DVD.

CHARLIE BROWN CHRISTMAS (1965): When you were a kid, didn't you always look forward to the night that this aired on TV? There's a great, boxed set of the *Peanuts* classics available on DVD.

EMMET OTTER'S JUG BAND CHRISTMAS (1977): This Jim Henson production, with songs by Paul Williams, is a clever adaptation of O. Henry's classic Christmas story *The Gift of the Magi* that never fails to remind us what is most important about the season.

THE RAYMOND BRIGGS' THE SNOWMAN (1982): This beautifully melodic adaptation of Briggs' book is a mesmerizing, wordless treat for young children.

Christmas Stories for Children ✳

Children's stories have a way of focusing the holidays and helping to set a mood. Some options:

THE BIRDS' CHRISTMAS TREE by Emma L. Brock (1946): A tree decorated with bird seed makes for a happy bird party at Christmastime.

THE LITTLE FIR TREE by Margaret Wise Brown (1954): The author of *Goodnight, Moon* wrote this sensitive story full of love and hope about a lame boy and a tree in the forest.

THE ANIMALS' CHRISTMAS by Anne Thaxter Eaton (1944): Poems, carols, and stories about the animals present at Christ's birth.

NIGHT TREE by Eve Bunting (1991): A touching story of a family who decorates and sings carols to a tree in the forest every Christmas Eve.

APPLE TREE CHRISTMAS by Trinka Hakes Noble (1984): An eloquent story about a family in the 1800s and their beloved apple tree.

THE CLOWN OF GOD by Tomie dePaola (1978): A retelling of the French legend of the little juggler who offers the Christ child the gift of his talent and the miracle that occurs.

Christmas Cards and Letters ✳

Christmas cards, which date back to the 1840s, were originally a way for less affluent Londoners to exchange a "gift" of remembrance during the holidays. Increasingly today, people are sending out Epiphany or New Year's cards and enjoying the leisurely week after Christmas to write thoughtful notes.

Christmas cards are a fun way to exert some seasonal creativity. Eric Kerns, for example, creates an annual card featuring his daughters in various, silly tableaux. Not a professional photographer, he shoots these scenes at home with a digital camera, a few hardware-store floodlights, and the assistance of his patient wife. The 2002 card showed one daughter discovering her three-week-old sister stuffed inside a Christmas stocking with the caption "Have yourself a very little sister!" Last year featured Eric in a Batman suit flanked by his two girls wrinkling up their noses in disgust; the caption simply said, "Jingle Bells, Batman Smells . . . "

Which brings us to the subject of the family Christmas letter. I won't mince words. I dislike photocopied holiday letters, which are mostly an excuse for people to brag about their year-to-date accomplishments and have little to do with connecting with the recipient or wishing them well. That people would send a generic letter to everyone on their Christmas list I find equally bizarre, considering that if they are close friends you probably know most of these details, and if they are not, you probably don't care. That said, there is one holiday letter I do enjoy receiving. It's from Joe's cousin Clay. He hates these letters too, and one year he decided to write one that gleefully lampooned the genre, but still managed to be informative about his family's activities—which is pretty hard to do. The result was hilarious. If you must send one, please make it worth reading, like Cousin Clay's on the following page.

Gift Giving ✳

Centuries ago, ancient Romans exchanged gifts during Saturnalia to celebrate the New Year. In early Christian times, children were told that baby Jesus brought gifts with his angels on the eve of his birth. In France, he was Le Petit Jesus, in Germany, Christkind or Christkindel, which eventually became Kriss Kringle. Gifts were delivered depending on

Dear Friends, Family, and Potential Subscribers,

This is the fifth annual Thompson Christmas letter (not counting the year we never got around to it). Due to popular demand and word-of-mouth, this letter now goes out to over 1,700 families, some of whom we've never met. Those who are not our close friends will find an invoice in the envelope. If you wish to stay on our mailing list, please pay up.

I know you're all dying to hear about our year. I am working for a small, very successful management consulting firm in Tulsa. They have quite a good reputation, and so far I haven't spoiled it (of course, they haven't let me out of the office). Our number is (812)-555-0631. I can be bought.

Melissa and I went to Boston and saw the Boston Pops, where the program was "Broadway Hits." When they started playing "Oklahoma!" I stood up, as all good Okies should. Melissa was mortified. The guy next to us (from England) had said he would stand up with me if I did. I don't think he thought I would go through with it. He was mortified, too. We also went to St. Croix, but nothing funny enough to mention happened. But on the way home, we sat next to Geena Davis, which excited Melissa. In case anybody wonders, she didn't look nearly as good as my lovely bride. (Melissa suggested I put that in.)

My brother and my sister got married (not to each other). One of them married way over their head. I'm not saying which one. We love both new additions to our family.

My parents decided to retire after more than thirty years, and are now in the process of a big "going-out-of-business" sale. If you want some terrific deals on great stuff, hurry to downtown El Reno. Please. My inheritance is at stake.

God has blessed our family greatly, and we pray He blesses you in the coming year. Although we know that we won't see as many of you as we would like, we value keeping in touch. We wish you a joyous Christmas and many blessings in the New Year.

The Thompsons

PS: For a limited time we're offering a bound collector's edition of all the Thompson Christmas letters. These masterpieces go back to 1989 (except for 1991—the lost year). You may get yours by sending cash payment (no checks) of $29.95 to the return address. Actually, we started in 1987 but no longer have 1987 or 1988, so if you've saved yours, they're probably worth a lot of money.

how well children had behaved—good behavior meriting a reward while naughty behavior was punished (providing an early introduction to theology).

St. Nicholas, who lived during the fourth century in what is now Turkey, was the inspiration for the Santa Claus figure. An orphan, Nicholas dedicated his life to helping the poor and often brought gifts to children. Also revered by sailors, he eventually became the patron saint of travelers and children. He was born on December 6, now the feast day of St. Nicholas. By the 1200s, St. Nicholas Day was a religious holiday in Holland, Germany, and France that focused on generosity and charity. By the 1400s, St. Nicholas was the third most-beloved religious figure, after Mary and Jesus, with over two thousand chapels and monasteries dedicated to him.

The Dutch continue to honor St. Nicholas (Sinterklaas) on the eve of December 6. They also observe Christmas, but strictly as a religious occasion. Sixteenth-century Dutch children were told that if they were good, St. Nicholas would appear in his red bishop's robe on the eve of his feast day and leave fruit and small treats in their stockings or wooden shoes. These were left by the hearth stuffed with hay for the horse or donkey that accompanied him. Dutch colonial settlers in New Amsterdam (New York) brought this custom with them, and Sinterklaas evolved over the years into Santa Claus in North America.

In 1822, Clement Moore wrote *A Visit from St. Nicholas* (also known as *'Twas The Night Before Christmas*), drawing inspiration from a description by a Dutchman who drove Moore home from a Christmas Eve party in Greenwich Village in a horse-drawn sleigh. Interestingly, though Moore is credited with conjuring the contemporary image of Santa as a jolly man in a red suit, the name "Santa Claus" does not appear in print for another year until James Fenimore Cooper's novel *The Pioneer*.

During the Civil War, cartoonist Thomas Nast, who created the Democratic donkey and Republican elephant, depicted a jolly Santa delivering presents to soldiers from a sleigh pulled by reindeer for *Harper's Weekly*. (It was Nast who invented the idea of Santa living at the North Pole.) Santa Claus is a mixture of many mythological figures: St. Nicholas, Saturn (the Roman god), the Holly King (the Celtic god of the dying year), Father Ice (the Russian winter god), and Thor (the Norse sky god). A Santa who arrives by reindeer-drawn sleigh and slides down the chimney is a purely American fabrication.

Today in Mexico, Spain, and South America, gifts are brought by the Three Kings on January 6 (Epiphany). Indeed, in Puerto Rico, the Epiphany—El Dia de los Reyes (The Day of the Three Kings)—is the highlight of the season rather than Christmas. Children receive their gifts on the Epiphany, leaving grass in their shoes for the Three Kings' camels, and it's a national holiday. In England and France, Father Christmas bears gifts, and in North America, of course, it is Santa Claus who leaves the loot. In thinking about Santa Claus, I'm reminded of a definition I once read, as told by a young girl. She said that a myth is a story that isn't true on the outside, but is real on the inside.

Letter to Santa ✳

In Germany, children leave letters to Santa between the interior glass and the exterior storm window or screen. An angel collects the letters at night, sometimes leaving behind a small gift. In England, children write letters to Father Christmas. Lucky were the children of J.R.R. Tolkien who, starting in the 1920s, received an annual letter *from* Father Christmas in response to their letters. The letters were filled with details about the North Pole, the elves, and the weather, and were beautifully illustrated by Tolkien.

Compiled in a book called *The Father Christmas Letters*, it's a gem to read and will perhaps inspire you to start your own letter-writing tradition.

Eric Kerns's father always put his letter to Santa in a red envelope, which the family ceremonially burned in the fireplace, the idea being that the smoke would carry it up to the North Pole. But his father would secretly switch the envelopes, so that on Christmas morning, the letter that had supposedly gone up the chimney miraculously reappeared by Eric's stocking with singed edges. Eric does this with his own little girls, and the look on their faces when they see the "burned" letters is priceless.

PLAYING SANTA My friend Molly Polk told me: "Family gatherings are ideal occasions to perform songs learned throughout the year and especially songs learned in preparation for the Christmas season." 'O Holy Night' and 'Ave Maria' are two of my family favorites. But right around 8 o'clock on Christmas Eve at my aunt and uncle's house, we switch to the secular when my uncle Martin plays 'Rudolph the Red-Nosed Reindeer' on the piano. This is the cue for whoever is playing Santa that year to come down the stairs, in costume, with a bag full of candy. Santa sits by the fireplace in the living room, and everyone takes turns telling him what he or she wants for Christmas. Santa has been played by my father, my brother, my husband (he was my fiancé at the time, so this was good for his credentials), all of my uncles, and even a family friend or two. I think it's about time a woman played the part, so I might volunteer this year."

It Is Better to Give ✳

A way to combat the commercialization of the season is to emphasize the origins of gift giving, by offering homemade gifts that express your values or feelings for the recipient with the latest expensive gadget:

✳ Picture frames decorated with shells, buttons, or rhinestones for photos of your child and her friends make wonderful gifts for close friends.

✳ Especially if you have young children, ask other parents to consider exchanging home-made gifts. Last year at my daughter's playgroup we drew names from a hat, and the kids and moms made the gifts. One was particularly inspired: a Baby Wipes box labeled a Snow-man-Making Kit, filled with buttons, painted pebbles, an old scarf, and a hat, which was used all winter by the lucky recipient.

✳ When our son was young, we found two rocks on the beach in the shape of a footprint. We paint-stamped them at home with an imprint of his foot and gave them to each of his grandfathers for paperweights.

✳ A gift of a poem or song that you've written is something your children will never outgrow. And if your kids wouldn't be mortified, ask them to perform a song, a dance, a poem, or skit for their grandparents. Children gain good skills by memorizing and per-forming, and their audience will love it.

✳ Try wrapping presents in recycled materials, like comics or cloth napkins or magazine pages. Challenge yourself to have it look great, and it will be a gift to the earth as well.

Giving When There's a Crowd ✳

If you have a lot of kids or relatives to shop for, or want to limit the volume of toys or token presents, there are some useful alternate strategies. One of my favorites is the Yankee swap: Each participant contributes one wrapped gift worth $10. Everyone sits in a circle, and someone starts by choosing and opening a gift from the pile. Next, the person to his or her right opens a gift, and can keep it or exchange it for gift #1. The next person opens a gift, and can keep it or exchange it for gifts #1 or #2. Usually the gifts are comical, so the exchanging becomes hilarious, with people fighting for the pink plastic back scratcher or tasseled toilet plunger. When all the gifts have been opened, the person who started gets his choice from among the whole pile. At this point, there's much shouted advice, as well as the attempted hiding of presents people don't want to relinquish.

My cousin Robin has a "Jack Horner" ritual on Christmas night, based on the nursery rhyme. In her variation, you pull out a gift instead of a plum. She makes a centerpiece with a bowl filled with gifts attached to ribbons. Each ribbon leads to a place setting. After dinner, everyone pulls a ribbon and receives the gift attached at the other end.

I know of one large family that has each child pick a sibling's name out of a hat, and that will be the one brother or sister they give a present to. When it is time to exchange gifts, the giver and receiver sit on the couch together and open the gift in front of the assembled family. With each child concentrating her or his effort on just one gift, there is a thoughtfulness in their choices that would likely be lost if they were pressured to select gifts for everyone.

And if you have a Brownie troop or chess club to host, organize a cookie exchange instead of a gift exchange. (Baking beforehand is half the fun.) Everyone brings their favorite Christmas cookies, wrapped in packages of six cookies each. If you bring three packages, you take home three packages, and so forth. Everyone ends up with a wide assortment of homemade treats to share for the holiday.

Giving to Others ✳

GIVING TREE Churches, firehouses, or other civic institutions will often set up a Giving Tree with paper ornaments, each one identifying a family or individual in need in the community. My sister-in-law Victoria takes her daughter to the local firehouse, chooses the name of a child her daughter's age, and purposefully selects several gifts that are on her five-year-old's wish list. Mother and daughter buy, wrap, and deliver the presents to the firehouse for the other little girl, prompting a discussion about the nature of giving. Victoria also makes sure that her daughter gets a few, but not all, of the items that she's requested for herself.

SANTA'S SECRET HELPER Do something helpful for someone on the sly. Maybe a neighbor needs firewood or to have her front yard raked or driveway shoveled. If your action might be misunderstood (after all, someone might be startled if a stack of firewood suddenly appeared on his lawn), leave a note signed "Santa's Helper." Children delight in the strategizing and secretive nature of this gift. A variation on this idea is to draw names within your family—the name you draw is the person you secretly do nice things for—it can be making a bed, ironing a favorite shirt, or leaving flowers by a bedside. The catch is that it must be done secretly, which is harder to do than you might think, but working out how to accomplish this is half the fun.

SECRET ST. FRANCIS Take cat food or dog biscuits to your local animal shelter or veterinary clinic, or donate old blankets or towels. Rather than throwing out your gingerbread house as the season winds down, leave it outside for small animals and birds to enjoy.

BE AN ANGEL TO A STRANGER After my first husband passed away just before Thanksgiving, I took the train to New York a few weeks later—an enormous effort—and while riding along the Hudson River we hit a bump and my soda spilled all over me and the floor. Today it seems preposterous that I'd be upset by such a trivial mishap, but when you're fragile, small problems can seem monumental. The train steward saw it happen, though I tried to hide my tears. He didn't say a word, but ten minutes later he returned with a fresh soda for me. I was so grateful and shall never, ever, forget that stranger's gesture. At the time, I thought, oh boy, I must really seem like a loser, but now I realize he had a finely tuned emotional antenna and he used it thoughtfully.

BE AN ANGEL TO OTHERS Christmas may not be much fun for those who work over the holiday, such as bus drivers, restaurant workers, building doormen, store clerks, or

SLEIGH BELLS RING When I was four, my Uncle Joe's family came to visit us for Christmas. We were living in Falmouth Foreside, Maine, at the end of a dead-end road that hugged a cove, and just after I was tucked into bed, Uncle Joe ran down the beach ringing a strap of sleigh bells. I still remember opening the window on that clear night, the sea in the cove almost black, the stars twinkling, and the air painfully cold in my lungs as I stuck my head out the window and inhaled. I wanted to race down the stairs to tell everyone, but my mother encouraged me to look out the window for more traces of Santa until my uncle had time to sneak safely back inside.

nurses. You might bake cookies for them, or think of other ways to acknowledge their contribution while passing along some holiday cheer.

Christmas Morning ✳

Though many parents get up in a state of semiexhaustion (having stayed up late stuffing stockings and wrapping presents only to be awakened in near darkness by overexcited kids), at this point the bulk of the holiday work is done, and everyone can relax and enjoy themselves. Consequently, it should come as no surprise that of all the Christmas traditions I asked people about, Christmas Day yielded the fewest surprises. Everybody does pretty much the same thing, with a few subtle variations.

An informal survey of friends suggests that most families allow children to dive into their stockings first thing in the morning but wait until the entire family is assembled, and slightly more awake, to open gifts. In some households, chaos reigns, with the children descending on the presents like a pack of wolves taking down a limping caribou. Many Catholic families attend one of two Christmas masses, the sunrise Shepherds' Mass or the Kings' Mass, later in the day, and a few even bake a birthday cake in honor of the Christ child.

Another common gift-opening scenario is one in which someone is selected to play Santa and pass out the gifts. Presents are then opened one at a time so that everyone can see what each person has received. Linda White's family takes this one step further and uses each gift as soon as it's opened. If someone gets a board game, the gift opening stops and the game is played then and there. If someone receives a new outfit, they must model it for the rest of the family. Linda enjoys how it keeps everyone together for the entire day.

As you may have experienced, small kids can take a long time to open their gifts. If one package contains a coveted new toy, the rest of the world disappears once that toy is in their hands. You might stash away any presents that are still unopened by Christmas afternoon and dole them out over the Twelve Days. . . .

At some point on Christmas day, there comes a beautiful time of peace, when everyone retreats to a little nest in a couch or armchair with a new book or toy. Take advantage of the lull, stop doing chores, curl up (or stretch out), and relax. Maybe even take a nap on the couch by the fire. You've earned it.

The Pageantry of Food ✳

By the eleventh century, the English were serving strange and magnificent dishes during the twelve days of Yuletide feasting. Preparations involved hunting expeditions for pheasant, grouse and, if the hunters were lucky, wild boar. Game birds were plucked, stuffed, roasted, and re-plumed before being served with much fanfare to guests at holly-strewn tables. Wild boar were difficult to hunt, so serving a boar's head in medieval times was a magnificent treat, and the sixth day of Christmas, December 30, became the day to "bring in the boar." An Elizabethan Christmas feast included swan, pork, and beef, as well as potatoes, which were a delicacy in those times.

To this day, the Christmas meal, while not as central as the Thanksgiving feast, figures prominently in most people's recollection. Roast turkey is a common main dish in the United States and Great Britain, but it's a relatively recent tradition, popularized in 1843 when Charles Dickens published *A Christmas Carol.* Christmas menus around the world include the following:

SEAFOOD EXTRAVAGANZA My cousin Bradley's wife Donna is not sure how her family's tradition of eating seafood on Christmas Eve began—maybe because a grandmother was from Naples (there's a Sicilian tradition of a seven-fish dinner on Christmas Eve, because Catholics weren't supposed to eat meat). The fish must be fresh, and there must be lots of it. Donna's father always overdoes it—so Donna has to swear not to tell her mother the cost—but that's his tradition, every year dreaming up a new fish menu to "wow" the crowd. Back from the market, the family spends the day cooking anywhere from seven to thirteen seafood dishes: poached salmon with cucumber scales, shrimp draped over ice bowls lit from underneath, lobster trees that spin, with the pièce de résistance, a seafood dish linguine with tomato sauce (fra diablo). The family eats and parties until midnight, when they kiss and exchange gifts. Hungry again, sausage and pepper sandwiches are served. (It's okay to eat meat, as it's after midnight, it's tradition). It's crowded and loud, and friends stop by after midnight since there wasn't enough room for them at the table (that seats thirty) earlier in the evening. (And this is the table Donna's father had extended just so there'd be no kids' table on this one night of the year.)

DENMARK Roast goose stuffed with prunes and apples is served with red cabbage, followed by apple cake.

ENGLAND Stuffed roast turkey with strips of bacon strapped across its back is accompanied by roast potatoes and other root vegetables, followed by a Christmas pudding soaked with brandy, topped with a white hard sauce. The person who finds the coin inside the pudding will have good fortune in the coming year.

FINLAND Boiled codfish, suckling pig, rye bread, and boiled potatoes are the Christmas staples.

SITTING AT THE KIDS' TABLE Is there an image more iconic of childhood gatherings than "the kids' table"? Those three words take me back to my grandmother's house at Thanksgiving, with all the adults sitting in the dining room around Great Uncle Wally's table, and us cousins at the kids' table in the kitchen on the speckled linoleum floor. It wasn't half bad—if you craned your neck you could see the adults through the doorway, and, truth be told, it was more fun in the kitchen; at the adult table we had to behave. Our table was a warped card table Dad had found at the dump, with one wobbly leg that was in danger of giving way if you put your elbows down hard and leaned forward. The lucky ones got first dibs on the green metal folding chairs—the rest of us had to make due with upturned milk crates, telephone books, or the swivel piano stool. The adults ate off the peony china; we got the orange Fiestaware and Dixie cups. "In our family someone had to die before you graduated from the kids' table," joked one cousin. "Hey, Aunt Myrtle's not looking so hot—now's my chance."

FRANCE While roasted goose or turkey is the principle entrée; it's the desserts that are the real stars—there is the *bûche de Nöel* (a cake that looks like a Yule log, frosted with marzipan), or *pithiviers*, a puff-pastry cake decorated with a crown (a nod to the Three Kings), with a lucky bean baked inside (whose recipient gets to be king or queen for the day).

RUSSIA From a vast country of varied traditions comes holiday specialties that emphasize sweetness: *kolach* (braided loaf) in the Ukraine and throughout Russia, *kut'ya* (steamed wheat, sweetened with fruit and raisins) and *vzvar* (a beverage made with stewed dried fruits).

On Christmas Eve, my Oklahoma in-laws always served clam chowder. (On the other hand, growing up on the New England coast, I've always had roast beef—go figure.) The

Fox family in suburban New York always serves lobster—even the grandkids get their own crustaceans. Judging by gourmet magazines and holiday recipe guides on the Internet, there seems to be a trend toward adventurous Christmas menus that incorporate dishes from around the globe, from linguine with gorgonzola and walnut sauce to Moroccan lamb kabobs to lobster thermidor. This is the time for a celebratory meal with expensive ingredients you might not be able to justify on a regular basis. Whatever the dish, people have vivid memories of their Christmas meals, as evidenced by the following:

As my friend Erik Bruun explained, the dessert of rice pudding, with a single whole almond hidden inside it, has been an annual source of amusement, suspense, and stability. No matter what calamities have struck his family (and he laughingly says there have been plenty), this was something from their Danish heritage that everyone looked forward to, for whoever found the almond received a special gift. And, he noted, it took his brother almost thirty years to win it. Past prizes have ranged from an ostrich egg to a waterproof camera.

Popular in Russia and Poland, especially with Eastern Orthodox Christians, the Svjatyj Vecer consists of a meatless dinner of twelve courses to symbolize the twelve apostles. The guests must take a bite of each course, which can be as simple as a dish of olives or as elaborate as stuffed-cabbage pastries. The meal starts when the first star is seen in the sky. Hay is often used as a table centerpiece, to remind celebrants of the manger in the stable.

For Christmas Eve, my cousin Steve's French Canadian wife serves tourtiere, a meat pie that is typically eaten after midnight Mass. Made by cooking and grinding a pork loin, then combining it with mashed potatoes and spices (heavy on the cloves) in a double-crust pie, tourtieres are typically served with bread-and-butter pickles, rolls, and a salad. They freeze well, and she makes at least a dozen before the holidays, to give away as Christmas gifts.

☀ The English set the table with little "firecrackers" that, when pulled (by two people), spill a tissue paper crown and a small gift. My friend Sue Hamilton would never think of having Christmas dinner without Christmas crackers—she used to have her parents send them from England, but now they're available in the States.

☀ The Raab family always has their big meal on Christmas Eve, with ornaments at each place setting for guests to take home. Christmas Day dinner is leftovers, with the same hors d'oeuvre served every year: shrimp marinated in a little olive oil, bread crumbs, and lots of black pepper, then grilled in their shells in the flames of the fireplace. You can eat the shells and all.

Twelve Days of Christmas ☀

I used to assume that the Twelve Days of Christmas led up to Christmas, not realizing they were the days between Christmas and Epiphany, on January 6. In 567, the Council of Trent proclaimed the twelve days to be a sacred season, and by the Middle Ages, Christmas was a twelve-day holiday:

DAY 1: CHRISTMAS DAY • DECEMBER 25 Christ's birth was honored on January 6 until the fourth century AD, when the Roman Emperor Constantine moved the date to December 25 in an effort to synchronize with pagan festivals.

DAY 2: BOXING DAY · DECEMBER 26 Boxing Day dates back to the Middle Ages, when collection boxes for the poor were placed outside church doors. It's a huge holiday in virtually every English-speaking country with the exception of the Unites States and nearly as important as Christmas in Britain. Since the 1600s, there has been a tradition of giving tradesman their Christmas box, or annual tip, the day after Christmas. December 26 is also the feast day of St. Stephen. Celebrated primarily in Ireland, where it's a national holiday, this is the feast day on which Good King Wenceslas looked out, and the carol is about generosity to those less fortunate. It's still a day to meet with family and friends, and some make an effort to donate time, money, or energy to helping others in need.

DAY 3: MOTHER NIGHT (ALSO KNOWN AS ST. JOHN'S DAY) · DECEMBER 27 Mother Night was so-called by Anglo Saxons, as it celebrated the Winter Goddess (shown in drawings as a woman on a sled drawn by dogs, dispensing gifts over twelve days). Known by different names in various mythologies, she was Frau Holle in Germany, Mother Carey in the United States, and Berchtl in the Tyrolean Alps. She can also be found as Mother Holle in the Grimm's fairytales, where snow was symbolized by the feathers that Mother Holle shook from her comforter. Catholics created a feast day on December 27 for the disciple John; in Germany and Austria, priests bless the wine on this day, and "St. John's wine" is thought to have healing properties.

DAY 4: HOLY INNOCENT'S DAY (IN ENGLAND, CHILDERMAS) · DECEMBER 28 Looking for the infant Jesus, King Herod ordered his soldiers to slay all the male children in Bethlehem under the age of two. The church referred to these massacred infants as the Holy Innocents. Celebrated in both Latin and Greek Churches, the Feast of the Holy Innocents is included in the Calendar of Carthage as early as the fifth century. It is not widely celebrated today.

DAY 5: FEAST OF FOOLS • DECEMBER 29 One of the oldest relics of religious theater, the Feast of Fools dates back to the twelfth century and was roaringly popular in the Middle Ages. For centuries, the clergy found it hard to control those who clung to the customs of the pre-Christian past, so the Church dedicated a feast day that allowed the common folk, in the diary of one doctor, to "exhale at least once a year . . . the folly which is natural to and born with us." The Feast of Fools was a peculiar feast day, with clerics and peasants cutting loose by inverting the social order: priests wore outlandish masks, clergy dressed as women and danced in the sanctuary, incense was made with stinky shoe soles, priests screeched chants and concluded the Credo with donkey brays. The Feast of Fools was outlawed by the Council of Basel in 1431 but didn't lose steam until the Protestant Reformation in the 1500s. Today, December 29 is a day for Morris dancers and mummers, general buffoonery, and a masquerade ball. In England, especially during the early Tudor period, the noblemen appointed a King of Misrule to preside over festivities at their great estates. This title dated back to Saturnalia, when Romans appointed someone to preside from Halloween to Candlemas, and spread throughout medieval Europe—he was called the Abbot of Unreason in Scotland and the Prince des Sots in France—with his reign lasting anywhere from twelve days to three months.

DAY 6: BRINGING IN THE BOAR • DECEMBER 30 Dating back to a time when Norsemen and Druids hunted wild boar for solstice parties; at Queen's College at Oxford University, students still carry in a roasted boar on a platter, singing a carol dating from 1521: "The Boar's head in hand bring I, Bedecked with bays and rosemary; I pray you, my masters, be merry, *quot estis in convivo* (so many as are in the feast)."

DAY 7: NEW YEAR'S EVE • DECEMBER 31

DAY 8: NEW YEAR'S DAY • JANUARY 1

DAY 9: SNOW DAY • JANUARY 2

DAY 10: EVERGREEN DAY • JANUARY 3 In pre-medieval times, trees were considered sacred because spirits were thought to live in them.

DAY 11: ST. DISTAFF'S DAY • JANUARY 4 In pre-industrial societies, this was the day people returned to work—the women at home, the men in the fields. They tried to make it fun by being silly: if the women were weaving, for example, the men might set fire to the flax. There is no St. Distaff—the distaff is a tool used in spinning.

DAY 12: TWELFTH NIGHT • JANUARY 5 Twelfth night not only ends the twelve days of Christmas, but begins carnival season, a riotous time, especially in the American South, that extends from Twelfth Night until Mardi Gras.

Epiphany ✳ January 6

Epiphany describes the bodily manifestation of the infant Christ to the Three Wise Men—from the Greek word *epiphaneia* (appearance). Epiphany was first mentioned in the writings of Clement of Alexandria in AD 200. The Feast of the Epiphany honors the Magi (the Three Wise Men). In Latin America, Epiphany is called the Day of the Magi Kings, and on this day children receive three presents, or presents in multiples of three. Since this was the day the Wise Men visited Christ, it is customary in some quarters to bake a cake in the shape of a crown.

In Oklahoma it used to be considered unlucky to remove Christmas decorations before Twelfth Night. Where my husband Joe grew up, neighbors on his block would toss trees in the street on the evening of January 6 and have a bonfire party. In Sweden people would "plunder the Christmas tree" on Twelfth Night, going door to door collecting the trees, then burning them in a bonfire in the village square, singing carols and "Auld Lang Syne" at midnight. This was also common in rural England: in Herefordshire it was called "the burning of the bush" (the bush being a globe made of hawthorn and mistletoe). To this day, it is considered bad luck to take down the tree before Twelfth Night.

WASSAILING

Wassail is an old English toast, with *waes hael* meaning to be whole or hale. But it also became the name of a winter punch of hot ale, nutmeg, sugar, and roasted apples. On Christmas Eve, New Year's Eve, and Twelfth Night, medieval carolers throughout the British Isles carried a wassail bowl with them from house to house, expecting it to be refilled, and toasting each other. You might consider inviting your friends to a wassailing party: send out invitations that explain the history and include a wassail song, a bonfire, and perhaps a cider-inspired menu.

TWELFTH NIGHT CAKE

In England and France from the Middle Ages through the 1800s, it was common to bake a cake on Twelfth Night and hide within it a dried bean, coin, or charm. The person who got the favor would be king of the festival, sometimes called the Lord of Misrule. In France, children still celebrate Epiphanie with La Galette des Rois (Kings Cake), and it's popular in New Orleans as well. With a paper crown, the king can choose his queen, and the royal couple presides over the merriment. You can sprinkle the top of the cake with the Mardi Gras colors (green for faith, gold for power, and purple for justice). Decorate with a gold crown frosting border.

Kwanzaa ✳ December 26 through January1

While many families are putting away their Hanukkah and Christmas decorations, millions of others will be getting ready for Kwanzaa, a secular holiday established in 1966 to celebrate and reaffirm African American identity and culture. Kwanzaa is traditionally held between December 26 and January 1, and the name Kwanzaa comes from the Swahili phrase *Matunda ya Kwanza*, which means first fruits of the harvest. (The second "a" distinguishes the African American celebration from the African word *Kwanza*.) Although Kwanzaa is still a relatively young holiday, its guiding principles lend themselves to a host of traditions.

Some critics of the relatively-rapid rise of Kwanzaa into the mainstream—and its perceived encroachment on the turf of more established winter holidays—try to dismiss it as a made-up holiday that borrows rituals and customs from other cultural celebrations. But that accusation could be leveled at most of the traditions currently enjoyed around the world. Yes, it's unconventional to hold a harvest festival in the dead of winter, and the multibranched candelabra does resemble a menorah. But as we've learned, most enduring traditions are hybrids that have evolved to adapt to cultural and geographical changes. It's fascinating to see that evolution at work in this new holiday.

SEVEN PRINCIPLES

The main focus of Kwanzaa is the Nguzo Saba, or seven principles, and each day of the celebration is devoted to one of these building blocks of self-awareness. According to the official Kwanzaa website maintained by Maulana Karenga (the creator of Kwanzaa), there are seven principles of the Nguzo Saba.

UMOJA (UNITY) To strive for and maintain unity in the family, community, nation, race, and the world.

KUJICHAGULIA (SELF-DETERMINATION) To define ourselves, name ourselves, create for ourselves, and speak for ourselves instead of being defined, named, created for, and spoken for by others.

UJIMA (COLLECTIVE WORK AND RESPONSIBILITY) To build and maintain a community together and make others' problems our problems and to solve them together.

UJAMAA (COOPERATIVE ECONOMICS) To build and maintain our own businesses; to control the economics of our own community and share in all of its work and wealth.

NIA (PURPOSE) To make our collective vocation the building and developing of our community in order to restore our people to their traditional greatness.

KUUMBA (CREATIVITY) To always do as much as we can, in the way we can, in order to leave our community more beautiful and beneficial than when we inherited it.

IMANI (FAITH) To believe in our people, our parents, our teachers, our leaders, and the righteousness and victory of our struggle.

KWANZAA SYMBOLS

Many families decorate their homes for Kwanzaa using the Kwanzaa colors of black, red, and green. Black symbolizes the face of the African American people, red represents the blood they have shed, and green stands for the hope and color of Africa. In addition, there are seven symbolic objects used in the Kwanzaa celebration:

MKEKA (MAT) The mkeka is typically made of straw or cloth and should be manufactured in an African country. This direct link to Africa—and its tradition, history, and many cultures—serves as the figurative and physical foundation for the other symbols in the Kwanzaa setting or centerpiece.

KINARA (CANDLEHOLDER) The seven-branched kinara is the center of the Kwanzaa setting and represents native African ancestry. The kinara can be any shape, provided the seven candles it holds are separate and distinct, like a candelabra. The kinara may be made from a variety of materials, and many families create their own from wood, clay, or other natural substances.

MAZAO (CROPS) The mazao represent the historical foundation for Kwanzaa. The gathering is patterned after African harvest festivals in which joy, sharing, unity, and thanksgiving are the rewarding fruits of collective planning and labor. Families place fruits, nuts, and vegetables on the mkeka to represent the labors of the year.

MUHINDI (EAR OF CORN) The muhindi represents fertility and symbolizes that through the reproduction of children, the future hopes of the family are brought to life. One ear is placed on the mkeka for each child in the household, and if there are no children in the home, then two ears are still placed upon the mkeka to symbolize the children of the community whose welfare is the responsibility of all.

MISHUMAA SABA (SEVEN CANDLES) These mishumaa saba symbolize the Nguzo Saba or Seven Principles.

KIKOMBE CHA UMOJA (UNITY CUP) The kikombe cha umoja is a special cup that is used to perform the libation, or tambiko, ritual during the Karamu feast on the sixth day of Kwanzaa. During the Karamu feast, the cup is passed to family members and guests, who drink from it in a demonstration of unity. The eldest individual present then pours the libation in the direction of the four winds: north, south, east, and west, to honor the ancestors. The cup can contain wine, juice, or water.

ZAWADI (GIFTS) When Imani is celebrated on the seventh day of Kwanzaa, meaningful gifts are exchanged with members of the immediate family to promote or reward accomplishments of the year. Handmade presents are particularly encouraged to show self-determination, purpose, and creativity, as well as to avoid the chaos of commercial shopping and consumption during the December holiday season.

Kwanzaa is not without its detractors, including members of the African American community, who maintain that Dr. Ron Karenga (the leader of the militant United Slaves Organization who created Kwanzaa while he was incarcerated for a violent felony) was using the holiday to preach a message of racial separatism and Marxism. Many of his original writings on Kwanzaa could be interpreted that way, and Dr. Karenga altered his message in a new Kwanzaa guide published in 1990 to make the holiday more inviting, especially to African American Christians, many of whom were put off by Karenga's assertion that Kwanzaa was to be celebrated instead of Christmas, not in addition to it.

African Americans who celebrate Kwanzaa consider it a time to reflect on principles of daily life and focus on family. Many families who observe Kwanzaa also celebrate Christmas, separating the two with the simple belief that Kwanzaa is not religious and Christmas is not cultural. To many, there is no conflict in observing Christmas as one of the High Holy days in the Christian church and then celebrating Kwanzaa, which honors family and community.

According to *Ebony* magazine, it is estimated that somewhere between five and ten million people celebrate Kwanzaa each year in the United States, and perhaps the best indicator of the holiday's increasing popularity is the appearance of Kwanzaa-related merchandise carried by mainstream retailers. It's now easy to find Kwanzaa greeting cards, wrapping paper, books, and other related products, and the U.S. Postal Service has issued a Kwanzaa stamp. Still, in the face of this commercialization, many families seem to embrace the holiday as a refreshing addition to the December holiday season.

Some Kwanzaa traditions to share with family and friends:

✳ Plan an activity for each of the seven days of Kwanzaa that reflects the principles. For example, work on a family craft project on the day that celebrates Kuumba (creativity), or tackle a project like cleaning out the attic on the day of Ujima (collective work).

✳ Discuss the meaning of each day during the candle-lighting ceremony. Give children a chance to share their thoughts about each of the seven principles. Keep a journal of what your children say each year, so they can reflect on it when they're older.

✳ Older children can make their own *kinara* (candleholder), and the whole family can make candles to decorate the house and celebrate the theme of light that is so central to Kwanzaa. Younger children can make simple candles by rolling sheets of beeswax around wicks (both available at craft stores), while older kids might like to make more elaborately decorated candles from kits.

✳ Let your kids contribute to the Karamu, or Kwanzaa feast, by making invitations, setting the traditional table, or helping to prepare favorite foods.

✳ If the unity cup used for toasts to the ancestors contains alcohol, fill a second special cup with juice for the children.

✳ During Kwanzaa week, visit a museum that features African or African American history or art.

✳ Watch films about the African American experience. Standouts include: *Amistad, Glory, The Color Purple, A Raisin in the Sun, Sounder, The Tuskegee Airmen, Something the Lord Made, Introducing Dorothy Dandridge, I Know Why the Caged Bird Sings, Native Son*, and *Roots*.

✳ There is a wealth of African American literature that is appropriate for the Kwanzaa celebration. Read passages from W. E. B. DuBois' *Prayers for Dark People* or Martin Luther King Jr.'s "A Christmas Sermon on Peace" around the Karamu table. The works of Toni Morrison, Jamaica Kincaid, Langston Hughes, Maya Angelou, and Ralph Ellison are excellent choices for Kwanzaa reading. Younger children will enjoy *The Gifts of Kwanzaa* by Synthia Saint James, *K Is for Kwanzaa: A Kwanzaa Alphabet Book* by Juwanda G. Ford and Ken Wilson-Max, and *Seven Days of Kwanzaa* by Ella Grier and John Ward.

✳ A New Year ✳

And now let us welcome the New Year
Full of things that have never been."
RAINER MARIA RILKE

Before people realized that the earth rotated around the sun, the beginning of a new year was determined by various natural phenomena—Egyptians, for example, calculated it by when the Nile overflowed. To this day, people throughout the world use different calendars, and it wasn't until 45 BC that Julius Caesar introduced the Western (or Julian) calendar that began with January 1 (partly because senators took office January 1). January is named for the Roman God Janus, from *janua* (door), who is always portrayed with two faces—one anticipating the future, the other looking back—in keeping with the spirit of many New Year's customs, bidding farewell to the old and ringing in the new.

New Year's Resolutions ✳

With the dawn of a new year, we often think of ways we can improve our lives, by starting good habits or ending bad ones. Silly as some of these resolutions can be, they can also be fun and help kids think along these lines:

✳ Ask everyone to make a list of whatever they want to let go of—habits, thoughts, or experiences. Everyone tosses his or her list into the fire and watches it burn.

✳ As a group, come up with a family resolution for the year. To get the discussion going, present broad categories, such as taking a vacation (when and where), tackling a home project (building a jungle gym or turning a spare room into a playroom), or launching a self-improvement project (everyone trying snowboarding, or learning Spanish).

✳ One family videotapes each other on New Year's Eve every other year—the adults talk about goals, jobs, hopes, predictions, the state of the world, or whatever is meaningful to them. The kids do the same. On alternate years, the family watches last year's video.

Old Celebrations ✳

✳ Making a racket at midnight harkens back to a time when people feared that evil spirits would ruin their crops, so they trumpeted on horns and pounded on drums to scare the demons away. Today, church bells peal at midnight, people set off fireworks, and in parts of the American South, guns are fired to ward off evil spirits.

✳ At the stroke of midnight, everyone holds hands and jumps from east to west into the new year. This is the favored childhood celebration of Tommy Webber, a friend who to this day finds the easterly point in the room wherever he is on New Year's Eve and insists that whoever he's with join hands and leap westward into the future.

✳ A pagan Scottish solstice celebration that went underground during the Protestant Reformation re-emerged in the seventeenth century as Hogmanay (new day). The party begins at the stroke of midnight and can last several days. According to Scottish lore, the first person who walks across your threshold in the new year—the first-footer—will bring good or bad luck to your household, depending on the person. There was a preference that it be a man, since if there was a maiden in the house, the first-footer might be her future husband. The first-footer always brought a symbolic gift. To this day, according to my friend Richard Criddle, a good Scot will always visit friends on Hogmanay to bring them good fortune, and will never appear without a piece of coal to warm the house and a bottle of whiskey to warm the hosts.

✳ Another Scottish custom involves unlocking the front door at midnight on New Year's Eve to let luck in while the back door is locked to trap it.

✳ A quirky but lovely eighteenth-century custom throughout rural Britain that I stumbled across was to stand on your front porch at midnight and sing "Auld Lang Syne" written by Scottish poet Robert Burns in 1788.

✳ For many African Americans, Watch Night (beginning at midnight) is a time to be in church greeting the new year with prayer and song. Some believe Watch Night began when abolitionists and slaves gathered in church the night before President Lincoln issued the Emancipation Proclamation on January 1, 1863. It remains a popular tradition today.

New Celebrations ✳

✳ A family in Georgia spreads out all the photographs they took during that year and talks about them—what they did, where they went, what mattered to them—and arranges them in an album. (When their teenager was old enough to go to a New Year's party, she ducked out early so she could be home with her family, going over the pictures.)

✳ My friend Will Dudley's parents began a tradition in 1968 with five other couples from the University of Virginia Law School. Since then it has grown into an annual event that no one wants to miss. One couple serves as host for a themed potluck supper where everyone comes dressed in costume. Sometimes the themes are related to a specific culture (Mexican, Indian, or African), and sometimes they are relevant to current events, such as a bicentennial or an Olympic year.

✳ As a banker, my father-in-law Jim worked late with his staff every New Year's Eve to close out the accounts by midnight, and so a breakfast party evolved at the Thompson's.

Other friends, on their way home from New Year's parties, also dropped by for eggs, coffee, and dancing. The party went from midnight until dawn.

✳ The Cathedral of St. John the Divine in New York has a renowned midnight candlelight Eucharist service and, earlier in the evening, a free New Year's Eve Peace Concert, launched by Leonard Bernstein, that features everything from medieval singers to a hip-hop theater group.

In the New Year, may your right hand always be stretched out in friendship and never in want.

CELTIC BLESSING

Throughout the World ✳

People have long regarded the passing of a year with anticipation and superstition:

✳ Armenian mothers bake bread to knead luck into the dough.

✳ The Danes bang on the doors of their friends' homes to "smash" in the New Year, sometimes going so far as to throw dishes at the doors for good luck.

✳ Ecuadorians create a scarecrow by stuffing old clothes with newspapers and lighting it at midnight, saying goodbye to *año viejo* (old year) with a cheerful blaze.

✳ South Koreans celebrate the lunar New Year with Seol-nal, a holiday when family members travel back to the towns and villages where they were born and their ancestors are enshrined. Seoul is virtually deserted during this three-day celebration; indeed, three months before, when bus and train tickets go on sale, people stand in line for hours to buy tickets for Seol-nal.

✳ Throughout Japan, people listen to the temple bells ring 108 times, signifying the 108 human emotions, before going to the temple to pray. Parents also give their children and neighbors' children a small amount of money on New Year's Eve, much as children in the United States are given candy by neighbors on Halloween. Families stay home the next day—to visit someone's house on New Year's Day would be considered impolite.

✳ Everyone knows about Carnival in Rio de Janeiro, but less known is Iemanjá, when Brazilians go to the beach on New Year's Eve, light thousands of candles, and ask Iemanjá, the goddess of the ocean, for her blessings. At midnight, hundreds of thousands of blue and white flowers are thrown into the waves as gifts for the goddess. The celebration includes fireworks, Afro-Brazilian drumming, and singing.

✳ In Iceland, New Year's Eve is a phenomenon. Friends and family dress up in the early evening and gather for dinner in each other's homes, and then, in a tradition dating back to the Middle Ages, move outside to enjoy the huge bonfires that are lit throughout the countryside and in the city of Reykjavik to symbolically burn up the problems of the previous year. The streets are lively—filled with music, the smell of wood smoke, and throngs of people. Most Icelanders then go indoors to watch a television show that satirizes the year's events and politicians (incredibly, close to 90 percent of the adult population watches the show). At its conclusion, everyone goes back out into the winter night to set off a mind-boggling number of skyrockets and fireworks. Since there are no trees and the landscape is snow covered, fireworks are a virtual free-for-all. Families and neighborhoods get into the act trying to outdo each other, and the skies of Reykjavik light up as midnight approaches; on a clear night you can even see fireworks of towns fifty kilometers (40 miles) away. "It's nothing unique," noted Magnus Bernhardsson. "We've just taken it to an extreme level." After midnight, the thriving Reykjavik music scene kicks into high gear.

✳ Russian children gleefully anticipate the arrival of Ded Moroz (Grandfather Frost) who appears with Snegurochak (the Snow Maiden). These figures are suspiciously similar in appearance to favorite relatives and give children *pryaniki* (sweet cookies) for a sweet year.

New Year's Day ✳ January 1

In the 1800s, it was customary for Americans to have a party on New Year's Day, not New Year's Eve. It was an important courting time, when unmarried girls waited at home for visits from bachelor suitors. Many food superstitions associated with New Year's persist to this day. Perhaps the best-known is the Southern dinner menu of ham, corn bread, and Hoppin' John, made with black-eyed peas for luck, rice for health, and collard or turnip greens for good fortune. A native Oklahoman, Joe still insists on cooking black-eyed peas on New Year's. Some food customs for both New Year's Eve and Day:

✳ Texans and Southerners in the low country serve the African-inspired Hoppin' John to bring luck to all who dine at their table. The person who finds the dime in his or her bowl of beans will have the best luck in the coming year.

✳ North Carolinians eat foods that swell when cooked, for prosperity, including turnip greens, black-eyed peas, rice, and peaches.

✳ Russians eat goose or chicken after midnight, while toasting the New Year.

✳ Germans eat fish for health, with carrots and white cabbage for wealth (symbolizing gold and silver).

✳ Albanians serve cake to bring in a new year of sweetness, with one slice containing a lucky coin.

✳ Louisianans cook collard or mustard greens and black-eyed peas (symbolizing dollars and small change).

✳ The American Dutch, from early colonial times through the mid-1800s, opened their homes on New Year's Day, and each would feature a different food. Neighbors went from house to house: at one they'd be served eggnog, at another, oysters, and so on.

*If you're working on New Year's Day,
you'll be working the whole year through.*

AFRICAN AMERICAN SAYING

Chinese New Year (Gong Hey Fat Choy) ✴ January and February

Lasting fifteen days, the Chinese New Year begins with the first full moon after January 21. This colorful celebration occurs in major cities throughout the world and has been celebrated for five thousand years. In traditional Chinese families, from the first day of the New Year until January 15, it is considered important to perform a different task each day. Each of the fifteen days has a theme: the first is Family Day, to welcome the gods of heaven and earth into your life. Everyone gathers for a symbolic meatless meal that includes lotus seeds to ensure many children and seaweed for wealth. The second day—the common birthday of all dogs, according to the Chinese—is a day to pray to your ancestors and your gods, and to be kind to canines. The third and fourth days are dedicated to in-laws. On the fifth day the house is scoured and the dust is taken to running water (such as a river). Beginning on the sixth day, you visit relatives and friends. The seventh day is when farmers show off their produce. The eighth day is given over to a family reunion, and the ninth through the twelfth days are spent in prayer, making offerings, and partying with family and friends. The thirteenth day is when you cleanse your system, and the fourteenth day is preparation for the fifteenth day: the Chinese New Year Parade.

In cities with large Chinese populations like New York and San Francisco, these parades are major events. In 2007, my family made an outing of it—lunch at a Chinese restaurant, followed by a walk through Chinatown (which included a stop at a Chinese candy shop for New Year's treats such as gold chocolate coins for luck and firecracker plum candies to scare away the spirits). We then enjoyed the frenzy that built as the parade worked its way through Chinatown: a panoply of dragons, lanterns, snakes, confetti-crackers, and a dazzling amount of confetti shot into the sky.

Throughout China, people serve whole fishes on New Year's to ensure good ends and beginnings. You are expected to eat it for good fortune, but you aren't supposed to finish; like many Chinese words that resemble others and suggest double meanings, "fish" sounds like "leftover" in Chinese, so you can't eat your leftovers or else you'll have nothing left for the future.

People also wear red for a bright future and put a penny under their pillows when they go to sleep during the Chinese New Year. Children go to their elders on New Year's, and are given a red envelope with money in it. The Chinese believe that if you cry on New Year's Day, you'll weep throughout the year. Children learn early that they can be rather mischievous on New Year's, since parents go to great lengths to avoid confrontations that could result in tears. At midnight, windows are opened to let the old year escape. In northern China there is also a tradition that when you open the front door for the first time on New Year's Day you should set off firecrackers to scare away evil spirits. People don't use scissors on this day, for they might cut off good fortune, nor do they sweep, for fear that they might sweep away their luck.

Super Bowl Sunday ✳ February

When people think about unifying American traditions, Thanksgiving feasts and Fourth of July fireworks spring to mind, but there's also that sporting event on the first Sunday in February that attracts 100 million television viewers, and forces the United States to release some of its Strategic French Onion Dip Reserve.

Does it really matter who wins or who's playing? There are thirty-two teams in the NFL and only two teams in the Super Bowl, so every year an overwhelming majority of the

My personal favorite was a Super Bowl Sunday spent with a visiting company of British actors from Shakespeare's Globe Theatre in London. The actors were in New York performing Two Gentlemen of Verona at the New Victory Theater on Forty-Second Street and I was their U.S. company manager. It was my job to look after them during their two-week run, and as they were at loose ends on Super Bowl Sunday, my then girlfriend (now my wife) and I decided to invite them all over to watch the game. We made big pots of chili and grilled bratwurst on the grill out on the fire escape, ordered in hot wings and generally created the iconic American Super Bowl atmosphere. Needless to say, if you ever have the opportunity to watch the Super Bowl with a houseful of foreigners who have no idea how American football is played, take it. Everyone had a blast. A group of these actors have, to this day, gotten together every year to watch the Super Bowl in London, in the middle of the night.

—Eric Kerns

people watching the game don't really care about the outcome. Getting together with family and friends to enjoy unhealthy but tasty food and scream at the TV is the main attraction.

✳ If your team isn't playing and you are indifferent to who wins, do as one friend does and divide your viewing room in half with masking tape, decorating each side with a team's colors. As your guests arrive, assign each person to a side, making sure to break up couples. The instant rivalry factor makes the game more exciting.

✳ Or have an NFL franchise potluck. Assign each guest or couple an NFL team and inform them that they must bring a dish that reflects the hometown of their team. If you get the Bills, bring wings, Chiefs, bring barbecue, Eagles, bring cheese steaks, and so on.

✳ You can also use the day as an excuse to do some good. Nearly 13,000 churches around the country make a special Souper Bowl Sunday offering that morning to support soup kitchens. One tavern in Wisconsin sponsors a football pool where the winner gets to keep a replica Super Bowl trophy at his or her house for a year and the cash winnings go to a local charity.

❋ After the Holidays ❋

With the swirl of activities over the holidays, it's hard to savor the quiet of winter until the season has really seeped in, around late January or February. Then you can enjoy the deep snow, starry evenings, cozy fires night after night, your warm bed, gatherings in the kitchen, good books, baking bread, sledding, and steaming hot chocolate. Here are some simple traditions:

❋ Test a favorite recipe with the kids. My kids love apple pie, and one winter every weekend for five weeks, I cooked an apple pie for them from a different cookbook. At the end, we all voted on our favorite recipe, and it's our standard now—a perfect pie every time. (Our winner was from Jeanne Besser's *The First Book of Baking*.)

❋ Incorporate a new hobby into your routine. Having a babysitter from El Salvador, we decided to learn Spanish; she helps us by speaking to us in Spanish, and we bought Spanish-word magnets (and have fun testing each other when we go to the refrigerator), watch a few Spanish videos, and play some Spanish games.

❋ Stock the pantry in preparation for the first big storm. No matter what your schedule, try to clear the decks on a snow day (you usually have a bit of advance warning about the weather). Wouldn't you rather your kids remember how you sledded with them and made chocolate chip cookies on a snow day, rather than how you were on the phone or nervously checking emails all day long?

✳ Force spring narcissus bulbs to bloom. It's an indoor gardening project that takes minutes, and the fragrant benefits are many. (I often buy old ceramic pots at tag sales and keep them in the basement; when I'm ready to do my bulbs I buy several dozen—enough for bulbs in several rooms of the house and to give to friends as gifts.)

A Season of Giving ✳

How do you teach young children about helping others? A friend has an idea:

✳ When her kids receive a gift of money, she lets them spend a portion of it, they put a portion into a college savings account, and they contribute a portion to a charity box. At the end of the year, they sit down as a family, talk about places in the community that need money—museums, schools, hospitals—and vote who will receive the money. (And if the desire to help others doesn't motivate you, consider the fact that a review of seventeen clinical studies found that people who help others tend to feel less depressed and anxious.)

YOUNGER CHILDREN

✳ Charity is most successful when it's tangible and has an achievable goal. Let's weed a friend's yard. Let's take soup to someone who just had a baby or who broke her leg. Our neighbor has a bad back, so let's shovel his walk. As children get older (at the age of four they may have to be coaxed, but by five they can do this), let's give baby toys and books to the hospital, or to the children's room at a correctional center.

※ You can leave a decorated box in the kitchen or hallway, in which each member of the family puts loose coins. Jewish families call this the *tzedakah* (righteousness or, loosely translated, charity) box. As one rabbi pointed out, piggy banks teach us the value of money, whereas the tzedakah box teaches us the obligation to our community. When Trainer was little, we decided as a family to split our charity money at the end of the year two ways: two-thirds went to a hospital, and one-third went to a local aquarium because, in the words of our four-year-old, "sick people need help more than sea creatures." When Trainer was six and Isabel was two, Joe lobbied hard—as he always does—for us to give the money to the children's program at Massachussetts Museum of Contemporary Art where we work, whereas Trainer wanted to give it all to victims of the 2004 tsunami. Trainer argued impressively that they needed it most, and, as we had to reach a consensus, was able to convince the rest of the family to give the full amount to tsunami survivors.

OLDER CHILDREN

As children get older, you can capitalize on their interests. Your children love the outdoors? Maybe they'd like to help clean up a hiking trail. A child who is interested in animals might want to help by exercising dogs at the animal shelter or by putting together a fund drive to raise money to train a seeing-eye dog. Your pitching in, too, sends a strong message to your child. Richard Criddle started working at a therapeutic equestrian school with his teenage daughter; she graduated from high school, but he's still there, mucking out the stalls one evening a week. Encourage your kids to donate part of their allowance by offering to match their gift and sending a check to a charity. Talk to them about acts of generosity through the years in your family—I'm proud that my children's great-grandfather—Joe's grandfather, a small town Oklahoma banker—loaned customers money personally over the years when they could not qualify for bank loans. Most of them were Native Americans, and when I talked to my mother-in-law recently to verify the details, I learned that the antique beaded moccasins that I have were from him—often the Native Americans would pay him in lovely beadwork. When he died, many Native Americans lined the streets for his funeral.

AS A FAMILY

Charity is something that is learned. Giving toys away is hard for young children; think if you were asked to give away your favorite piece of clothing. When I feel as though we are about to be overrun by toys, I sit down with my kids and see if there are toys that they feel comfortable giving away. Sometimes we make a project of picking three items to give away. Or I wait until the eve of an occasion when we'll be inundated—Christmas, birthdays, grandparent visits—and we talk about giving and try to choose things that others might want or need more than we do. Of course, children learn best by example. Here are some ideas:

✳ Do good deeds together. Work on a community project, like building a playground or a Habitat for Humanity house. Pick up litter at the park. Take a meal to someone who just came home from the hospital.

✳ Rather than taking off Martin Luther King Day, do as King's widow Coretta Scott King requested: use the holiday to engage in community service.

✳ The first thing Joe told me about his college roommate was that the Besser family had always taken a two-week vacation in the summer on an Indian reservation. Rich Besser's father was a doctor in Princeton, New Jersey, and every summer he'd volunteer his medical services. Other friends have done similar charity; a friend with a plane has gone to Indian reservations throughout New Mexico every year to fly medical supplies to remote locations.

✳ Give money yourself. One philanthropic family I know wrote 442 checks to various charities last year.

✳ There is an organization in New Orleans called Young Aspirations/Young Artists (YAYA). A woman artist had observed city kids hanging around without much to do, so she bought furniture at tag sales and set up a studio in a hard-hit neighborhood. She invited kids to paint the furniture as wildly as they wanted, and she set up a storefront where they could sell the work. The profits were split in thirds: one-third went to YAYA for operations, one-third went into the children's college accounts, which they could access if they graduated from high school and went to college, and they got one-third immediately.

Anybody can observe the Sabbath,
but making it holy surely takes the rest of the week.
ALICE WALKER

CONCLUSION

*Let us put our minds together and see what kind of
life we can make for our children.*

CHIEF SITTING BULL

This morning you woke up to the sound of birds singing. There's still snow on the ground, but you can hear the steady drip as snow melts and tiny, green shoots peek through the remaining ice crystals in the garden. The cycle has made another complete revolution, and we're back, ready to rise from winter's slumber to greet the renewing light of spring. Throughout the changing of the four seasons, over the course of a year we've preserved cherished traditions and created new ones that may become part of our family fabric.

Judith "Miss Manners" Martin once wrote that "Ritual, or at least a common share of peculiar habits, is what gives a family identity." For people raising children in a complicated time when individualism is prized, the quest for collective family identity takes effort, but it's worth it. Beyond the capacity to nurture and support and provide a center of gravity for individuals, strong families are the building blocks of healthy communities, which, in turn, combine to form a robust, enduring culture. By observing traditions that link us with the past, ground us in the present, and prepare us for the future, we—if we're lucky—can help establish a context for the human experience and honor our own cultural evolution. Plus, they're fun.

SELECT BIBLIOGRAPHY

Abramowitz, Yosef I., and Rabbi Susan Silver-
man. *Jewish Family Life: Traditions, Holidays,
and Values for Today's Parents and Children.*
New York: Golden Books, 1997.

Adler, Margot. *Drawing Down the Moon: Witches,
Druids, Goddess-Worshippers, and Other Pagans
in America Today.* Boston: Beacon Press, 1986.

Alban Gosline, Andrea. *Welcoming Ways.* San
Rafael, CA: Cedco Publishing Company, 2000.

Ausubel, Nathan, Ed. *A Treasury of Jewish Folklore:
The Stories, Traditions, Legends, Humor, and
Wisdom of the Jewish People.* New York: Crown
Publishers, 1990.

Ban Breathnach, Sarah. *Mrs. Sharp's Traditions.*
New York: Scribner, 1990.

Ban Breathnach, Sarah. *Simple Abundance: A
Daybook of Comfort and Joy.* New York: Warner
Books, 1995.

Bane, Mary Jo. *Here To Stay: America Families in
the Twentieth Century.* New York: Basic Books,
Inc., 1976.

Berg, Elizabeth. *Family Traditions: Celebrations for
Holidays and Everyday.* Pleasantville, NY: The
Reader's Digest Association, 1992.

Berkow, Ira. *Hank Greenberg, The Story of My Life.*
Chicago: Triumph Books, 1989.

Broussard, Antoinette. *African American Holiday
Traditions.* New York: Citadel Press, 2000.

Burland, C. A. *Echoes of Magic: A Study of Seasonal
Festivals Through the Ages.* Totowa, NJ: Rowman
and Littlefield, 1972.

Christopher, Doris. *Come to the Table.* New York:
Warner Books, 1999.

Cohen, Hennig and Tristam Potter Coffin. *The
Folklore of America Holidays.* Detroit: Gale
Research Inc., 1991.

Costa, Shu Shu. *Wild Geese and Tea.* New York:
Riverhead Books, a division of G. P. Putnam's
Sons, 1997.

Cox, Meg. *The Heart of a Family.* New York:
Random House, 1998.

Dobler, Lavinia. *Customs and Holidays Around the
World.* New York: Fleet Publishing Corporation, 1962.

Eklof, Barbara. *For Every Season: The Complete
Guide to African American Celebrations—
Traditional to Contemporary.* New York: Harper
Collins, 1997.

Exley, Helen. *Mother Quotations: A Collection of Beautiful Paintings and the Best Mother Quotes.* Watford, U.K.: Exley Giftbooks, 1993.

Eyre, Linda, and Richard Eyre. *Three Steps to a Strong Family.* New York: Simon & Schuster, 1994.

Foley, Daniel J. *The Christmas Tree.* Philadelphia, PA: Chilton Company, 1960.

Frazer, Sir James George. *The Golden Bough.* New York: The Macmillan Company, 1940.

Fulghum, Robert. *From Beginning to End.* New York: Villard Books, 1995.

Greenaway, Kate. *Language of Flowers.* New York: Gramercy Publishing Company, 1978.

Hamerstrom, Frances. *Walk When the Moon Is Full.* New York: The Crossing Press, 1975.

Ickis, Marguerite. *The Book of Festival Holidays.* New York: Dodd, Mead & Company, 1964.

Isaacs, David. *Character Building: A Guide for Parents and Teachers.* Dublin: Four Courts Press, 1981.

Jenkins, Emyl. *The Book of American Traditions.* New York: Crown Publishers, 1996.

Jones, Julia, and Barbara Deer. *The Country Diary of Garden Lore.* New York: Summit Books, 1989.

Kightly, Charles. *The Customs and Ceremonies of Britain.* London: Thames and Hudson, 1986.

Krythe, Maymie R. *All About American Holidays.* New York: Harper & Row, 1962.

Lang, George. *The Folklore Calendar.* Detroit: Gale Research Company, 1970.

Lieberman, Susan A. *New Traditions: Redefining Celebrations for Today's Family.* New York: Farrar, Straus and Giroux, 1991.

Matthews, Caitlin. *The Celtic Book of Days.* Rochester, Vermont: Destiny Books, 1995.

Matthews, John. *The Winter Solstice: The Sacred Traditions of Christmas.* Wheaton, IL: Quest Books, 1998.

Mueller Nelson, Gertrud. *To Dance with God.* New York: Paulist Press, 1986.

Murphey, Sallyann J. *The Metcalfe Family Album.* San Francisco: Chronicle Books, 1999.

Nanda Anshen, Ruth. *The Family: Its Function and Destiny.* New York: Harper & Brothers, Publishers, 1959.

Panati, Charles. *Sacred Origins of Profound Things: The Stories Behind the Rites and Rituals of the World's Religions.* New York: Penguin Arkana, 1996.

Peroni, Laura. *The Language of Flowers.* New York: Crown Publishers, 1984.

Pickels, Dwayne E. *Ancient and Annual Customs.* London: Chelsea House Publishers, 1998.

Pollock, Penny. *When the Moon Is Full: A Lunar Year.* Boston: Little, Brown and Company, 2001.

Reed, Bobbie. *501 Practical Ways to Teach Your Children Values.* St. Louis: Concordia House Publishing, 1998.

Robinson, Jo, and Jean Coppock Staeheli. *Unplug the Christmas Machine: A Complete Guide to Putting Love and Joy Back into the Season.* New York: Harper Paperbacks, 1991.

Schafer, Louis S. *Best of Gravestone Humor.* New York: Sterling Publishing Company, 1990.

Skarmeas, Nancy J. *The Traditions of Christmas.* Nashville, TN: Ideals Publications Incorporated, 1997.

Spencer, Paula, *Everything Else You Need to Know When You're Expecting.* Irvine, CA: Griffin Publishing, 2000.

Starhawk, Diane Baker, and Anne Hill. *Circle Round.* New York: Bantam Books, 1998.

Trafton O'Neal, Debbie. *The Family Hand-Me-Down Book.* Minneapolis: Augsburg Fortress, 2000.

Treasured Traditions. *Health Magazine,* (2003).

Tuleja, Tad. *Curious Customs.* New York: Galahad Books, 1999.

Van Renterghem, Tony. *When Santa Was a Shaman: The Ancient Origins of Santa Claus and the Christmas Tree.* St. Paul, MN: Llewellyn Publications, 1995.

Walsh, William S. *Curiosities of Popular Customs.* Philadelphia, PA: J. B. Lippincott Company, 1898.

Wigginton, Eliot. *Foxfire 9.* New York: Anchor Press, 1986.

WEBSITES
www.peabody.harvard.edu
www.isleofavalon.co.uk/avalon-arthur.html
www.candlegrove.com
www.orkneyjar.com
http://marriageandfamilies.byu.edu/issues/1999/December/traditions.htm
www.webwinds.com/yupanqui/apachesunrise.htm
www.cin.org

INDEX

A

Abbot of Disobedience, 63
Adoption anniversaries, 114
Advent, 206–207
Advent calendars, 207–209
Advent wreaths, 207
African tree planting, 97
African American
    literature, 248
King Ahashveros of Persia, 37
Alcott, Louisa May, 114
All Fools' Day, 59–60
All Saint's Day, 46, 151
All Soul's Day, 46, 151
American Indian Religious
    Freedom Act (1978), 124
Anniversaries, 168–171
Annual excursions, 90, 92–94
Appalachian Trail hiking, 90
Apple harvest, 140 (box)
April Fools' Day, 59–60
Arbaeen celebration, 73
Armenian Easter, 56
Ash Wednesday, 32
Atwood, Margaret, 50
"Auld Lang Syne," 251
Aurealian (Emperor), 204
Autumn, about, 130
Autumnal Equinox, 133–134
Aztec festivals, 151

B

Baby booties, 103–104
Baby gifts, 101–104
Back to school day, 134–135
Balanchine, George, 216
Bar Mitzvah/Bat Mitzvah, 121–
    122, 127
Baseball season, 84–86
BBC April Fools' Day joke, 59

Bedtime rituals, 117–118
Begay, Mandy, 124, 125 (box)
Beitzah, 53
Bel (god), 62
Beltane, 46, 62–63
Bernstein, Leonard, 252
The Best-Loved Poems of
    Jacqueline Kennedy
    Onassis (Kennedy), 27
Bird albums, 49
Birth celebrations
    China, 95–96
    Christian, 99
    Hindu, 102
    Iceland, 100–101
    Jewish, 99–100
    Korean, 100, 113 (box)
    Muslim, 102
    Thailand, 114
Birth flowers, 107 (box)
Birth stories, 98–99
Birthday certificates, 112
Birthday elf, 111–112
Birthday letters/books, 112–113
Birthday parties, 108–109
Birthdays
    celebrating, 104–105, 110–111
    milestones, 109–110, 115
    rituals, 105–108, 111–114,
    111, 127–128
Blessing of the animals
    tradition, 136
Bly, Robert, 128
Boxing Day, 239
Bradford, William, 186, 205
Bridesmaid dresses, baby
    quilts and, 103
Bringing in the Boar day, 240
Brit habat ceremonies, 122
Buddha Purinama, 70
Burning Man, 130–131
Butter festival, 36

C

Calendars
    Christian, 29
    Gregorian, 59
    Islamic, 30
    Jewish, 29
    Julian, 59
    lunar, 30
    Russian Orthodox, 36
Calle Ocho, 35
Candlemas, 22–23, 46
Canoe expeditions, 86–87
Carnations, symbolism of, 68
Carnival season, 32
Carnivals, 35. See also specific
    carnivals
Carson, Rachel, 73
Celtic festivals, 22
Chapter books, for bedtime
    reading, 118
Charity, teaching, 260–263
Charles II, 64
Charles IX, 32, 59
Charoset, 53
Chaucer, Geoffrey, 25
Chihuahuas, 65
Children's Day, 117
Chinese New Year, 256–257
Christianity
    calendar, 29
    pagan festivals and, 22
Christmas, 46, 238
    candles and, 215–216
    caroling during, 217
    Christmas trees, 206,
    209–211
    decorations for, 211–216
    food and, 234–238, 235
    giving ornaments, 210–211
    history of, 203–206
    as legal holiday, 205
    stepchildren and, 219–220

Christmas cards/letters, 223–
    224, 225
A Christmas Carol (Dickens),
    206
Christmas Day traditions,
    233–234
Christmas movies, 221–222
Christmas music, 220–221
"A Christmas Sermon on
    Peace" (King), 248
Christmas stockings, 214–215
Christmas stories, 223
Chuseok (Korea), 138–139
Cinco de Mayo, 65–66
Civil War. See Memorial Day
Claudius II (Roman Emperor),
    24–25
Clinton, Bill, 69
Collections from My Childhood
    (Alcott), 114
Coming of age ceremonies
    Apache, 123–124
    Navajo, 123
    Sunrise Ceremony, 124, 125
    turning fifteen, 126–127
    turning thirteen, 122–123
Community service, 262
Continental Congress, 84
Coolidge, Calvin, 79
Council of Nicaea, 29
Cross-country trips, 89

D

Dairy products, 35
Danson, Ted, 169
Dartmouth College, 32
Day of the Dead, 46
Daylight Savings Time, 60–61
Decoration Day. See Memorial
    Day
Dia de las Madres, 68

Dia de los Muertos, 150–152.
    See also Day of the Dead
Dickenson, Emily, 25
Ditmas family, birth
    traditions, 96
Diwali festival, 199
Dodd, Sonora Smart, 79
Dong Zhi (China)196
Dreidel, 200
Druids, 131

E

Easter, 29, 46, 54–58
Easter bunny, origin, 55
Edwards, John and
    Elizabeth, 171
Egg balancing, 47
Egg dying, 54, 56
Egg hunting, 57, 58
Egg painting, 54–55, 56–57
Egg rolling, 55
Eggs-in-a-Nest dessert, 57
Eid ul-Fitr, 30
Election Day, 153
Elijah (prophet), 52
Eostra (goddess), 54
Ephron, Delia, 154
Epiphany, 241–242
Epitaphs, 76–77
Esther. See Purim
Evergreen Day, 241

F

Fall equinox, 45, 46
Fall Harvest Festivals, 46
Family communication
    conferences, 116
    dinnertime discussions, 116,
    172–174
    "Five-Facet Review," 116–117
Family Hibernation Day, 24

A Family of Poems: My Favorite
    Poetry for Children
    (Kennedy), 27
Family picnics, 87
Family trips, 88–89, 93–94
Fasting, 30–31, 35
Fat Tuesday (Mardi Gras), 31,
    32, 33–34
The Father Christmas Letters
    (Tolkien), 227–228
Father's Day, 79–80
Feast days, 139–140
Feast of Fools, 33, 240
Feast of San Gennaro, 140
Feast of the Blessed Sacrament
    (Portugal), 139
Festival of the Breaking of the
    Fast, 30
Festivals of Light
    Diwali, 199
    Hanukkah, 198–202
    Loi Krathong, 198
    St. Lucia day, 198
Festus Fatrorum (Feast of
    Fools), 59
Fire in the Belly (Keen), 128
The First Book of Baking
    (Besser), 259
"Five-Facet Review," 116–117
Flor de Nochebuena, 213
Floralia, 62
Florence, Italy, Easter in, 56
Francis, of Assisi, St., 204–205
Franklin, Benjamin, 60, 189
Frost, Robert, 58
Funny Sauce (Ephron), 154

G

Ga people (Ghana), birth
    traditions, 96
Garden journals, 49
Gelasius (Pope), 24–25

Gift giving, 230
    Giving Trees, 231
    history of, 224, 226–227
Gift-of-Self night, 202
Godparents, 101
Golden birthdays, 106–107
Goldwasser, Rabbi Jeffrey, 53
Gong Hey Fat Choy (Chinese
    New Year), 256–257
Good Friday, 55
Goodman, Ellen, 179
Grandparents, 109
Gray, Francine Du Plessix, 173
Great American Cleanup, 48
Green Man, 63
Greenberg, Hank, 143–145
Greenberg, Steve, 143
Greenwood marriages, 62
Groundhog Day, 23–24, 46
Guatemala, Easter in, 55–56
Guest, Edgar, 145

H

Haggadah, 51
Halloween, 46, 146–150
Haman. See Purim
Hannukah, 46, 199–202
Harvest festivals, 135–136
Harvest Moon Festival/
    Zhongqui Jie (China),
    137–138
Haymarket Riot, 63
Heirlooms, giving, 115–116
Herrick, Robert, 213
Hoffman, E.T.A., 216
Hogmanay celebration, 250
Holly, 212
Holy Innocent's Day
    (Childermas), 239
Home nights, staying in,
    180–181
Hot cross buns, 55

Howe, Julia Ward, 68
Howland, Esther, 25
Human sacrifices, 62

I

Iceland, New Year
    observations, 253–254
Ides of March, 40–41
Iemanjá celebration, 253
"If Ever I Cease to Love"
    (Leybourne), 34
Iftar, 30
Imbolc festival, 22, 46
Independence Day, 83–84
International Women's Day, 39
International Workers' Day, 63
Intihuatona, 45
Irish Hunger Memorial, 42
Irish Olympics Festival, 43
Iron John (Bly), 128
Iroquois prayer of thanks, 189

J

Jamaica, birth traditions, 96
Janus (Roman God), 249
Jarvis, Anna M., 68
Jefferson, Thomas, 187
Jesus. See Candlemas
Johnson, Lyndon, 79
Ju Dong (China), 196
Judaism, calendar, 29
Julius I (Pope), 204
"Jumping the broom," 170
Juno (Roman goddess), 24

K

Kant, Immanuel, 67
Karpas, 53
Keen, Sam, 128
Keillor, Garrison, 187–188
Kennedy, Caroline, 27
Kennedy, John, 27
Kentucky Derby Day, 66
King of Unreason, 63

Kings Day, 33
Kitchen, 175–177
Knocking on wood, 62
Koran, 30–31
Kwanzaa
    activities, 247–248
    literature, 248
    seven principles, 243–244
    symbols of, 244–246

L

La Quinceañera, 126–127
Labor Day, 63, 91
Lammas, 131
Lang, Gerhard, 207–208
Latke *vs.* Hamantasch
    debate, 38
Lent, 31, 35
Leybourne, George, 34
Liberal, Kansas, 35–36
Lincoln, Abraham, 187
Little Women (Alcott), 135
Logan, General John, 70
Loi Krathong, 198
Longfellow, Henry
    Wadsworth, 64
Lord of Misrule, 63
Louis XI, 32
Lughnasad, 46, 131
Lullabies, 117
Lupercalia festival, 24, 32
Lupercus (fertility god), 24
Luther, Martin, 215, 217

M

Maccabees, revolt of, 199
Machu Picchu, 45
Madison, Dolley, 55
Maeshowe, 45
Mardi Gras, 33–34. *See also*
    Purim
Maror and chazaret, 53

Martin, Judith "Miss
    Manners," 265
Maslenitsa (carnival), 36
May Day, 46, 62–64
May Day baskets, 64
Maypoles, 62
Memorial Day, 70–72
Menorahs, 200–201
Metcalfe, Anna, 206
Mexico, Easter in, 56
Miccailhuitl festival, 151
Miccailhuitontli festival, 151
Michael, Moina, 71
A Midsummer Night's Dream
    (Shakespeare), 83
Midsummer's Eve, 46
Mistletoe, 202
Moon festivals, 137–139
Moon walks, 183
Mooncakes, 138
Mother Balls (Taiwan), 197
"Mother" church, 66–67
Mother Night/St. John's
    Day, 239
Mothering Sunday, 67–68
Mother's Day, 66–69
Mourning periods, 73
Movie nights, 181
Ms. Foundation, 61

N

Naming traditions, 99–100
Nast, Thomas, 227
National Holiday Act, 71
National Hunting and Fishing
    Day, 141–142
Nativity scenes, 218–219
New Grange, 45
New Orleans, 32
New Year, 46
    Celtic blessing for, 252
    Chinese parades, 256

food customs of, 254–255,
    257
observation of, 248–249,
    250–251, 252–254
resolutions, 249
New Year for Trees. *See* Tu
    B'Shvat
New Year's Eve Peace Concert
    (New York), 252
Nine Night (Jamaica), 73
Nixon, Richard, 79, 141
Noatak River exploration, 87
Norouz, 44, 47
North Adams Steeplecats, 86
Nutcracker Suite (Tchaikovsky),
    216

O

"Ode to a Turkey" (Franklin),
    191
Oktoberfest, 136
Olney, England, 35–36
Orkney Islands, birth
    traditions, 96
Outward Bound, 120

P

Pancake Tuesday, 35–36
Parades, 43
Passover, 46, 50–53. *See also*
    Easter; Tu B'Shvat
Paz, Octavio, 151
Pepys, Samuel, 64
Persian New Year Festival, 44
Philadelphia Athletics, 85
Pi Day, 40
Piazza della Signoria ritual, 32
Pierce, Franklin, 206
Plimoth Plantation, 185
Poinsett, Joel, 213
Poinsettias, 212
Poppies, 71
Los Posadas, 197–198

Prayers for Dark People
    (DuBois), 248
Puebla, Battle of, 65
Purim, 37–38

Q

Queen of the May, 63
Quing Ming, 73

R

Ramadan, 30–31
Remembrance rituals, 73–76
Richard II, 25
Rilke, Rainer Maria, 248
Rimmon, Eyal, 110
Rio de Janeiro, 32
Road games, 89
Roadside historical markers, 88
Roosevelt, Franklin, 187
Roosevelt, Theodore, 141, 209
Rosh Hashanah, 142–143
Rossetti, Christina, 19
"Rudolph the Red-Nosed
    Reindeer," 221
Russian Orthodox Easter, 56

S

Samhain, 46. *See also*
    Halloween
Santa, playing, 228
Santa Claus
    letters to, 227–228
    origins of, 227
Santa Piñata, 197
Saturnalia, 46, 203, 212, 224
Scent and memories, 75
Scents, power of, 20–21
School, last day of, 78
School of Lost Borders,
    120–121
Scotland, April Fools' day, 60
Seder, 27–28, 51–53. *See also*
    Passover
Seol-nal holiday, 253

1776, 84
Shabbat, 177–178
Sham al-Naseem, 49–50
Shivah, sitting, 74
Shrove Tuesday, 31, 32, 35
Shrove Tuesday Pancake Race, 35–36
Shunpiking, 88
Silent Night (Stille Nacht), 217
Sitting Month, 95–96
Sol Invictus, 204
Sol-ya-lang-eu ceremony, 197
"Speaking of Greenberg" (Guest), 144
Spring, about, 20–21
Spring cleaning, 47–48
Spring equinox, 22, 45, 46. *See also* Passover
Spry, Contance, 25
St. Brigid's Day, 22
St. Clare of Assisi, 55
St. Distaff's Day, 241
St. Francis of Assisi, 136
St. John's Day, 46
St. Lucia Day, 198
St. Nicholas Day, 205, 226
St. Patrick, 22, 41–42
St. Patrick's Day, 41–43
St. Valentine's Day, 24–27
Steenburgen, Mary, 169
Stepmother's Day, 69
Stonehenge, England, 83
Stones, as remembrance token, 73
Sugaring-Off Party, 50
Suhoor, 30
Sukkoth, 132–133
Summer Harvest Festivals, 46
Summer solstice, 46, 82–83
Summer vacation, 86–89
Sunday night traditions, 178–180

Sunrise Ceremony/Sunrise Dance, 125
Super Bowl Sunday, 257–259
Svjatyj Vecer, 237
Syrup making, 49–50

T
Taco Bell April Fools' Day joke, 59–60
Taft, William Howard, 85
Tailgate parties, 137 (box)
Taily Day, 60 (box)
Take Our Daughters to Work Day, 61
Tchaikovsky, Pyotr I., 216
Thanksgiving, 184–192
    family toasts, 190
    family traditions, 190, 192
    first thanksgiving, 185–187
    inclusiveness of, 184
    three kernels story, 185
The Nutcracker and the Mouse King (Hoffman), 216
Toledo Mudhens, 86
Tolkien, J.R.R., 227–228
Tree planting, 74, 80, 97–98
Triangle Shirtwaist Factory fire, 39
Trillin, Calvin, 189
Trips
    grandparent-and-grandchild, 120
    heritage exploration, 121
    parent-and-child, 119–120
    without parents, 120–121
Tu B'Shvat, 27–28, 46
Tudor, Tasha, 26
Twelfth Night, 31–32, 241
Twelfth Night cake, 242
Twelve Days of Christmas, 238–241
Tzedakah box, 261

V
Vacation "books," 94
Vacation retreats, 181–182
Valentine cards, 25
Valentine's Day, 46
Valentine's Day crafts, 26
Valentinius (Valentine), 24–25
Vernal equinox, 29, 44–45, 47
Vesak, 70
Veterans of Foreign Wars, 71–72
"Virtual" trips, 93
Visakha Puja, 70
A Visit from St. Nicholas (Moore), 206

W
Walk When the Moon is Full (Hamerstrom), 182–183
Walker, Alice, 263
Wampanoag Indians, 185–186, 187
Washington, George, 187
Washington Senators, 85
Wassailing, 242
The Waste of Daylight (Willett), 60–61
Watch Night, 251
"We Shall Keep the Faith" (Michael), 71
Weddings. *See also* Anniversaries
    about, 154–155
    Apache wedding prayer, 154
    best man, 159
    bouquet tossing, 158–159
    bridesmaids, 159
    China, 162, 164–165
    date selection, 155–156, 156
    dress lore, 157–158
    Eastern Orthodox, 165
    "encore weddings," 167–168
    Hindu, 166
    Jewish, 165

Korea, 162, 165
Mexico, 166
Muslim, 166
Native American traditions, 158
North Africa, 162
rice throwing, 161–162
Sikh, 166
wedding cakes, 160
wedding gifts, 168–169
wedding rings, 162–164
wedding songs, 161
Weekend family trips, 92–93
Wesak, 70
"Wet the baby's head" celebration, 96
Whine/No-Whine Zones, 88
White, E. B., 174
Whittier, John Greenleaf, 193
Willett, William, 60–61
Williamstown Theater Festival, 84
Wilson, Woodrow, 68
Winter, Paul, 195–196
Winter solstice
    about, 22, 194–196
    ancient peoples, 45, 46
    Persian traditions, 197
Witherspoon society, 208–209
Women's suffrage, 39
Woodchucks, 23
Wordsworth, William, 21

Y
Yom Kippur, 143, 145–146
Young Aspirations/Young Artists (YAYA), 263
Youth sports programs, 91
Yule log, 213–214

Z
Zeroa, 52